Atlas & Co.
New York

Inside the
Stalin Archives

Discovering the
New Russia

Jonathan Brent

for Franny

Atlas & Co. *Publishers*
15 West 26th Street, 2nd floor
New York, NY 10010
www.atlasandco.com

Distributed to the trade by W. W. Norton & Company

Printed in the United States

Atlas & Co. books may be purchased for educational, business, or sales
promotional use. For information, please write to info@atlasandco.com.

Sections of this book are based upon articles that have appeared in
The New Criterion and *The Chronicle Review*, published by *The Chronicle
of Higher Education*.

Library of Congress Cataloging-in-Publication Data is available upon
request

ISBN: 978-0-9777433-3-9

13   12   11   10   09   08   1   2   3   4   5   6

Contents

Introduction

I threw myself at the hangman's feet,
You are my son, my horror.
Everything's mixed up for me forever,
And who is a man and who a beast
Will never now be clear . . .

—Anna Akhmatova, *Requiem*, 1937

At the funeral of Josef Stalin on March 9, 1953, Vyacheslav Molotov, Stalin's comrade since the revolution, bid farewell to his beloved *vozhd*, his leader, with the words: "The immortal name of Stalin will always live in our hearts, in the hearts of the Soviet people and of all progressive humanity." Even though Stalin had imprisoned Molotov's wife in 1949 and sent her into exile; even though Molotov had seen many signs that he himself was out of favor with the master and in imminent danger of being purged and possibly executed, his complete devotion to Stalin never wavered to the end of his long life in 1986.

Molotov was not alone. Two days later, on March 11, Ilya Ehrenburg, the Jewish journalist and writer who found himself on the verge of arrest many times in the 1930s, wrote in *Pravda*:

These words of Stalin were uttered at his grave: "We are the true servants of the people, and the people want peace and hate war. Yes, all of us are dedicated to the desire of the people not to allow the spilling of blood of millions and to safeguard the peaceful structure of a happy life." These were the thoughts of Comrade Stalin, his care, his will. . . . These words touch every simple person and together with us they say: "Stalin lives."

"Stalin lives"—something mesmerizing shines in those words. On February 3, 1940, Nikolai Yezhov, the man who had directed the secret police during the height of the Great Terror and who knew intimately all of Stalin's secret methods and designs, begged the court at the end of his trial—during which he had been falsely accused of, among other things, being an English spy—to "tell Stalin that I shall die with his name on my lips." "I am a victim of circumstances and nothing more," he told the court, "yet here enemies I have overlooked may have also had a hand in this." He was shot the next day. It was incomprehensible to him that he could have been abandoned and betrayed by the very man for whom he had executed so many so ruthlessly, and Yezhov clung to the belief that only "enemies" he may have overlooked could have been responsible for the judgment against him. "At the preliminary investigation," Yezhov told the court, "I said that I was not a spy, that I was not a terrorist, but they didn't believe me and beat me up horribly. During the twenty-five years of my party work I have fought honorably against enemies and have exterminated them. I have committed crimes for which I might well be executed." What were these crimes? "My great guilt lies in the fact that I purged so few [from the security services]." Yezhov arrested and executed some 3,800 security officials in 1937 and 5,600 in 1938, including criminals, police, and firemen, along with millions of Communist Party members and ordinary people. Estimations of the number of Stalin's victims over his twenty-five-year reign, from 1928 to 1953, vary widely, but 20 million is now considered the minimum. He has been called the greatest mass murderer in European civilization.

Yet fifty-five years after Stalin's death, the place of Stalin in Russian life remains enigmatic, and many in Russia and around the world might utter the same words as Yezhov at his trial; there are many for whom "Stalin lives." How can this be? After Khrushchev's secret speech in 1956 denouncing the cult of personality, Stalin's crimes became public knowledge and his body was removed from the Lenin Mausoleum; after the revelations of glasnost, outrage against the cruelties and stupidities of the Soviet police state was publicly aired; after the 1991 collapse of the Soviet Union, the nation that Stalin had killed and tortured so mercilessly to construct seemed a thing of the past. How could anyone believe any longer in Stalin's vision of the "peaceful structure of a happy life"? Facts and figures do not explain it.

When I recently asked an officer from the the Russian Federal Security Service (FSB; one of the successor organizations to the KGB) whether he thought Stalin could be rehabilitated, he looked at me in horror. "No," he said. "Impossible. It would be like rehabilitating Hitler." He spoke for many, yet the numerous books published in Russia and elsewhere in recent years praising Stalin signify something else. While new extremist political groups make undisguised use of Stalin's image and accomplishments, and his picture can be found on a box of chocolates today on sale at the duty-free shop at Sheremetyevo Airport outside Moscow, few would wish a return to the dark days of the 1930s. Nevertheless, it is fair to ask whether an airport in Berlin, Frankfurt, or Munich could sell a box of chocolates bearing Hitler's image. Though long ago removed from public buildings, Stalin's name and sayings remain on the lips of ordinary people, and in remote districts busts and statues of Stalin can still be found.

Could the legacy of Stalin be on the verge of a rebirth, and if so, in what form? Did it never die in the hearts of "progressive humanity?" Would it be like "rehabilitating Hitler"? If we follow the long road Russia has traveled since the Soviet Union was dissolved by Boris Yeltsin in December 1991, do we end up close to where we began? These questions have haunted the history of the "new" Russia and bear upon Yale University Press's sixteen-year project of publishing material from the Soviet archives—a task that has now culminated in the Russian government's approval to publish Stalin's personal archive.

When Yeltsin decreed that the previously secret Soviet state and party archives would be opened, researchers from around the world began to flock to Moscow in anticipation, and ordinary Russian citizens along with scholars, politicians, partisans—victimizers as well as victims—impatiently awaited the opportunity to scrutinize these secret books and files, gain access to KGB dossiers and interrogations, and read for the first time speeches, diaries, and letters of Kremlin leaders. Secret Central Committee decrees, deliberations of the Communist International (Comintern), and directives of the intelligence organizations, along with the daily traffic of the inner party bureaucracy that once determined so much for so many lives would now be openly studied.

With these perhaps naively euphoric expectations, I flew to Moscow in January 1992 to initiate the Annals of Communism project for Yale University Press. My purpose was to publish documents from the Soviet period that would help explain abiding questions of twentieth-century Soviet history: Was the 1934 murder of Sergei Kirov (first secretary of the Leningrad Regional Committee and secretary to the Communist Party Central Committee) the work of a lone assassin or a conspiracy that reached to Stalin? Was there a rupture between Lenin and Stalin or was there continuity? Did the U.S. Communist Party (CPUSA) engage in espionage? What was the real role of the Soviet Union in the Spanish Civil War? Why did Stalin not act on the intelligence he received daily before the Nazi invasion of June 1941? Who initiated and controlled the Great Terror of 1936–1938? How and why did the tragedy of the Katyn massacre of Polish officers take place? Was the 1932–1933 famine in the Ukraine and elsewhere a natural disaster or a politically motivated, state-sponsored mass murder? These were among the questions I hoped the Annals project would answer.

Answers were, inevitably, not easy to produce. The Central Party Archive alone held some 250 million documents, very few of which might be considered "smoking guns." Many essential high-level decisions were never written down; some documents had been destroyed. All this pointed to the need for a long-term program of painstaking research and integration of materials from many disparate sources. Over time, a larger question began to take shape: what was the mechanism by which the Soviet system operated as a whole? Understanding that mechanism eventually became the over-riding goal of the Annals series. The project continues to this day and has now published over twenty-five separate volumes with many others still under contract.

"Everything should take place slowly and incorrectly so that man doesn't get a chance to start feeling proud, so that man is sad and perplexed," Venedikt Erofeev reflected in his masterpiece, *Moskva petushki* (*Moscow to the End of the Line*), through his tragicomic hero, Venechka. I have kept these beautiful words before me over the past sixteen years of working in the Soviet archives, and I remain humble before the immensity of reconstructing the history of the Soviet period. During this time the situation in Russia itself has been perplexing and often sad. The slow and difficult rebuilding of the Russian nation has left many in despair, and while events often seem to have overtaken all predictions, the country finds itself poised in what Alexander Yakovlev evocatively called a "twilight"—the threshold between old and new, past and future, authoritarianism and freedom, between dreams of past glory and the reality of its present difficult economic and geopolitical place at the beginning of the twenty-first century. Though much has changed, much remains unchanged in fundamental outlook, or what the Russians call "mentality," prompting one Russian scholar to warn me that total disclosure of the Soviet period is simply not possible at the present time because of a fear of "analogies" between past and present. What analogies? Whose fears? No one can say with certainty.

What's clear is that Soviet Marxism simply did not work. By 1987 the Soviet Union couldn't support its army or its social welfare programs; it couldn't raise the standard of living of its people beyond a certain base level. Pragmatists understood this, and soon after Yeltsin declared the end of the Soviet Union in December 1991, many people, both in Russia and abroad, believed that the country could become a Western-style, liberal democracy with a flourishing economy.

But for many the goal of the Soviet system was not merely to "work"; it was to achieve the greatness and power that Stalin had envisioned and once had been theirs. Lines were soon drawn between the remnants of the Communist Party, who had joined with various nationalist groups, and reformers like Alexander Yakovlev, who developed the concept of perestroika during the Gorbachev period. Yakovlev wished to purge the country of its Bolshevik legacy, atone for the crimes of the Soviet system, and develop a society based on the rule of law. He and others hoped this transformation would be publicly institutionalized through the trial of the Communist Party begun in September 1992. Their efforts did not succeed, and Russia's equivalent of the Nuremberg trials was abandoned less than midway through the process. Today the Communist Party of the Russian Federation, or KPRF, remains a legal Russian party. No other state-sponsored project of national introspection and reconciliation has ever taken place. Unlike Germany, de-Nazified after World War II, Russia has never been completely de-Bolshevized. Instead, a widespread effort is underway to "normalize" the Soviet past.

According to provincial church records, Josef Vissarionovich Djugashvili was born in Gori, Georgia, on December 18, 1878 (December 6 by the old calendar), in the aftermath of the disastrous Russo-Turkish War, a time that marked both the height of imperial Russian power and the onset of its twisting pathway into impotence and eventual dissolution. Unlike his mentor, Vladimir Lenin, whose family was bourgeois and well-educated, Josef Djugashvili was born into impoverished circumstances, the son of a shoemaker given to heavy drinking and violent outbursts against both his son and his wife, and who was left by them to die alone in a Tiflis apartment. According to Stalin's biographer, Dmitri Volkogonov, after 1903, when Stalin became a revolutionary, he may not have seen his mother more than four or five times. He did not attend her funeral in 1937.

Stalin stood five feet four inches tall. Two toes on his left foot were fused. His sallow complexion was heavily marked by the smallpox he suffered as a child. But he possessed penetrating black eyes and the confidence of a man possessed by history. To the end of his life he wore his thick, black hair combed back, revealing a prominent widow's peak. Whether from childhood accident or disease, he had a slightly withered left arm, which he generally kept less exposed to public view, and his left hand often curled inward like an injured paw.

Stalin's life was marked by contradictions and continuous efforts at self-reinvention. In 1912, Djugashvili became Stalin, the "Man of steel." He became general secretary of the Communist Party in 1922, and then, after Lenin's death in 1924, he and Leon Trotsky struggled for control of the Soviet state. Trotsky was expelled from the party in 1927 and exiled from the Soviet Union in 1929. Stalin, victorious, changed the date of his birth to December 21, 1879, possibly so that his fiftieth jubilee could be celebrated in 1929, after he had firmly consolidated his rule. By 1937, together with Marx and Lenin, the image of this small, pockmarked son of an illiterate shoemaker billowed on giant banners over Moscow's Red Square during parades or floated in the sky on giant blimps; by 1953, the year of his death, his visage was identified in the minds of people all over the world with political terror on an unprecedented scale. As he reinvented himself, he reinvented Russia, transforming his nation into a military power with the ability to reach around the globe. Unlike Hitler, Stalin died in his bed.

The image of Stalin's strength, however, always seemed paired with the fact of his withered limb, and it may not too great an overstatement to suggest that it was this often invisible hand that held so much of Soviet and world history in its grasp.

Toward the end of 1930, Stalin wrote to Maxim Gorky, the world-famous Russian writer who emigrated to Italy after the revolution, hoping to lure him home:

Things aren't going badly here. In industry and in agriculture the successes are undeniable. Let them, each and every medieval fossil, caterwaul there in Europe, at the tops of their voices, about the "downfall" of the USSR. They aren't going to change our plans or our affairs one iota that way. The USSR is going to be a first-rate country with the biggest technically equipped industrial and agricultural production. Socialism is invincible. There's not going to be any more "*beggarly*" Russia. That's over! There's going to be a mighty and plentiful *vanguard* Russia.

Not long after Stalin's confident vision of "a first-rate country with the biggest technically equipped industrial and agricultural production," the writer Isaac Babel returned to Moscow from a tour of the famine-stricken Ukraine. He confided to a friend that he had witnessed things impossible to speak or write about—cannibalism and inhuman destitution. After a similar trip, Boris Pasternak wrote to a friend, "There was such inhuman, unimaginable misery, such a terrible disaster, that it began to seem almost abstract, it would not fit within the bounds of consciousness. I fell ill. For an entire year I could not write." What made it worse was the suspicion that this "inhuman, unimaginable misery" was somehow being engineered or at least managed by the government, by Stalin, for reasons no one could understand. Stalin's "vanguard Russia" would never be realized.

But the cruelty underlying that vision was not Stalin's alone. Lenin invoked it in 1922 when he ordered a final assault on the Orthodox Church for the purpose of confiscating its immense wealth. The document issuing this order was discovered by Richard Pipes in the secret Lenin archive in Moscow; it was published for the first time in 1996 in the Annals of Communism volume *The Unknown Lenin.*

I think that here our enemy [the church] is committing an enormous strategic mistake in trying to drag us into a decisive battle at a time when it is particularly hopeless and particularly disadvantageous for him. On the contrary, for us this moment is not only exceptionally favorable but generally the only moment when we can, with ninety-nine out of a hundred chances of total success, smash the enemy and secure for ourselves an indispensable position for many decades to come. It is precisely now and only now, when in the starving regions people are eating human flesh, and hundreds if not thousands of corpses are littering the roads, that we can (and therefore must) carry out the confiscation of church valuables with the most savage and merciless energy, not stopping [short of] crushing any resistance.

We must, come what may, carry out the confiscation of church valuables in the most decisive and rapid manner, so as to secure for ourselves a fund of several hundred million gold rubles (one must recall the gigantic wealth of some of the monasteries and abbeys). . . . All considerations indicate that later we will be unable to do this, because no other moment except that of desperate hunger will give us a mood among the broad peasant masses that will guarantee us the sympathy of these masses or at least their neutrality.

The state must assert its full power "with the most savage and merciless energy." It can hope to triumph with "ninety-nine out of a hundred chances of total success" only when "people are eating human flesh" and "hundreds if not thousands of corpses" litter the roads. This is the paw inside the sleeve of Soviet power. Neither personal cruelty nor the desire for revenge explains these actions of the Bolsheviks. Rather, they had been prepared by a way of thinking based upon an ideology that freed Lenin and the Bolshevik state from both the substance and the vocabulary of traditional morality—from the "medieval" fossils caterwauling in Europe, as Stalin put it. But what gave Lenin this freedom paradoxically also gave him no options: "we can (and therefore must)," he writes. Sixteen years after Lenin's secret decree to confiscate church valuables, at the height of the Great Terror, Andrei Vyshinsky, procurator of the Soviet Union and later ambassador to the United Nations, described his recent inspection tour of various camps in the gulag. In a 1938 memorandum to Nikolai Yezhov, the head of the NKVD (the KGB at the time), he wrote:

> Among the prisoners there are some so ragged and lice-ridden that they pose a sanitary danger to the rest. These prisoners have deteriorated to the point of losing any resemblance to human beings. Lacking food . . . they collect orts [refuse] and, according to some prisoners, eat rats and dogs.

Vyshinsky quotes the chief procurator of the Bamlag camp:

"In the infirmary, there are prisoners lying naked on long bunks, literally packed like sardines in a barrel. They are not taken to the bathhouse for weeks owing to the lack of underwear and bedsheets. In some rooms, women are lying on the bunks in the same room as men. A syphilis patient lies side by side with a tubercular patient. In a common room, there are patients with erysipelas (infectious) packed with stomach patients. . . . Those who arrive have no underwear, nothing but rags. The terrible thing is that there is not a single change of underwear, boots, or clothes in the Bamlag. Their bodies are covered with scabs, but they do not take a bath, because they are not provided with underwear. Their tatters are full of hundreds of lice. There is no soap. Many have nothing to put on to go out to the bathroom. . . . They resemble humans or, more likely, savages, or people of the Stone Age. . . . And new trainloads of people without clothes keep coming, and people go on the road barefoot, unclothed, and we have minus twenty to minus fifty degrees centigrade here."

These people only "resemble humans"; they are "savages, or people of the Stone Age." A member of the Central Committee, Vyshinsky was able to put into words what Isaac Babel could not and concludes that "somebody—obviously hostile—is arranging for people to die en route and to die upon arrival." It could not occur to him that it was the system itself that was producing this horror. Belief in the ideology was so strong that, like Yezhov in 1940, it was inconceivable that the party itself, rather than hostile enemies, could have produced these results. The great experiment of "progressive humanity"—to create a vanguard nation according to scientific laws of dialectical materialism and become a "first-rate country"—could fail only as a result of enemies from without; as a consequence, the system created endless waves of such enemies and drove numberless masses to destitution and death.

In October 1952, Stalin called in the head of the security services and the interrogators who had failed to make significant progress in obtaining confessions in the so-called "Doctors' Plot." Many doctors were arrested and tortured when Stalin claimed that the Jews among them had led a conspiracy to murder Politburo leaders. After Stalin's death, the Soviet government repudiated the "plot," blaming it on renegade security officers and releasing the doctors from prison. At the 1952 meeting, Stalin demanded that the interrogators beat the physicians:

> "Beat them!"—[Stalin] demanded from us, declaring: "What are you? Do you want to be more humanistic than Lenin who ordered Dzerzhinsky to throw Savinkov out a window?"

They did as Stalin demanded, and one interrogator stated after Stalin's death that during a torture session the elderly Dr. Vasilenko "lost his entire human aspect" begging for mercy. Days and nights of physical and mental torture, sleeplessness and humiliation had reduced him to one of those Vyshinsky observed in the gulag in 1938—literally a nonperson.

Exercising "the most savage and merciless energy" against those who have been reduced to "nonpeople" or creatures from the Stone Age was possible once they were identified as enemies. This process of identification was not simple, but once accomplished it was lethal and irreversible. The mechanism of this process lies at the heart of the Stalinist state. It fused a way of thinking, a way of seeing, with a set of powerful political ideas. At the heart of this way of thinking is Josef Stalin.

Part One

Connections

Chapter 1

Descent: January 1992

The Aeroflot flight had been delayed three times and nearly six hours before takeoff on a dreary January day in New York. Communication with Jeffrey Burds, a young American historian and my sole contact in Moscow with the directors of the Soviet archives, had been impossible from JFK as delay after delay had been announced. I had gotten in touch with Burds through Ivo Banac, a professor of history at Yale University who had directed Burds's graduate work and was one of the first academic advisers to the Annals of Communism project. I knew Burds only through correspondence and telephone conversations, and I was not at all certain that anybody would be waiting for me when I landed.

And now, after some nearly twenty hours, feeling a backwash of fatigue I had never before experienced, I gazed in amazement out the window of the airplane at a jagged gash in the frozen ground that seemed to rise toward us as we swept downward. Fence posts protruded along its edges like teeth that had come in wrong. Beyond it and just coming into view was the empty runway leading to the terminal of Moscow's Sheremetyevo Airport.

My first thought as the wheels hit the ground was, How could this actually be the Moscow airport? How could this be the airport of the capital city of the second greatest superpower in the world? It seemed much smaller than JFK, LaGuardia, O'Hare, or any other major American airport. Where were all the other planes? Where were the technicians in jumpsuits waving fluorescent batons? Where were the baggage trucks speeding under the wings of 747s? A few planes, largely from other East European countries, were parked at the hangars—but they seemed at odd angles to each other and to the terminal gates, as if hastily abandoned with no thought of whether anyone would ever get on or off of them again. Something was missing.

As Burds had directed, I had brought ample supplies of Jack Daniel's, salami, biscuits, chocolates in the shape of the Statue of Liberty, and cartons of Winston cigarettes, along with strategic quantities of *valuta*—one-dollar bills and several hundreds (nothing in between, I was told, would be accepted either on the street or in the currency exchanges). Meetings had been arranged; people were expecting me. But looking out at the empty terminal I had the fleeting apprehension that I was in the wrong place and that all the arrangements I had imagined had already been forgotten.

It is an odd sensation to be in a place that is new but somehow known, that feels like a return but is so foreign that the simple words *"Kofe? Chai?"* spoken by the stewardess coming down the aisle made my heart jump. The simple signs *vykhod* ("exit") and *vkhod* ("entrance") took on a vibrant new meaning. Like most in my generation who grew up in the Cold War, I had formed my ideas about communism and the Soviet system largely from books, reinforced daily by violent images on television and in film: images of Khrushchev banging his shoe on the podium at the UN, the U.S. naval blockade of Cuba, confrontations at the Berlin Wall, and endless columns of Soviet tanks and missiles parading through Red Square were all most Americans actually knew of the world that the words *kofe* and *chai* now brought to life for me.

We touched down on Monday, January 9, 1992, in a dull, gray light. Somewhere between sleep and wakefulness, I could not tell whether it was morning or afternoon. As we gathered at a set of sliding glass doors at the end of the exit ramp, a lethargic young soldier with a blotchy white complexion unwound himself slowly from a chair and ushered us down a corridor. A submachine gun was casually slung at his waist. Shunted by our sleepy guard down a wide staircase into a large holding area leading to *Pasportnii Kontrol*, we joined hundreds of other worn-out human souls. Some seemed half-asleep in heaps on the stairs. Cigarette smoke filled the air. Copper-colored cylindrical lighting units that honeycombed the ceiling seemed to absorb rather than emit illumination. "I am line," a tall, elderly man in a gray overcoat growled in heavily accented English to a little gray-haired woman who kept jumping up and down like a bird in a cage demanding from anyone who would listen: "Ver is line? Ver is line?" There was no line. The rapidly accumulating mass of humanity pressed forward.

A cluster of Texas oilmen standing in front of me, with heavy satchels at their feet, spoke eagerly of making their way to the drilling fields of Siberia and the Far East. There were grandmothers anxious to be reunited with families left behind, awkward new *biznes* men clutching flimsy attaché cases, and large numbers of merchants from the

Far East pushing forward unwieldy shipments of unknown merchandise wrapped in brown paper or sealed in plastic. A long delay resulted when one of them reached the control point. The young female border guards, in olive uniforms and wide-brimmed hats, checked and rechecked documents, made telephone calls, and then seemed quite willing to wait forever for authorization from some unidentified and unreachable authority higher up before letting them pass through. The next time I came, in July, a sign for something called *BeeLine*, the first Russian cell phone company, was installed above the glass inspection cubicles.

Once I was finally beyond the flimsy gray barrier, my passport duly stamped, my baggage indifferently inspected, I felt my heart race from the jolt of having made it. I was through. But as I pushed my way toward the waiting area of the terminal, the exhilaration turned to nausea from the dizzying human stink that enveloped the main building and stunned the senses. The ventilation had not been working for days, and no one, I was told, knew when it might. With many degrees of frost on the thermometer, opening doors and windows was impossible.

The sour, sullen stench seemed to mark you with each breath and draw you somehow down into itself; it became part of you against your will, regardless of the force of "history" driving events on the streets and squares and in the government buildings of Moscow. I could feel my will to resist begin to seep away when a tallish, stocky young man in a green parka suddenly appeared before me. The hood was thrown back, revealing a mass of unkempt fair hair and a bluff, friendly, boyish face.

"You're Jonathan Brent," he announced, like a theater director handing out a part. Then he added, "We've been back and forth twice!" There was no time for explanations. "Nikolai's here. The car is waiting. Let's go." This was Jeffrey Burds.

Before I could reclaim my large duffel bag, it had already been seized from behind and lifted away by someone I hadn't noticed before. The man was taller than me and had what I took to be a military bearing. With a shrug of his shoulder, he signaled that I was to follow. He was a powerful man with broad shoulders, a symmetrical face and a well-trimmed, chestnut mustache. Leading the way, he kept his eyes straight ahead.

"Watch out!" Jeff yelled. "They'll slam you in the face if you're not careful."

Careful of what? There was no time to ask. The terminal's glass door caught me off guard, and I lurched, narrowly escaping its violent backswing, into the frozen air of Russia.

As we waited at the curb for the car, I asked Jeff how he knew who I was.

"Not hard," he replied. "There aren't many Americans. You looked lost. Anyone can tell—your shoes, your coat, your haircut. Were you hassled? Never take a taxi. Never let anyone carry your luggage. Do you speak Russian?"

"Not well."

"Then say as little as possible."

Jeff's energy was hectic, explosive, and filled with urgency, as if at any moment the tragic and beautiful events unfolding in this country would blaze into an epiphany. "You'll love Mariana," he assured me, once we were safely in Nikolai's small gray Russian car that smelled of gasoline and grease. He explained that he had arranged for me to stay with Mariana, the mother of his friend Lyonya. When he stopped to pay the parking fee, Nikolai dimmed the lights and shut off the engine. He shoved some orange ruble notes into the bare, cupped hand of the parking lot attendant, a little man in overalls. The attendant went around to the gate and unstrapped the end that was held in place with what appeared to be a single leather or rubber thong attached to a concrete stanchion. The long wooden pole rose smoothly and we made our way out onto the congested thoroughfare. Military trucks blew exhaust directly into the window of the car as they passed by. Unable to crank the window up all the way, I lowered it to let in fresh air. It was bitter cold.

Nikolai said something in Russian. "Nikolai says to raise the window. You don't have a hat." Another military truck rolled past, spitting exhaust. My head was swimming. "Ne rabotai bez upora" was printed on the hood. "What's that mean?" I asked, pointing. Jeff translated: "Do not operate without support."

"It's the Old New Year," Jeff said, adding that most people had nothing to celebrate. "Lyonya is there, but his wife has moved out for a few days to visit her parents, so Mariana has some extra space. It's safer this way for you, and cheaper."

"Who's Lyonya?"

"He's an archivist for the Orthodox Church. He's converted to Russian Orthodoxy and has recently convinced Mariana to convert as well." Jeff had met Lyonya through his work in the Moscow City archives, and through Lyonya, Mariana. Staying in a private apartment would be much preferable to one of the former Inturist hotels, where the bugging may be gone but there were still plenty of bugs. When Jeff mentioned my trip, Lyonya immediately volunteered his mother's apartment. Eventually, Lyonya would also become a coeditor of a volume in the series on the Bolshevik revolution and the Orthodox Church.

Jeff explained that I would meet the heads of the archives tomorrow and with any luck Nikolai could arrange a meeting with the head of the entire archival system for some point during my stay. KGB representatives had heard I was coming and wished to meet me.

"Did you bring the Winstons?" Jeff asked.

"Yes, but I don't smoke."

"Doesn't matter. Open a pack, take one out, light it, then slide the pack across the table." I looked skeptical. "Just do it. Whoever's opposite will push his pack toward you. Take one, put it in your mouth, light it—don't inhale if you don't wish—then slide it back. It's a first step."

That evening we would sit down and plan out the strategy. The most important aspect of making this deal, Jeff stressed over and over again, was to demonstrate respect for those across the table. Don't come on like a conquering hero; don't be a smug American; don't look down on them because their system failed and ours triumphed. Nikolai Petrovich would be an intermediary with the archive. He would also drive us around. As a historian and head of an important department at the Russian State University for the Humanities, he knew everybody.

"That's the marker of the farthest Nazi advance toward Moscow," Jeff said, pointing to the massive steel monument of a tank trap by the roadway. "But now, of course, it's actually inside the city limits."

"So they got to Moscow after all," I thought, not certain I could say such a thing out loud.

Chapter 2

Mariana

Recently widowed, Mariana had been married to a Soviet army general; she had taught the piano for many years and lived, Jeff told me, in one of the better apartment complexes in Moscow, on Kutuzovsky Prospect by the Square of Victory. She spoke a smattering of English and a trace of Yiddish. In her youth she had been a beauty, judging by the small oval photograph hung on the wall of my modest bedroom, in which a dark-haired young woman gazed upward over the camera with romantic longing in her dark eyes. The Mariana who stood before me in her thin housecoat had gold-plated teeth, bleached hair, and the sagging skin of an old woman. She had the sensitive hands of a pianist, but now only her lively, inquisitive eyes seemed to link her to the picture on my wall. She had a small black poodle that she called her *chyornaya idish sobaka*—her "black Jewish dog."

Communicating with Mariana didn't strike me as a problem when she came in to see how I was doing shortly after Jeff and Nikolai departed.

"Chai?" she asked, peering in from the doorway.

"Da," I answered, as if it were the easiest thing in the world. *"Spasibo."*

So far, so good.

I followed Mariana back into the small kitchen, where a small gray kettle such as I had not seen since the 1950s was already heating up on the small gas stove. Everything seemed small: The ceiling seemed low, the windows struck me as narrow, the blinds paper thin. The ceiling electrical unit had four bulbs but only two were on and they seemed only marginally incandescent. The wooden chairs seemed light and just barely glued together. There were no paper towels or napkins. Jeff had cautioned me to bring my own toilet paper, and now I understood why.

On the shelf above the sink was a can of Nescafé Gold instant coffee. Two or three globelike orange flowers hung from their dry stalks in a clear glass vase. Beside them was a wooden box with the word *sol* on it—"salt." Above the shelf was a shiny picture of fresh fruits and vegetables—a cornucopia of tomatoes, carrots, peas, beets, and string beans, surrounded by an aurora of shining apples, pears, bananas, and oranges. Cracks ran along the top of the wall amid large fragments of peeling paint. Above the kitchen door was a shelf with boxes and glass jars that contained dried seeds, nuts, stewed or pickled vegetables.

A pleasant coolness emanated from the window over the radiator and behind the window was the rushing of wind. Outside, a single courtyard light reflected on the snow. It was already dark.

Mariana put a dish of apple slices on the table with brown bread. Tomorrow, she promised, she would make a real Jewish meal. She poured a dark liquid from a small china bowl into my cup and filled it with boiling water.

She was acutely interested in the United States, particularly the price of a good lock for her front door and the price of an apartment. She wanted to know how many rooms there were in my house, what kind of people I lived among, how much food and vitamins cost. She had heard of welfare. Is it a lot or a little? A friend of hers had written from the United States that it was a lot, but Mariana was sure it couldn't possibly be anything but *nishchii*—"beggarly." I confirmed her suspicion, and she looked pleased. She took a spoon from a drawer and held it up.

"Skol'ko?" she asked, waving the spoon over the teacup.

"Skol'ko?" I repeated.

"Da."

"How much?"

She nodded, smiling. "Yes, yes . . . khow?"

"In America?"

"Da, v Amerike."

"This spoon?" I reached out my hand to take it. It was as light as a feather, made of some aluminum alloy and clearly a relic of the 1950s or even earlier: as with the kettle, I recognized something about it from my childhood, some indeterminate but unmistakable stamp of scarcity, frugality and want that had been left over from the deprivations of the war but by the mid-1950s had become a thing of the past. Here all those household objects discarded in the course of my family's ascent into a better material life had not been discarded at all. I held the almost weightless utensil in my hand with a mixture of pity and the joy of finding something I never expected to see again—though what this was precisely I could not have said.

"Ne znayu," I had to admit. I didn't know. But when I saw Mariana's face drop, I added that I thought it might cost about a dollar, which I demonstrated by taking a one-dollar bill from my pocket and holding up a finger.

"Eto mnogo?"

"A lot?"

Mariana nodded.

"In America?"

She looked puzzled.

"In America it's okay. It's the right amount."

"Eto malo," she said, disappointed, putting the spoon down.

"No, no, it's not little. It's fine. It's what it should be," I tried to explain, but she had turned back to the stove. In the silence, I searched for ways of repairing the situation. Nothing came to me. Eventually, Mariana sat down without attempting conversation, and we remained that way for a long time at her little table in her kitchen with yellow walls and steamed-up windows, facing a calendar with a sliding red plastic square to mark the date.

"What do you think about the future?" I asked in some kind of mixed-up way. Mariana seemed to understand, but only shook her head. *"Ne dumayu, ne dumayu,"*—"I don't think"—was all she could answer.

The refrigerator next to the stove was the sort we had discarded when I was a child, though it remained in our garage for many years. From time to time I would visit it with no specific intention except to see it again, perhaps because my mother had used it and after her death it was somehow connected to her. It was our "icebox," as my father called it. Once, I worked up the courage to open the door and was repelled by the stench inside. Holding my nose, I glimpsed the stained and yellow walls, the flimsy shelves caked with black. A thick black spot seemed to grow at the bottom. I slammed it shut and raced out, vowing never to look inside again.

But now, here in Mariana's little flat in Moscow, I found that little refrigerator again next to her little stove with its familiar four gas burners and chipped enamel. I felt at home with the sound of its flame and the surge of the refrigerator's engine that, as a child, I would listen to at night pretending to be asleep in the next room. All these discarded things became dear again in a flash, even as a moment later Mariana held up a knife and asked: *"Skol'ko?"*

The objects in Mariana's apartment had to be approached in a particular way—not as I was used to at home, where I could grab a kitchen chair by the back and drag it across the floor or push it with my foot under the table to the right spot; or where I could come into the bathroom late at night, groggy, and twist on the hot water without restraining the force of my hand; or where I could pull open a door without first thinking of the degree of pressure the handle might take.

In Mariana's apartment, I threw myself sleepily into the chair in my bedroom and for a precarious second it seemed ready to collapse beneath me. When I put a book down on the low table by my bed, I sensed that a heavier object set down harder might cause it to collapse. I decided to leave my duffel bag on the floor. On my first trip to the bathroom, I turned the knob on the left, thinking it would be hot water only to discover it was cold, while the knob on the right was hot. But when the hot came out boiling hot, I pushed the spigot away from my hands with such force that the water shot up out of the sink. I turned the hot-water knob off, but again with such force that the knob twisted far past the point at which the water shut off and, to my horror, started flowing again. My god! In my first hour I had already destroyed Mariana's plumbing. Despite the scalding of my hand, I delicately adjusted the knob to the precise point where the flow of water ceased and delicately moved the wandlike spigot back to the center of the sink. I waited. The water had stopped. I breathed in deeply. The next day, when Mariana said nothing about the sink, I realized that the disaster I had seemed on the brink of was for her the normal state of affairs.

I went to bed the first night wrapped in the thick blanket Mariana provided, looking in the semidarkness at the low table by my bed. It seemed as if none of the objects in this room had ever been new but had come into the world already used and broken. A word floated up into my consciousness from where it had lain for some twenty years: *"Rykhlyi,"* I said over and over to myself, not even sure of its meaning. I pulled myself out of the warm coverlet determined to find my pocket dictionary. But I no longer remembered which way the bed faced, where the door was, or where my briefcase might be. I stumbled forward terrified of crashing into one of the already half-destroyed objects in the room. I stopped. Listened. Where was I? Alone in this dark room. There were no sounds except the tap of water in the kitchen sink. I waited. Suddenly the refrigerator engine revved and kicked in like something I remembered. I felt my way along the wall to the door, running my hand against the picture of Mariana as a young woman. It came loose but blessedly did not fall off its nail. At the door I reached up high and then low; I moved my hand in circles, but couldn't find the light switch. I went to the other side of the door. No switch. A lucky thought came to me. The toilet down the hall. I could go down the hall to the toilet. Surely I'd find the light switch for that. I opened my door carefully and peered into the black hallway. All was quiet, and to my unutterable relief I discovered that Mariana had left a small light on at the end of the hallway, no doubt anticipating such an eventuality. I returned to my room, felt my way to my briefcase that I remembered was placed strategically at the foot of the bed, reached inside, and to my delight found something that had the right thickness and size. In the light of the single naked bulb at the end of the corridor I looked into my pocket dictionary, and after a couple of mistaken spellings discovered what I wanted: *rykhlyi*, "friable, loose, porous." "Friable"? Easily crumbled, but not easily broken. A *rykhlyi* world.

I awoke well before dawn, which did not come until about nine o'clock. I went to the window and pulled back the drapes. The sky was still quite black, but on the other side of the wide courtyard a square of yellow light appeared. A figure stood in the square of light—I couldn't tell if it was a man or a woman. Getting up at this time of day—to do what? I wondered. What was there to do? I looked more closely at the figure across the courtyard. A man in his undershirt stood at the window looking down. That was all.

I returned to my bed and sank back into an uncomfortable, jet-lagged, and uneasy sleep.

As the sun slanted through the window, I noticed that the back of my room was piled high with bundles of one sort or another that I hadn't noticed when I first arrived. There were three television sets, a refrigerator identical to the one in Mariana's kitchen, a large wardrobe, and several smaller cabinets stacked on top of each other and shoved under tables. And as I looked at the boxes that no doubt contained other odds and ends, I understood what had bothered me from the moment I set foot in the apartment: the ceiling seemed very low. In retrospect, I suspect this feeling of being closed in had something to do with the cardboard boxes piled everywhere in the apartment, often reaching to the very top.

In the shower again, I feared that if I stretched out my hand or turned suddenly, I would be in danger of breaking something I couldn't sense in advance. The one-piece plastic shower curtain came only part of the way across the tub, and by the time I had figured out how to use the shower nozzle, I had sprayed the entire bathroom with water. Where to put my toothbrush without bringing the thin glass shelf down with a crash? Where to put the toothpaste tube while brushing and the shaving soap while shaving? And where to put my feet, which I turned degree by degree as if enveloped in infinitely brittle glass threads.

I finally left off trying to clean myself up, returned to my room, and put on fresh clothes. I went hesitantly into the kitchen, where Mariana stood just as I had left her the night before at the stove in her thin housecoat. Her body shook with a deep, bronchial cough.

After "Good morning" and "How did you sleep?" I pointed to my throat. Mariana nodded. I coughed. *"Da,"* she said. Her voice was hoarse. I ran back to my room and brought out a packet of Sudafed cough tablets and offered her two of the red, seedlike pills.

"Malenkii," she scoffed.

"Mariana," I urged. "Please take them. They look small, but they're strong and will help with your cough." I pointed to my throat.

She looked skeptical.

"Take them," I said, and in a rush, *"prinimayete, pozhalusta."*

She smiled doubtfully, but allowed me to place the pills in her open hand, then let them slip into a small white saucer on the kitchen table.

"Djonatan," Mariana smiled, as she pronounced my name. "Djonatan. *Eto yabloko.*"

"An apple?"

Mariana nodded.

"My name," I suddenly realized. "It's true, it's an apple." I had agreed to meet Jeff Burds in Revolution Square outside the Kremlin. It was getting late. "Take them," I repeated on my way out the door, holding out my hand. But Mariana dashed after me from the kitchen and caught me by my coat sleeves.

"No, no, no!" she cried. "No! *Shapka, gdye shapka?*"

"Shapka?"

She pointed to my head.

"Hat?"

"Da."

"No hat."

"*Pochemu?* Must . . ."

"I don't wear hats," I said reaching behind me for the hood of my parka.

"No, no, no! *Ochen kholodno.* Cold. Very cold. Get seek, seek. No good."

She slammed the door shut and I stood amazed as she raced to her bedroom and brought out a woolen ski cap for me to put on.

"Khed?" she pointed to my head.

"*Da.*"

"Now, put . . ."

But before I could take the cap from her hands she came close to me and slipped it over my head and ears.

"*Khorosho,*" she nodded approvingly. "Go."

Chapter 3

Into the Archive

Outside Mariana's door, the fishy smell I had tried not to notice the day before lay waiting. The smell of Moscow—flat, unwashed, sour—an accumulation of fifty years without sunlight or cleansing breeze, as if inhering in the things themselves—under them, around them and from within, from the ripped-open mailboxes, the broken plaster, the seeping pipes and twisted electrical cords of Mariana's building's entrance. From the old shoes and twig brooms, the broken shovels and spilled pails shoved into corners; old beer bottles, wrappers, and rags that had been tossed aside.

Jeff had informed me that the elevator didn't stop on the third floor, but since Mariana lived on the sixth, I could safely use it. I remembered this vaguely as the elevator pulled up with a clang, shaking the black metal grid that enclosed it. I waited for the door to open. It did not and in a minute began to descend. Should I knock on Mariana's door, I wondered, to let her know it's not working? But before I could make up my mind, Mariana appeared. Had the door not been shut and locked? Was it not a thick, heavy door? How had she divined the problem? She offered no explanation as she pushed the button on the wall plate summoning the elevator once more. Eventually, it came clanging back. When the door again did not open, I felt vindicated. But before I could point this out, Mariana simply seized the handle and pulled it back. *"Vot, vot,"* was all I could make out as she waved me inside. Turning around in the small compartment, I saw a worried look on Mariana's face, as if she doubted she would ever see me again.

Jeff had written down very specific directions on how to take the *trolleybus*, which I could pick up at a stop on Kutuzovsky Prospect, not far from the monument to Prince Mikhail Kutuzov's victory over Napoleon in 1812. But when I eventually found my way through the frozen courtyard of Mariana's building onto the Prospect, where masses of people already waited for *trolleybuses* that might or might not ever come, I decided to risk my ability to communicate and stuck out my hand for a taxi. Taxis were everywhere, completely unregulated by the city and informal. Anyone with a car could give you a ride for a negotiated rate. One immediately pulled up.

"Ploshchad Pobedi, pozhalusta," I said. The young man inside smiled and looked around at the monument to Prince Kutuzov's victory. Of course. We were in Ploshchad Pobedi—Victory Square.

"Ploshchad Revolutsii," I corrected myself—Revolution Square.

He waved me inside.

"Amerika!" he said, slipping a tape of the Beatles' "A Hard Day's Night" into his tape deck and turning up the volume. As the little Zhiguli rattled along Kutuzovsky, I tried to make out the storefront signs, but with little success. Crowds waited patiently in the bitter cold, pyramids of ice were piled

high on the sidewalks, and strings of colored lights swung from bridges and overpasses—the Old New Year lingered or had not yet begun, I didn't know which. Plastic bags could be seen dangling from apartment windows. Later someone explained that the bags kept the food cold so people could turn off their electricity. A trolleybus rumbled to the curb and a mass of people pressed into its center doors.

Like Nikolai the day before, when my young driver stopped in traffic, he shut off his engine and dimmed his lights. The windshield had no wipers; one of the backseat doors had no handle; a long, thin crack ran the entire length of the windshield. The driver wore no seat belt and had a cigarette in his mouth. Cardboard had been placed on the floor. At a light, a truck idling beside us belched a thick cloud of black smoke into the front passenger window that could not be completely closed. No one could explain why the exhaust pipes of Soviet trucks aimed their smoke directly into the windows of passing cars. The smell of exhaust, gasoline, and grease made my head swim. Again I read over and over on the hoods of the numerous military vehicles: *Ne rabotai bez upora*—Do not operate without support.

When we arrived at Revolution Square, I held up the one-dollar bill I had ready in my hand; the driver nodded and pocketed it gratefully. I had no idea how much such a cab ride might cost, and it seemed neither did he, but one U.S. dollar covered it.

The first meeting at the Central Party Archive was set for 11:00 A.M. The director of the archive would be present, along with the deputy director and some archivists.

Anxiously checking my watch, I wondered whether the clocks in Moscow were seven hours ahead of New York or eight—in which case I had already missed the appointment. But as I glanced around, looking for a public clock, Jeff once more appeared.

"I've been searching the square for you," he said. "Come on. Do you have your visa and passport? The Winstons? Now listen, open a pack and keep it ready."

I showed Jeff the bottle of Jack Daniel's.

"Wait with that," he said. "First we've got the Central Party, then the Russian State Archive of the Economy, then GARF, the State Archive of the Russian Federation. We'll have lunch at the Spanish Bar. Then, if Nikolai can set it up, a meeting with some KGB officers. We'll take the metro. It's the fastest way. Nikolai will meet us at the archive. The director is Vladimir Petrovich Kozlov, a Gorbachev democrat. They're anxious to meet you. I'll translate. I want you to meet a great friend of mine, Fridrikh Igorevich Firsov, head of publications of the Comintern archive—a great scholar and a great man. He's come under attack in the archive because of his anticommunist views and possibly because he's Jewish. His mother was Jewish. It's disgraceful. And you have to meet Andrei Konstantinovich Sokolov, one of the few truly progressive historians in Moscow."

Jeff said all this as if in one breath as we darted through alleyways, up staircases, through underpasses, and along sidewalks that had as much as six inches of ice on them.

"Everyone is unhealthy here. Everyone smokes. People get old earlier than in the States. Did you give Mariana the salami?"

In fact, I hadn't. Giving my host a salami as if it were a care package seemed a hopelessly awkward thing to manage, particularly without being able to offer any kind of explanation. I had given her a bottle of whiskey, however, and a box of chocolates, which she accepted without comment.

"It's okay," Jeff assured me. "I'll take care of that. Remember the most important thing is to show respect. Listen. Learn from them. Their physical circumstances are poor, but many are great scholars."

Militiamen in army fatigues with submachines slung over their shoulders stood on almost every corner, while officers in wide-brimmed military hats and greatcoats strode past, mixing with ordinary pedestrians in a way I had never seen in any American city. The faces of the young recruits maneuvering through the streets around the Kremlin area had something wolflike, ravenous, and skittish about them.

We approached the Central Party Archive from a side street, amid the congestion of cars and trucks. *Militsiya* stood with submachine guns in front of every government building. Three high gray pilasters separated three panels of windows at the front of the boxlike structure fronting Bolshaya Dmitrovka Street. Above the pilasters, resting upon a red lintel and embossed on rectangular blocks of black granite, the images of Marx, Engels, and Lenin gazed into the distance, while at eye level on the left-hand corner of the building's front entrance, a poster of a Nepalese or Tibetan beauty wrapped in colorful traditional headress and robes gazed out at the viewer with hypnotic eyes. The poster contained no text.

The guard checked our passports, visas, and *propusk* (entry permit) and signaled that we could go up for our meeting. At the top of a short flight of stairs, a white stone Lenin sat at ease on a dais in a dimly lit, slightly recessed, but central space in the corridor leading to the elevators. With one leg crossed over the other, this youthful Lenin leans forward watchfully, modest, yet charged with energy—patiently yet keenly peering over the heads of everyone who comes to his archive as if to challenge them with a question: *Can you see what I can see?*

In one of his marvelous stories, Andrei Platonov captured the essence of that challenge when he wrote of "the great worldwide hope which had now become the central idea of their still-small lives which had had no clear goal or purpose before the civil war" that had followed the revolution. Lenin's quiet but firm, private but public gaze would give the people this purpose. He would show them the way toward that "great worldwide hope." At Lenin's feet was a small glass vase of fresh violets.

Over the next ten years, the same small vase of violets was there every time I arrived. About five years ago the fresh flowers were changed to plastic. Today they are gone. Throughout Soviet history and particularly over the tumult of these last sixteen years, this archive has undergone its own transformations. Originally founded in the 1920s as the Institute of Marxism-Leninism, in the 1930s it was renamed the Institute of Marx, Engels, Lenin, and Stalin; but after Khrushchev's Secret Speech in 1956, Stalin's name was removed; in the 1980s, it became The Central Party archive and in 1991 became The Russian Center for the Preservation of Documents of Contemporary History (RTsKhIDNI); in 1999 it became The Russian State Archive of Social and Political History (RGASPI). Throughout all these changes, Lenin's searching expression has not altered. Does he await a return to his rule, as the remnants of the royal family in exile did after the revolution of 1917? Yet his exile is an odd one, for he has inhabited precisely the same space since he was first installed there in 1981—a replica of another statue of Lenin in the archive's rear, outer courtyard.

Though this Lenin with eyes like an eagle is now in exile in his own house like Tsar Nicholas II before him, he has not been exiled from the hearts and minds of millions of Russians, whether they still derive their "clear goal or purpose" from him or not. Fewer and fewer do, and soon enough children will be born who will know his name only from text books. Already, on one side of the entrance to the archive, which in 1992 was an empty, drafty, gray reception space, is a shop selling photocopiers, something Lenin surely had not foreseen. On the other side of the entrance, a bookstore now sells a wide variety of history books from many publishers, many of which contain documents stored in the archive. The archive must rent this space to pay for its heat and light. But in 1992, neither the photocopier outlet nor the book kiosk existed, and the dank, unheated entrance reminded me of the abandoned hangars at Sheremetyevo. The great archive of Lenin was not alone. At another archive, the director reached into the top drawer of her desk, took out a bulb, stood on a chair, and screwed the bulb into the fixture in order to turn on the lights.

After some hesitation at the elevators—there were two and it wasn't clear which of them worked—the three of us—Jeff, Nikolai, and I—squeezed into the small lift, and then realized we didn't know which button to push. We knew to go to the third floor, but the elevator showed two number 2s—the sequence being 2, 2, 3. Either the first 2 was a 1, or the 3 was a 4 with an unmarked "one" as a kind of subbasement. In the end, we pressed 3 and found ourselves on the correct floor when the black square of the elevator button snapped back and the lift came to a jarring halt.

We went down a dimly lit corridor carpeted with what were once fine oriental runners. There were private offices on one side; each bore the name of its occupant on a ruby red plastic plate with gold lettering. Several of the oak doors were sealed with a three- or four-inch piece of thread embedded in red wax and drawn across the crack between door and frame, a method of security that must have been left over from the 1930s. The colorful carpet down the otherwise empty hallway was worn through in many spots, and the stale smell of Moscow I had first encountered at Mariana's pervaded the entire building.

Various archivists and their assistants had assembled in the anteroom to the director's office. Two secretaries were at their desks opposite each other at the far end. Each desk had two rotary telephones—one white and one black—along with large manual typewriters. On the wall under the clock that read five o'clock, although it was eleven, was a large wall calendar for 1992 with Tuesday, January 10, framed by a sliding plastic marker. Above the dates was a picture of a Russian village girl in traditional peasant dress carrying water from a well as her bright-eyed suitor watches with a carefree smile on his handsome, symmetrical face.

"This is Fridrikh Igorevich Firsov," said Jeff, introducing me to a man in a gray Soviet suit. What made such a suit "Soviet" I could never identify precisely, but it was a combination of cheap fabric, washed-out colors, old-fashioned, wide lapels, and a cut that was always slightly too big or too small. "Professor Firsov is a very great scholar and is head of publications of the Comintern archive."

"Ochen priyatno," I said, reaching out my hand and repeating what I had been told to say. Firsov shook my hand warmly. Bald, about my own height, he had penetrating almond-shaped eyes and wide, expressive lips.

"Ochen priyatno, ochen priyatno," he repeated.

"He wishes to cooperate. Fridrikh Igorevich will do everything he can," Jeff said under his breath, bending close to my ear. "We have to build this project from the bottom up. This is the place to start. With sufficient pressure from below, the administration will come around to what we propose. He has the goods on Stalin and the Comintern."

As we waited, unidentified people came and went from the room, and I had the distinct impression of being on display: *So this is what they look like*, the darting glances seemed to say.

A severe middle-aged lady glared at the floor without acknowledging Firsov, Burds, or me as she passed by and then disappeared into a closed room to the right. Nikolai stood by impassively, as though everything were going according to schedule.

"S. Firsov's boss, a Stalinist. She's not happy with all this. But we'll deal with it. Firsov's confident she can be contained," Burds assured me. "We're waiting for Kozlov. Maybe she went in to get him."

A moment later, a tall, middle-aged man with brown hair came through the door S. had entered, dressed in a suit and tie. Beside him was a shorter, younger man with coal-black hair and wide, observant, black eyes. Everyone waited. The tall man beckoned us inside.

"Kozlov," Jeff whispered to me. "It's important he's here." Vladimir Petrovich Kozlov, formerly the director of the Central Party Archive, had just been appointed deputy director of the entire Federal Archival Service of Russia, known as Rosarkhiv.

On one end of the room was a desk piled high with papers; on the other was a closed door above which hung a portrait of Lenin with the look of a kindly if strict teacher who would correct your mistakes, as opposed to the statue in the foyer downstairs, in which he seemed to peer searchingly into the hearts and minds of the people. There were many Lenins.

I was motioned to be seated in the middle of the the long table in the center of the room. The seating was significant, but I didn't at first know why. Though the most powerful man present, Vladimir Kozlov did not occupy the middle seat across from me. Instead, he sat one or two places to my left. The younger man with black hair took his place opposite me, but clearly waited for some signal to begin the proceedings. Jeff sat to my left opposite Firsov; Nikolai to my right opposite a younger man with a notepad. As we were getting settled, I took out my pack of Winstons and lit a cigarette. My counterpart across the table did the same. I smiled and slid my pack across to him. He took it after a moment, withdrew a cigarette, and started to push the pack back toward me. I held up my hand and shook my head. So he pushed his own cigarettes toward me instead. The transaction was complete, and everyone but Firsov had a cigarette in his mouth. Since neither Jeff nor I smoked, our side was relatively clear, while the other was soon engulfed in thick haze.

After another moment or two, Kozlov began to speak in Russian. Jeff translated for me. The government of Russia, Kozlov said, hoped that we had entered a new period of cooperation and understanding with the United States, a period of openness and truthfulness; in short, that a new historical epoch was being inaugurated. A sign of this was the willingness of the new Russian leadership to explore the archives of the Soviet Union and to enable foreign researchers and publishers to make use of the materials they found there to establish a true historical record. Such work, he emphasized, must be done in a purely scholarly, disinterested, and balanced way, without the prejudices and the simple black-and-white formulations of the Cold War. In this spirit, Kozlov welcomed Yale University Press to the archive and looked forward to fruitful discussions. He paused.

I felt the need to respond, but had no speech prepared, no vision to unfold. I began with no clear end in sight but understood that I had to say something. I spoke in English and Jeff translated. After thanking Kozlov for welcoming me and Yale University Press, I expressed the hope that our discussions would be productive and I wanted to explain why I had come. Like all of us around the table, I said, I had grown up under the sign of the Cold War; I had hid under my desk as a child in fear of a nuclear attack from an unknown enemy; I had watched on television the U.S. and Soviet ships off the coast of Cuba in their fateful standoff; I had gone to bed many nights fearful of the invisible particles of radiation raining down on us continually from the skies from our atom bomb testing; I had protested the Vietnam War and had spent a night in prison as a consequence; as a child, I had ridden the bus to school every morning trying to make out the import of the words, "We will bury you," that were printed on an advertisement for the United Nations along with a picture of a small, round man standing at a podium with one fist raised as if in anger. Yet his expression was not unkindly. Why would he wish to bury us, and would he? These were the questions I wrestled with as I rode the school bus every morning. I had grown up listening to my father's record of the Red Army Chorus and had marched around our apartment to their glorious melodies. People who could sing such songs, I thought, could not possibly be my enemy. I had studied Russian in college in part to read Tolstoy and Dostoevsky but principally because I wanted to learn the lyrics of the Red Army Chorus songs. Now I had come to Moscow with the hope that we could negotiate in good faith and reach an understanding that would enrich both sides of the table.

I may have gone on too long, but I wished to make clear that for me this was not simply a business deal: it was a quest for understanding an enigma that was not a set of academic or political questions but the context of my life experience and that of my generation of Americans. How little I understood what drove my hosts on the other side of the table. How facile my account of the traumas of my generation must have seemed to those who had been touched by the terror of the 1930s, the monumental sacrifices of World War II, in which 20 million Russians had died, the so-called stagnation of the 1970s and 1980s, the exhilaration and deep despair that followed upon the "collapse" and loss of empire. To me, this experience had come through the media. To them, it had come like a whirlwind.

When I had concluded, Vladimir Petrovich stood up and announced that he had to leave for a meeting in the Kremlin, but that Oleg Vladimirovich Naumov, the recently appointed acting director of the archive in the wake of Kozlov's transfer to Rosarkhiv, would carry our discussions further. Fridrikh Firsov and others watched anxiously as Kozlov departed and the table rearranged itself to prepare for what would follow. But what would follow? The cigarette exchange had eased a moment of awkwardness, but suddenly I realized I needed more than cigarettes, Jack Daniel's, or memories of the Cold War. Before me lay a blankness I would have to fill.

The silence was broken when Naumov, the dark-haired man seated across from me, asked in Russian what an American publishing contract might consist of. Jeff continued to translate, and I suggested that perhaps it would be a good idea to begin with a description of the kinds of projects I was interested in and which I thought, after consulting with American specialists, might prove of general interest in the United States:

The Great Terror of the 1930s

The church and the revolution

The Comintern and the repressions of the 1930s

Daily life through the letters of peasants and workers of the 1920s

Daily life through the letters of peasants and workers in the 1930s

These were the topics Jeff, Nikolai, and I had discussed the evening before, though I had heard of such treasures as the diary of Georgi Dimitrov and possibly a new collection of previously secret materials on Lenin. How would such projects be managed? Naumov asked. I knew from my preliminary discussions with scholars in the United States that the Soviet archives were vast, with many hundreds of millions of files; each file might contain hundreds of documents, and each document might contain hundreds of pages. So I had envisioned that Yale would sponsor teams of researchers under the direction of both an American and a Russian scholar to go into the archives and find all the materials thought relevant to a particular topic. These would then be sifted through for the most important documents. Of the thousands so chosen, perhaps a hundred would be published in any given volume. Each document would then be carefully annotated and set in its historical context, and the whole would be framed with an essay on Soviet history by a noted scholar.

Naumov asked whether we might consider adding another project to the list, something already fairly far along on the Russian side. Would we perhaps be interested in the letters of

Stalin and Molotov from the late 1920s to the mid-1930s? I jumped at this. Of course, we would be.

After considerable discussion of the nature of the projects, how the research teams would be assembled, and the need to keep the list open-ended so that we could add to it as the project went along, I thought it time to return to the subject of how the deal might be structured and what a university press might be able to offer the archive and the researchers.

This would be a scholarly project, not a commercial one. Some of the books might sell five thousand to ten thousand copies; some might sell no more than five hundred or a thousand. We must therefore treat individual titles in different ways. The standard terms of a university contract . . . I paused as I noticed a burst of attention at the word "contract." What sort of contract? Naumov wished to know.

Thinking quickly, I suggested there would need to be different contracts. I took out a piece of paper and began scribbling terms for one contract with the archive; and then another with the editors of each volume, both American and Russian; and yet a third with the researchers. The editors would have their own contract? Yes, I said, of course. Here's what it would look like, I said, holding up the folded sheet of paper I'd been writing on and passing it across to Naumov.

Whoever does the work must be paid for it. And the researchers, too? Absolutely. And how would you pay them? The researchers according to their work, the archive for the right to publish. People would be paid in stages as work was completed. And then I said something that I think also caught their attention: the Russian editor would be paid the same amount as the American. And how much would that be?

This brought me back to my kitchen conversation with Mariana: the difference between *mnogo* ("a lot") and *malo* ("a little"), but now I couldn't weigh the teaspoon on my finger. I outlined the maximum I thought Yale University Press could afford, split three or four ways: the archive, two editors, up to six researchers, a translator—the lion's share of which would go to the archive. The sums I offered the editors seemed palatable, I believe, because I stressed that the Russian and American editors would receive a joint contract and equal pay. Whether *mnogo* or *malo*, it was *something*. Plus, I said that the press would pay for travel to the United States for consultation by the Russian editor and travel to Moscow for the American. We would also pay for photocopying, paper, toner, and shipping costs. In the end, we also paid for photocopying equipment and computers.

In the back of my mind expenses were adding up and I had no firm commitments for funding any part of this, except an informal promise from George Soros, with whom I had been in touch in 1991, for a modest amount of seed money. At this moment, the entire project could have gone out like a candle. What sustained it was the conviction shared by the heads of the archives and Yale that the value of publishing these documents was greater than the money it would take to publish them or the revenue we might realize from their sale, that these documents possessed *essential* historical value that was not simply academic or commercial. They were somehow at the center of what gave us a shared life in the twentieth century and would take us further toward understanding that life than any other means in our possession. Not science, not the books already in our libraries, not philosophical, economic, or sociological speculation, not memoirs or psychology or the study of political systems could advance our understanding of the heart of Soviet communism, with the same power and scope, detail and penetration, as these documents when set in context and fully annotated.

At the beginning, many researchers and journalists were searching for the smoking-gun document that explained everything, that set everything straight, provided the key insight, the missing, secret detail. Such smoking guns were rare, almost nonexistent. They had to be.

Kafka's Josef K found such a document in *The Trial*, when he bribed the custodian's wife to allow him to read the secret books that the judges had been studying throughout the course of his trial. He expected to discover the charges of which he was accused or some clue as to their reasoning. Instead, he found

> an indecent picture. . . . A man and a woman were sitting naked on a divan; the obscene intention of the artist was obvious, but his ineptitude was so great that in the end there was nothing to be seen but a man and woman, emerging far too corporeally from the picture.

" 'So these are the law books they study,' said K. 'I'm to be judged by such men.' "

The obscene secrets of power K discovered seemed to anticipate the discovery made seven or eight years ago, when an archivist working in RTsKhIDNI came across a cache of caricatures and obscene cartoons drawn by members of the Politburo usually during official meetings, ridiculing, provoking, or lambasting each other. Many of the best are by Bukharin; one bears Stalin's caption; many are viciously sardonic; some are pornographic and outright sadistic.

Perhaps the most grisly is a cartoon, dated April, 5, 1930, of N. P. Bryukhanov, former People's Commissar of Finances, who was shot in 1938. Stalin writes: "To the members of the PB [Politburo]. For all the sins, past and present, hang Bryukhanov by the balls. If the balls hold out, consider him acquitted by trial. If they do not hold, drown him in the river. I St."

One of the last is dated February 1937, with a caption that reads "At the Dead End." It depicts a murderous scene. G. L.Piatakov (1890–1937) and Lev Kamenev (1883–1936), risen from the dead (both had already been shot), are pointing fingers at two lynxlike figures with the heads of Nikolai Bukharin (1888–1938) and A. I. Rykov (1881–1938). At the top of Bukharin's erect tail twirls a swastika. A swastika is also drawn on the ground before a crowd that enters what is clearly a prison yard, holding the banner: "The School of Bukharin." The entire country was, in the words of K, "to be judged by such men" as drew these caricatures. Eventually, they judged each other. Both Rykov and Bukharin were shot in 1938. The word *tupik*, or "dead end," had a resonance the artist, V. Mezhlauk, could not have known. In the drawing it referred to Bukharin, Rykov, and their followers; from this distance it might well refer to the entire system that had reached a dead end.

The obscenities in the secret books of Josef K's judges and the secret cartoons of the Soviet Politburo reflected the betrayals that were an accepted feature of daily life under Stalin and that included relations between fathers and sons, mothers and daughters, husbands and wives, friends, lovers, bosses and employees, teachers and students, chitchat on the street, and the Sunday-morning banter among friends. But it also included the invented worlds of Soviet intelligence. In 1950, Lammot DuPont was named by Stalin's secret police as a conspirator, along with his brother, Pierre DuPont, President Truman, General Omar Bradley, and others in a plot to launch a nuclear strike against the Soviet Union. The plot was largely an invention of the MGB, the forerunner of the KGB, at Stalin's behest. Stalin's purpose was to intensify cold war tensions and push the United States into a nuclear confrontation with the Soviet Union. The fact that Lammot DuPont had died in 1884 meant nothing to those concocting this conspiracy. When the head of the MGB informed Stalin that the forced testimony of their principal witness in this affair was "difficult to believe" (because it had been coerced and patched together like Frankenstein's monster), Stalin declared that "one could expect anything from the Americans, and therefore if the confessions . . . are unconvincing, then . . . the MGB must make them convincing for the trial."

Stalin died before the plot could be fully set in motion, and after his death nearly everyone involved was either imprisoned or shot. But before March 1, 1953, when Stalin was found unconscious on the floor of his dacha, the world—and particularly Soviet Jews—had braced for another period of repression that would have included arrests, trials, executions, deportations, and setting the country on a war footing with the United States. How did *this* obscenity make its way into the "normal" world? How was it ingested into the consciousness of the people and normalized, such that many arrests had already been made, executions ordered and fulfilled, and purges undertaken by March 1953?

Fridrikh Firsov once said to me that he assumed most documents to be false until he could corroborate them from other sources. Building up this base of source material had to become the overriding ambition of our project, rather than searching for the single explosive document, which in most cases would turn out to be just another indecent amusement such as the "law books" K found in the judges' chambers. Neither Oleg Naumov nor I had any idea, as we sat together at the long oak table in his office, what picture of Soviet history would emerge from our collaboration, but I think we both suspected it would be one that Lenin, gazing down from his portrait on the wall, would likely not approve of.

"Here's what a publishing contract looks like," I said, enumerating the parts: the grant of rights, the royalties, the advance, the number of words in the book, the delivery date, and some other peripheral matters. I mentioned that the royalties would determine the size of the advance in conjunction with the price of the book and the discount at which it would be sold to customers. I had jotted all this down on a sheet of paper using two different models: specialized academic works with limited print runs; and works for a more general readership. After much clarification about the nature of royalties and how they would be paid, Naumov asked for the piece of paper, which I gladly handed him. He said that they would consider all this among themselves and that I should come back tomorrow for further discussion. We shook hands and I gave Naumov the bottle of Jack Daniel's.

On the street, Jeff was extremely animated. Endless possibilities. Pikhoia was next, but how to get through to him? Then there was the big archive of the Russian Federation—Romanov materials. If we couldn't get in to see Pikhoia, we'd be missing a step. By tomorrow the news would be all over Moscow—wait and see. By tomorrow everyone would know about our meeting. Everybody would know about a "royalty" and contracts for the researchers as well as the archive.

Why was this such a big deal? I asked. In Soviet times, Nikolai explained, the author would be paid a flat fee and then all other profits would go to the publisher—whether it sold a million copies or a thousand. They stole everything. Nobody got anything for his own work.

Pikhoia will know soon enough, Jeff jumped in. Probably from Kozlov. We must try. All this was conveyed in bursts, almost telegraphically. Nikolai would manage the meeting for tomorrow in the Central Party Archive (now RTsKhiDNI—an acronym nobody liked)—but Pikhoia? Perhaps, thought Nikolai—*mozhet byt'*. Generations of Russian archivists, Jeff assured me, would see that piece of paper on which I scribbled the outline of a business contract with the word "royalty."

"It's already part of the archive," Jeff said, and in the next breath moved on to Firsov. "You have to see Firsov. He'll come to the apartment, or we'll go to his. Mariana's a wonderful woman, but she needs help"—Jeff would help her, no need for me to worry about that. No need to get involved, in any case. He had to work this out with Mariana herself. Work out what? I had no idea.

Jeff circled back to the archive. Kozlov was there. *Kozlov.* Pikhoia is in with Yeltsin, but Kozlov's the rising star. Everybody knows that. It wasn't certain he'd be there. Not at all. It meant something. All the senior archivists were there. There's definite interest, but we had to work fast. Germans and Italians are snooping around. Even some Japanese. But the Japanese know nothing and are satisfied with trinkets. And the Germans and Italians are research institutes. Yale's the only real publisher right now. But who knows? If we stick with the archivists, push up from below, make them believe in the project as we do, we can make something stick, even without money. Pressure from below and recognition at the top. But we have to act fast. You never know and there are rumors about the Hoover Institution and the English publisher, Chadwyck-Healey. But those would be microfilm deals. Huge, but not books. They have money, lots of money. There's talk about big deals—but whoever sees the money? There's endless gossip. And then the nationalists are claiming the archives are the national treasures of Russia, its legacy—and the foreigners are coming in to steal everything. We have to protect Yale from this. Their venom will be directed mainly at Hoover, no question about that. Firsov is vital. Goodwill is vital. Clearly defined goals. Personal relationships. *Znakomstvo.* The meeting was a success all the way around. No question. Remember this word, *znakomstvo*, Jeff told me. It means "acquaintance," but it actually stands for much more: not only who you know but who knows you. It stands for the relationships that bind together a community of interests.

Chapter 4

Mariana, Continued

When Jeff and I returned to Mariana's apartment it was already dark. She looked me over from head to toe before letting us in, as though fearful that some essential piece might be missing. She questioned Jeff closely.

"She wants to know if you wore your hat."

"Da, da," I said, pleased that I had remembered to put it on before coming upstairs.

Jeff took the large end of a kolbasa wrapped in paper from his briefcase and handed it to Mariana.

Without taking it, she turned and walked into the kitchen. Jeff followed, holding the kolbasa in front of him. I heard raised voices. She was critical and unhappy.

"What's the problem?" I asked when Jeff returned still holding the kolbasa.

"She's insulted," Jeff said. "I didn't want to insult her, but she thinks I'm treating her as if she were poor. She told me to leave. She didn't want charity."

Mariana did not return from the kitchen. Calling out his deep apologies, Jeff put the kolbasa back in his briefcase and left.

Once he was gone, Mariana began coughing, almost choking in the kitchen. Her eyes were filled with tears. Her breathing was labored. She patted her throat.

"Lekarstvo, lekarstvo," I insisted. *"Gdye?"*

"Vot," she said, pointing to a small dish on the kitchen table. Sure enough, the two small red Sudafed pills were where she had put them in the morning.

"No, no, no, Mariana. You must take them, take them. Swallow." I gulped. "Medicine, *lekarstvo*. Please. *Pozhalusta*."

She gave the pills a dismissive glance and began speaking rapidly. I made out the word for doctor but little else. She began to cough again in short, hacking bursts. *"Chai? Vodka?"* she asked. *"Vodka?"*

I nodded and sat down. I distinctly thought I heard her say something like *labadan*, but no one I have asked since ever heard of such vodka. The darkish bottle had no label and seemed to have some sort of leaf in it, or perhaps she told me that the color was from the leaves in which the vodka fermented. The tea-colored liquid she poured into a small glass had a sharp, almost bitter taste. Nevertheless, I drank it eagerly. It hit like a trap springing shut inside me, while releasing something light and thin, a silken ribbon that spiraled upward to my head. A quiet warmth, unfamiliar yet somehow intimate, pervaded my body and spread instantly to the farthest reaches of my limbs. It was my first vodka in Russia. "Djonatan," Mariana said cheerfully, but watching me closely from the stove where she was heating something in a saucepan. "Djonatan."

"Da?"

"Kak yabloko," she said.

"Apple?"

She nodded.

"Yes," I answered. "Like the apple."

Mariana was very pleased with her joke, saying she could remember my name because I was an apple.

"Kushat'," she urged as she ladled the contents of her saucepan out onto my plate.

I gratefully ate the rice mixed with bits of onion and colorless pieces of what seemed like hot dogs with the unexpectedly light fork and knife that came from a drawer in Mariana's kitchen, but also from a past I thought had vanished forever but which now seemed to be winding itself around me with the vodka's silken ribbon. A past that was not past and not present. A past that was in the tender swelling under Mariana's jaw, in the fine touch of her fingers, in the eyes—the color of her *labadan*—that peered as if from the crack of a door. I thought ruefully of Jeff's kolbasa as I picked the pale bits of former hot dogs out of the oily rice, remedying the blandness with another shot of vodka and a piece of aromatic black bread called Borodinsky, flavored with coriander. There were no napkins at the table, but I managed to extract a Kleenex from my pocket and wipe my hands while Mariana's back was turned.

After tea and a plate of hard, almost tasteless, star-shaped cookies, we said good night. I retired to my room, but couldn't sleep. *Ne rabotai byez upora* spun around in my head before a wild stream of incomprehensible Russian broke through like an endless flow of cars and trucks through a tunnel. What awaited me the following day, I could not imagine, and I drifted back to the morning at the curb, hailing a taxi to take me to Ploshchad Revolutsii, with masses of dull-colored people surging from all sides toward the trolleybuses that creaked and moaned along Kutuzovsky Prospect, and feeling again that my heart seemed lifted up as on the point of a sword.

Chapter 5

The Little Man

We found each other easily on Revolution Square the following morning and Jeff told me excitedly that he'd spoken with Nikolai, who confirmed that word of our meetings had indeed already gotten around the archives and now I would have appointments at the largest of the federal archives—GARF, the State Archive of the Russian Federation—as well as at RGAE, the Russian State Archive of Economy, and perhaps one other if it could be quickly arranged. The KGB couldn't see me this time, but might the next. I would be leaving on Sunday, but how many days away that was I couldn't have said. Today was not a day. It was an action, a task. Sunday seemed irrelevant—a million miles away. As for Pikhoia, Nikolai was still trying to arrange a meeting, but this involved at least a day's wait for the *propusk* and visa clearance.

"Here," Jeff said, "I brought you something. I think you'll be interested." He put a copy of *Russkoe Voskresenie* (Russian Resurrection) in my hand.

"What is this?" I asked, staring at the cover. I'd never seen anything like it. The cartoon could have appeared in *Der Stuermer* from the 1930s. It included a caricature of a man with a long tail, a hooked Semitic nose, bulging eyes, and rapacious three-fingered hands holding a leash with two leads: one attached to a collar around a beastlike figure on all fours with the head of Boris Yeltsin; the other attached to a collar around a similar figure with the head of Mikhail Gorbachev—both eerily portrayed like the lynx figures in the 1937 caricatures of Bukharin and Rykov. The devilish Jew holding the leash is dressed in the Stars and Stripes. In the top right-hand corner of the front page is a boxed caption that reads: "'When government power uses all the means at its disposal to lead the entire nation to destruction, then it is not only the right, but it is the responsibility of every son of the nation to revolt.'Adolf—Hitler, *Mein Kampf.*" Inside the six-page issue is a long article on the relations between Hitler and Stalin, explaining that in fact they had many shared values, that Hitler was a man of the highest morality, and that they would never have gone to war with each other had the Jews not dragged them both into it.

"You can pick this up and many like it in just about any kiosk in the metro," Jeff said, reading my mind. "Here's something else you'll want." Jeff held up a copy of *The Protocols of the Elders of Zion*. I'd never seen it before in any language.

"Isn't this illegal?"

"You can buy it right outside the Kremlin. It's Russian democracy. It's the other side of the liberation." The edition bore a prefatory note by Henry Ford.

Nikolai drove us to GARF, some twenty minutes from the center. Again the streets were clogged with military trucks blowing exhaust into the windows of passenger cars, and again at every stop Nikolai turned off the ignition and dimmed his lights. Gasoline fumes and exhaust filled the car. My throat was cracked and I felt dizzy. When we got to the Moscow River Bridge, I felt sick. The arches and railings of the bridge still bore festive strings of lights to mark the Old New Year, like an old lady dressed up for her birthday, but forgotten by her children. Litter from last night's revels was strewn across the walkway and unlit bulbs hung limply from their electric cords.

According to Jeff, GARF would be an important source of materials on the social history of Soviet Russia—letters from the countryside, activities of outlying village soviets, as well as materials on the revolution itself. Sergei Vladimirovich Mironenko was a historian, very affable. He spoke some English and would be sure to want to explore any interesting possibilities; but you had to remember, he wouldn't take a step without the participation of the former Central Party Archive (RTsKhIDNI). Of course he knew everything already about the meeting with Kozlov. That was huge. That Kozlov stayed—my God, you had no idea what an impression it made on people. It meant, well, it meant they were interested. No, intrigued. It meant that they were seriously considering it and this would go all the way up to the ministerial level. That's why the meeting with Pikhoia was vital. Even so, we had to work below the radar as much as possible. Pikhoia's wife worked for Yeltsin. Some said she was his mistress.

"Nikolai," Jeff asked in Russian. "What do you think?"

"*Normalno,*" Nikolai answered, gripping the steering wheel and staring straight ahead into the gray morning. "*Vsyo normalno.*"

"What's that?" I asked.

"Everything's normal. You have nothing to worry about."

GARF is not a building, but a compound; corridors link various repositories and offices surround a courtyard with multiple entrances and passageways. The mazelike configuration required that we walk from the car through what appeared to be a vacant and frozen garden with birch trees and empty benches to an unidentifiable, narrow ramp more suitable for a warehouse shipping complex than one of the most important archives of the history of the Soviet Union going back to imperial times. After opening the door and checking with those inside, we discovered we were at the wrong spot and had to go back around to a door that felt like a neglected rear entrance.

The grimy façade of the building was badly pock-marked in many places where the plaster had worn off or been eaten away; inside, we immediately came into a small, drafty guard station where an Interior Ministry officer with a submachine gun at his waist asked for our documents. Two others stood on either side. He looked me over carefully and told us to wait. *Amerikanets?* he asked. Nikolai explained our business. No *propusk* had come down from the director's office. Nikolai explained that Mironenko was expecting us. He may be expecting you, the guard answered, but without the *propusk* we could not pass. Call him, the guard advised. Who is this American? He's here to see Mironenko about publishing. Call him. Nikolai got on the phone in a nearby alcove. After several minutes, he returned and said the secretary would come right down, and I couldn't tell whether the guard, a young man with a splotchy red face, was pleased or displeased at the result.

Soon we were being ushered by a young woman through narrow hallways in which the pastel blue paint had long ago faded, chipped, and cracked, up dusty flights of stairs, around corners, through unlit offices of some sort with many closed doors on all sides but without the red placards and the formal carpeting of the Central Party Archive. No portraits of Lenin or busts of Marx and Engels guarded our way. No scowling archivists bustled around us.

After numerous twists and turns, we came out into a hallway with a large office at one end. Both the interior and exterior of the building had an unfinished appearance, as though caught in the middle somewhere between being remodeled and falling apart. The same smell of Moscow was here. It was everywhere. It seemed to inhere in the material objects rather than surround them.

I had never quite thought of places having smells. On my father's farm in Wisconsin, there is the smell of Lake Superior and the pine forests, the smell of the horses and the land after a rain; in New York, there is sometimes a sweet smell in early morning with a bright sun or the stink of sewage or garbage left on the curb or the particular odor of a particular apartment building. But here in Moscow, the smell was not like this. It didn't emanate from any one source, or even from multiple sources; it wasn't the smell of the sewage system or the river or car exhaust or smog that had settled in. It was not smell of anything in the refrigerator; it was the smell of the refrigerator itself.

When we entered the office, the young woman asked us to please sit down and take off our coats. The director would be with us shortly. In a moment, a large, amiable, dark-haired man with a powerful handshake led us into his office. Sergei Vladimirovich Mironenko is an energetic, ambitious figure, a scholar in his own right and now a television personality. I found him instantly welcoming, warm, and personable. Seated at the table in his office, so crammed with boxes and files that there was hardly room for a visitor, was his deputy director, Vladimir Alexandrovich Kozlov—no relation to the former head of the Central Party Archive. Kozlov could speak English and was working on modern Soviet history, while Mironenko's area was the late imperial period.

The feeling here was more relaxed and Mironenko made no speeches. After some preliminary discussion, he asked his assistant to bring in tea and cookies. I explained as best I could my interest in Russian history and culture and in the Soviet period. He had heard that we had sketched out three or four projects with RTsKhIDNI and would like an equal number with his archive. I was eager to oblige, but didn't know what his archive might contain that would be suitable. Might I be interested in the documents connected to the fate of the Romanov family and the last tsar? he wondered.

Was there anything of interest still to know about the subject? I asked. Nobody has ever read all the tsar's letters to his wife; nobody has read the depositions of the man who shot the tsar and his family; nobody has ever seen the tsaritsa's last diary; nobody has ever seen all the documentation about the execution, including Lenin's telegram stating that the tsar and his family were safe and sound that he sent just before the execution. There was much here that might well answer the question of whether Lenin ordered the execution, whether the tsar was the weak and effeminate leader he had been made out to be—and whether the *entire* family had been shot or whether Anastasia had somehow miraculously escaped.

Twenty years before, in 1972, just home from college, I had horrified my girlfriend with my conviction that the tsar and his family—yes, even those pretty young girls and his helpless, hemophiliac son—deserved to be executed for the crimes they and all they represented had committed against the people of Russia, against the Jews, against humanity, reason, justice, and truth. When conditions become intolerable you must take action. It was his own fault that his beautiful family perished. It was his fault that he allowed himself to be pushed around by his dominating wife and the grotesque fraud Rasputin; it was his fault and the fault of his advisers and his heritage that enslaved Russia rose up justifiably against them for the sake of universal ideas of equality and justice. It was the fault of the capitalist masters that indigent servants and slaves lived without the basic necessities of life. But they killed the children, my girlfriend protested in tears, and the children were innocent. Innocent! Innocent! I'd heard enough of that. Nobody is innocent—or everybody is. They lived a life of privilege and took full advantage of their papa's wealth, prestige, and power. They were beautiful but imperious—all of them. They had to go. Pity, as I had learned from Dante, is a dangerous emotion. It draws you into the sins of others. Pity eats out your heart and compromises all principles. You must be pitiless to change. You must have no pity. You must "reach for the shoemaker's knife" in your boot, as Mayakovsky put it in *The Cloud in Trousers*, when the laws of your character and history require it.

"This is the most complete set of documents anywhere in the world," Mironenko was saying. "I think you will find this interesting. Call down Khrustalyov," he instructed his assistant, the young woman who had brought us up and now sat at the end of the table, taking notes.

"Khrustalyov has devoted his life to these documents," Kozlov said. "They are his life. He knows more about the royal family and what happened to them than anyone in the world."

"And he worked on these documents during Soviet times?" I asked.

"Alone, quietly, in obscurity. Yes. You'll see. He is a very specific kind of person."

"And it was tolerated by the authorities?"

Why not? Kozlov explained. As long as he published nothing, said nothing, and stayed more or less out of sight. No one paid any attention.

When he had finished speaking, we all looked around at a diminutive man framed in the doorway with a great stack of books and manuscripts in his arms. He seemed barely five feet tall. His head was completely covered in grizzled gray hair, but he had the awkward, crumpled look of a sickly child. The pile of books, albums, and folders in his outstretched arms came up to his eyes. How long he had been standing silently in the doorway nobody could tell.

Mironenko motioned him to the table, but he didn't move, like a serf at the door of his master's house. Mironenko spoke gently, coaxing him forward. As the little man limped toward the table, it became evident how great was his burden of manuscripts and books. When he got to the edge of the table he heaved them up over his eyes and slammed them down. He did not look up, and I couldn't tell if he was angry or sorrowful. His narrow beard reached below his waist; his eyes were inflamed, his lips were swollen, and the grayish skin of his face, lips, and hands were strafed with rash. His bony fingers had long, pointed nails. He wore an ill-fitting gray jacket with a narrow tie pulled slightly askew. He said nothing. When Mironenko introduced him, he bowed, but did not speak. He kept his eyes down and his hands firmly at his sides.

"You have a great collection of material," Mironenko said, encouragingly.

The gnomish little man nodded.

"And you have been working on them a long time."

He nodded again, closing his eyes, which seemed to well with tears.

"He has worked alone," Mironenko said, turning to me. "In his little office on the top floor. He has scoured all the archives and assembled everything himself. It has taken years of patient research."

The little man stood expressionless as if before an interrogator.

"This man from Yale University in the United States is interested in your work."

He nodded, but didn't take his eyes from the floor.

"He wishes to see some of the material in your files. You may show him what you have here."

His eyes flicked up at me as though I were a ghost or had come from another planet. But his brief look wasn't from another planet at all; the look in his face, in that flickering half-second, was simply from another time. I had come from the future into his past. I inhabited a zone he could not touch and dared not look at, like a beautiful woman. Nor could I touch his. He held his eyes down with stoic pride. I would disappear soon enough, but his documents would remain, his face said to me. I would pass away, but the truth was in his hands. And it was a sacred truth.

"He is very religious," Kozlov added, in his booming English, his voice coming up from the depths of his diaphragm. "This is not just history," he said, confirming what I had suspected. "This is his sacred duty. Look at him. He has nothing but this."

"Tell me what is here," I said to the little man.

Without acknowledging the request, he buried his glance deeper into the folders on the table and spoke almost inaudibly to the corner of the table near where Mironenko was sitting. He opened the cover of one large binder as Mironenko transmitted Khrustalyov's words to Jeff, who translated them for me.

"Vladimir Mikhailovich says that these documents tell the complete story of the last days of the tsar, they are the true record of his relationship with the empress, they contain materials nobody has ever seen before about the execution, how it was done, who did it, and why. If you are interested, he would be pleased to assemble the documents into a book with commentary. These letters between the tsar and the empress have never been published. Nobody knows these secrets. This is the true account of the martyring of the imperial family." Khrustalyov did not look up, but merely stepped backward toward the doorway, like a faithful steward.

"I am very interested, deeply honored that you would make such an offer, and I look forward to working with you," I responded. I explained that the terms of our discussion with the Central Party Archive were that each volume would have both an American and a Russian author. I said I would be delighted if Vladimir Mikhailovich would take this role upon himself; however, he would need to work together with an American to ensure that the final book was constructed to satisfy the needs of American and Western readers, both scholarly and general. Khrustalyov nodded without looking up. He whispered something to Mironenko, who told him to leave the materials on the table in his office for the time being. Without turning, he stepped backward across the threshold of the room and disappeared.

"He has health problems and would be grateful for some work. Now, everything costs money. How will you pay and how much?" Kozlov asked with surprising directness, and I couldn't tell if he was asking for himself or for Khrustalyov.

I said I didn't know yet—this was something I'd have to discuss with the management of Yale University Press, and in any case we needed to work out the larger terms of the contract. However, I could say that the working principle was that the American and the Russian editors would receive equal payment; researchers, if necessary, would be paid on a monthly basis for their work, and the archive would receive a royalty on the books as well as an advance. I would pay directly whoever did the work.

"Melochi," Mironenko commented dismissively. I looked at Jeff.

"Details."

"If you're truly interested, we have something of possible special value, although to be honest many people here think it of little significance. Maybe a separate publication or maybe just for the other book," Mironenko said in an offhand manner.

"What is it?" I asked.

"Volodya," Mironenko said to Kozlov. "See if the 1918 diary of the tsaritsa is here."

After some digging, it was discovered that the tsaritsa's diary was not among the materials Khrustalyov had brought down.

"Tell Vladimir Mikhailovich to bring down the diary," Mironenko directed his assistant.

After a short time, Khrustalyov again stood silently in the doorway clutching a small volume in both hands.

The small booklet—no more than four inches by six inches—was bound in a pale greenish cloth. At the top of the front cover was a reverse swastika that Kozlov quickly pointed out was an ancient Zoroastrian symbol rather than a Nazi insignia. The empress had also decorated the door frames of her house in Tobolsk with such imagery.

"What is this?" I asked.

"Open it."

When I did so, I discovered a frontispiece decorated with what I knew to be the Old Church Slavonic alphabet. Below each letter was a number. There was a dedication in English:

> To my sweet darling Mama dear with my best wishes for a happy new year. May God's blessings be upon you and guard you for ever.

> Yr own loving girl
> Tatiana
> Tobolsk. 1918
> *Gubernatorsky dom*

The diary was a gift to the empress from her daughter Tatiana. Though she was the empress of Russia, Alexandra, the granddaughter of Queen Victoria, wrote her diary in English, sometimes flawed. It begins on page 2.

On Monday, January 1, the temperature was minus four degrees celsius. At "7¼"—that is, 7:15 A.M.—Empress Alexandra Fyodorovna "got up. At 8 went to church." Her daughters Olga and Tatiana both had fevers: 37.3 and 38 degrees celsius, respectively, from German measles. The tsarevich, Aleksei, was "alright again." The empress "sat with the girls, sowing [*sic*]." Then she lunched with them in their bedroom at 12. The weather was beautiful and sunny. At "4½" (4:30 P.M.) Kolya Derevenko "also took tea" with them. At 6, she rested until 8, reading and writing. Olga's temperature went up 0.1 degrees; Tatiana's went up 0.5 degrees. At 8 she dined with her daughters. At 9, she took their temperatures again. Before bed, she played bezique with Nicholas, who then read to them while the empress knitted.

"This is all there is," Kozlov stated. "Nothing but dates, times, temperatures. Very little else." Yet there was something else—a silence in between all these dates, times, and temperatures, a silence that told more than words could of an obsessive need to note just where and when everything happened as the entire world was turning upside down. "I want it," I said. "What it doesn't say is as important as what it does. Let's put this on the list."

On January 3, the empress begins noting the date with both the old calendar and the new: January 3 is now also January 16—the Gregorian calendar, which Lenin adopted for the new Soviet state, was thirteen days ahead of the Julian—thus the oddity that the October Revolution in Russia occurred on November 7 in the rest of the world. Henceforward, every day in the empress's diary would bear both dates—old and new—as if she needed constantly to orient herself in the new time by reference to the old.

The utterly quotidian acts of caring for her ailing daughters and her constant attentions to Aleksei, taking tea, playing bezique with "N.," knitting and nightly readings unfold within these grotesque dislocations of time and space. Once the doomed family is moved from Tobolsk to Yekaterinburg to "the house of special purpose" where they would be executed, another shift occurs, duly noted by the tsaritsa:

22 May/4 June, Tuesday:
Baby [the tsarevich] slept well, but less so than the night before.

Fine, bright morning.

Baby spent the day in my room—apetite [*sic*] still not good.

The others went out in the afternoon . . .

Knee much less swollen (3 cm.) he may be carried out tomorrow.—

I had a bath at 10

Lenin gave the order that the clocks have to put [*sic*] 2 hours ahead (economy of electricity) so at 10 they told us it was 12.

"At 10 they told us it was 12." For the royal family, time truly was out of joint. Revolutionary time had overwhelmed them. It had overwhelmed all of Russia. The disjunctions and disruptions were exhilarating—as in the poems of Mayakovsky—and catastrophic—as in the ruminations of the empress. Psychologically, socially, politically, this rupture has incalculable importance in understanding all that followed. Yet in her diary, the three centimeters' difference in the swelling of the tsarevich's knee had the same significance as Lenin's order. Perhaps it had more. The centimeters measuring daily life and the millennia measuring civilizations collide here with almost unimaginable precision and power. This was not a document; it was a fossil. Time's "petty pace," signifying nothing, was etched here as if in limestone.

Not long before the execution of the tsar and his family, which took place in the early-morning hours of Tuesday/ Wednesday 3/16 – 4/17 July, 1918, Lenin received an anxious inquiry from a Danish newspaper, *National Tidende*:

Rumor here going that the exczar has been murdered.
Kindly wire facts.

At 4:00 P.M. on July 16, as the empress read spiritual literature with friends and "tatted" (embroidered), a reply was
issued:

Rumour not true exczar safe. All rumours are only lie
of capitalist press. Lenin.

Nine hours later the family members were shot and their
bodies were dumped into a mine shaft. They were covered
with corrosive lime, and the skeletons lay untouched for
almost seventy-five years until they were exhumed in the
early 1990s and identified by DNA analysis.

The image of that execution must have lacerated the heart
of Vladimir Mikhailovich Krustalyov as he assembled his
documents bit by bit over the decades, reading for himself the
murderers' own accounts of how the bullets ricocheted off
the diamonds sewn into the bodices of the grand duchesses
in the killing room; repeating for himself the tsaritsa's last
words, "What, there isn't even a chair? One isn't even allowed
to sit down?" and then as the guns were drawn, hearing the
tsar exclaim, "What? What?" as he finally understood why
the family had been hastily awakened at one o'clock in the
morning. Silently and obscurely, Khrustalyov had built for
himself and for generations to follow a picture of the true
fate of the Romanov family, with little hope that it would
ever see the light of day—a loyal servant of two masters.

Chapter 6

Mariana, Continued

When I knocked on Mariana's door around six thirty that night, the unfamiliar voice of a young woman asked who I was.

"Eto Djonatan," I said, hoping I was not at the wrong door or apartment complex.

The door opened immediately, and before me stood a well-dressed, attractive woman in her thirties with short blond hair. Papagena? I wondered. Mariana transfigured?

"Vrach," I heard the young woman say.

"Doctor?"

"Da."

Mariana's voice erupted from her bedroom and the young doctor went to see what she wanted. I took the opportunity to put my things down, shed my coat, and go to the toilet. After I turned on the light and closed the door, I noticed a difference in the small room, but couldn't make out what it was. It seemed slightly larger and brighter. When I finished, I went into the kitchen for a glass of water. Here, too, I noticed a change. At the kitchen table the night before I had rubbed my finger along a greasy film on the edge of the window while Mariana was busy at the stove. The grease was gone. I looked into the corners of the room—they were free of the dust balls and cobwebs I had seen the night before.

Who had done this bit of cleaning up? When the doctor reappeared, I asked how long she had been tending Mariana. Since around eleven was the reply. Since morning?

"*Da.*"

And Mariana? Mariana wished to see me. I went down the hall to her room and stood outside the door. I said hello through the closed door. Mariana shouted. I looked back quizzically at the doctor, who waved me forward. I should go into Mariana's room?

"*Da.*"

I cracked open the door and peeked inside. Mariana lay facedown on the bed, completely naked. She looked up hopefully and motioned me inside. As I entered, she pushed herself up with both hands from the mattress, arching her back, and gestured to close the door. She had a strong figure, well preserved. Her graying blonde hair was scattered over her naked shoulders, and her eyes were wide with expectation. The muscles tightened in her arms and stood out in taut striations on her back. When she saw my astonishment, she rose higher yet off her stomach and, shifting her weight, pointed with one hand to her back. Several large glass balls like Christmas ornaments were dangling from her skin, attached, it seemed, by some kind of suction. I drew closer. There were large, deep red spots all over her back. When she rose to an almost sitting position, the balls jingled and clinked.

In the kitchen I had noticed a large pot of water boiling on the stove with several such balls in it. At first I thought she might be canning preserves or pickles, but then the Yiddish expression came to mind: *Es hilft azai vi a taten a bankes*—"It helps as much as cupping a dead man," a phrase from a different century. These things dangling from Mariana's back were the *bankes*. *Bankes!* Once heated, these glass balls, open on one end, create a kind of vacuum when placed against the skin. They draw the blood to the surface and thereby aid circulation. As a child I had heard of these mythical objects, often in the same context as the *krysteers* (enemas) without Fels-Naptha of my father's childhood, which implied the harshest possible treatment for persisting in one's mischief. These *bankes*, once evoked only as jests or threats, were now here before me swinging from Mariana's strong back, while she beamed with pleasure at this demonstration of the power of *her* medicine. Russian medicine, as she put it. Strong medicine. From a little china cup by her bed she removed my two little red pills and held them out to me in the palm of her hand.

"*Malenki,*" she insisted—little ones. *Malo.* Of no value. Then she produced the pills her doctor had given her. Each was about an inch long and looked like pills you give a horse. This was Russian medicine. Strong. She laughed, motioning for me to take mine back.

I was speechless. I tried to show that I was thoroughly beaten. Her medicine was stronger than my medicine. Her god was stronger than mine. Mariana enjoyed her triumph. I shook my head in wonder and withdrew, not daring to turn my back.

Later, and now in her housecoat happily busying herself in her newly cleaned kitchen, she made a point of showing me how much better her breathing was, no more pain or congestion in her chest, no more swelling in her throat—and emphasized her point by placing my hand on the soft area on either side of her windpipe, just beneath her chin.

Chapter 7

Day Two in the Archive: The Only American

Through connections I was never able to discover, Nikolai managed to arrange an appointment with Pikhoia for the day after next—the day before I was to leave Moscow. "You have no idea what a coup this is," Jeff assured me. "It's ceremonial. He won't do anything that isn't already prepared. But it's a signal. It means they're interested. Maybe they'll do business. They want to find out who you are. Everybody knows the name Yale. But a lot of others have started showing up: Germans, Italians, some Japanese I've heard about, the Brits are over here, the French. Right now you're the only American. You're not commercial and they like that. That is a key, but maybe not the only one. You have to work fast."

"They don't want to make money?" I asked.

"Of course they do," Jeff answered, "but they're also afraid of it. They're happy to have it come to them but not eager to do what is necessary to get it. There's a term people are starting to use here, *delovoi*. It means someone who can deal with business affairs, but they don't really have the notion of a businessman or of making money. They understand stealing—that's what the superrich do, or the state; but making it is a very foreign idea. Most people don't even know what an office is—they don't really have a word for what we consider an 'office,' so they just use the word—*offis*—and the same goes with business—*biznes*."

I began to understand the impression I had on my journey down Kutuzovsky Prospect in the cab on my first day. There was a difference between this street and a street in North America or Europe. What was it? I began to realize that the shops along the wide boulevard were not advertised as in the West. They had no public persona or image. A shoe shop was simply "Shoes," a clothing shop was simply "Women's Clothing," a restaurant was simply *Restoran*, and so on. Nowhere could you find a Johnston's Shoes, a Saks Fifth Avenue, or a Louis' Lunch.

The absence of a person's or a private company's name denoted the line between public and private space. In 1992 this line was still observed with some precision: in the public area the private could not intrude, and nearly everything seemed public, except of course places like Mariana's bedroom. The name of an individual person or private concern was nowhere to be found in public. To offer a contract to an individual who would then also receive a royalty was somehow connected to the problem of this public space, but I did not yet clearly see how.

The anonymous quality of the public space was also in keeping with the absence of advertising along the roadways. A private face in a public place could be reserved only for government officials or the bronzed visages of great poets or statesmen. Where banners with Stalin's or Lenin's faces once dominated the skies, there was still grave uncertainty about waving a banner with that of Ronald McDonald or Colonel Sanders, let alone a private Russian merchant. It would not be easy to fill this vacuum. Public space was reserved for heroes and emblems of power. The dirty little business of making money had no place in it.

Though I had heard that a Pizza Khat had moved in somewhere and a much anticipated McDonald's had opened in 1990 in Pushkin Square and another would soon open not far away, it would not be easy to contend with the totemic presences of Pushkin, Gogol, Tolstoy, Prince Mikhail Kutuzov, hero of the War of 1812, or Prince Yuri Dolgoruky, a twelfth-century founder of Moscow who had gazed over the teeming Moscow streets since 1954. These were real people, leaders, geniuses, but who *was* Colonel Sanders or Ronald McDonald? What was their relationship to anything around them? Why were they so happy? Why was this space, once filled with images of Soviet power and Russian culture, now being threatened with flimsy images of money and pleasure? Who owned this space? Who commanded it? Who was in charge? It was disconcerting, but perversely comforting at the same time to find on my first trip down Kutuzovsky Prospect, not far from Mariana's apartment complex, the familiar but hugely magnified face of the Marlboro Man, painted over the blank side of an apartment building. In red shirt, cowboy hat, and tapaderos, lighting up a cigarette and grasping the reins of his horse, the Marlboro Man seemed irrefutable proof that the West had finally come to Russia.

The necessary *propusk* was waiting for us when we arrived at the Central Party Archive. We made our way quickly past Lenin's questioning gaze into the worried corridors of his institute, up to the anteroom of the vacant director's office on the second third floor (according to the buttons in the elevator), and then into the acting director's office, where a delegation similar to the one the day before was awaiting us, but now without Vladimir Petrovich Kozlov.

Acting Director Naumov produced the piece of paper from the earlier meeting with my explanations of royalties and discounts and asked that we go over the concept of the discount: Why was it necessary? What was it for? How did we sell our books? To whom? The principle of parity between Russian and American editors was acceptable. But how would we actually do what needed to be done? Who would do the work? How would they be paid? How would the concept of copyright apply to the work done by the editors?

When I suggested that money could be transferred by wire into personal bank accounts, the archivists opposite me looked stoically down at the table and Naumov explained that that probably would not work because no one had a bank account, the banks were unstable, nobody trusted them, and if money went into such an account there would be nothing left after the taxes were taken out. We would need to find another solution.

We discussed the idea of "rights." If we purchased certain rights, we needed to know that these would not be sold to anyone else. Could researchers not connected with the project use these materials while we were in the process of selecting them? My first answer was no, but it was clear this caused problems—or would cause problems for the "nationalists," already suspicious of foreign intruders. Russian researchers could use them. But not others? Why not? We decided on an arcane formula whereby they could research and quote from the materials for their research, but not publish the documents qua documents. But can they use 20 percent of a document in one place, and then 20 percent someplace else, and then another 20 percent, and so on? Who would do that? Who knows? But if they did . . . Okay, we'll have to figure out a way of delimiting such usage; otherwise a wily researcher could quote 100 percent of a document in five succeeding publications, thereby effectively violating our exclusive right to publish it in its entirety. There is something called fair use, I pointed out, that is universally accepted and when I returned to the United States, I would fax them a copy of the guidelines.

But with all this said, Yale University Press will need to have exclusive *publishing* rights; otherwise, we wouldn't be able to sell the rights to foreign publishers who might be interested. But why should Yale sell these rights when the archive could sell them itself? Because Yale has a whole network already set up to do so; the archive doesn't. Yale's name is known throughout the world as a guarantee of quality and reliability. We'll split the sale in an appropriate way, but we can probably do a more effective job all around. And what if you make a lot of money with these rights—do the editors benefit? If we make a lot of money it will be a miracle, but we can find a formula to cover this as well. Well, miracles do happen, especially in Russia. What about a Russian edition of these documents? What about it? You certainly can publish whatever you like. But we have no money and it will create a great deal of opposition if certain nationalistic elements find out that the documents are being published abroad before they're being published in Russia. The archive and the archival agency, Rosarkhiv, will be accused—fairly or not—of selling out to the Americans. Well, how much will it cost to publish such a volume in Russia? *Nado podumat'*—we must think about it. There's a lot to think about. Yes. We must draw up a protocol of understanding to enumerate all the things we intend to do and all the things we must think about. We must show the protocol to Rosarkhiv and then once we have a preliminary go-ahead, we can work out the details and begin to prepare a contract. Can you write out a protocol of understanding before you leave? Yes, I said. But I was unsure of how I could accomplish this without a computer or typewriter. We will try.

In Naumov's view, the only thing that would protect Yale's position in the archives was speed—to get there first. *"Bystro, bystro,"* the Russian soldiers were said to have urged their French prisoners of war after Napoleon's debacle: "Quickly, quickly." When these soldiers returned to France, they remembered those words, which in turn were used to name the popular new French bistros offering quick service. We, too, must work *bystro, bystro*. Nothing was certain; things changed everyday. There were so many competing interests and little means of controlling events in a country in which men were stronger than laws. Nobody knew what to expect. The courts were generally corrupt. Only the work would remain.

I objected to this strategy at the time because I wanted to ensure maximum legal protection for our side, but time has proved Naumov right.

"That's why Pikhoia is key," Jeff whispered. "Let him see you're a responsible businessman, but also a scholar who understands the needs of the archives and scholarship."

We had conferred for almost two hours and it was time for lunch.

"I can't sincerely recommend Trotsky, but it's convenient," Naumov said.

"Trotsky?"

"Our canteen. Our cook—his name is Lev Davidovich, so we call him Trotsky, come back to poison the remnants of the Communist Party. The party is gone, but the food is the same. Such is life. Unfortunately, I have some business but Fridrikh Igorevich can accompany you, if you so decide."

Fridrikh Igorevich Firsov led us downstairs to the commissary, where we ate whatever dishes the ghost of Trotsky could summon for us: rice with bits of onion and greasy sausage, sauerkraut with black bread.

"Tell me what is in your archive," I asked Fridrikh after I had consumed as much as I could of the unappetizing mixture on my plate.

"Documents from communist parties from around the world."

"From the Germans?"

"Yes."

"And the French?"

"Yes."

"And the Italians?"

"Konyechno."

A light went on in my head. "And so you also have material from the American communist party?"

"Of course, but nobody really cared much about the American party. It's not one of our important holdings. As a consequence, we don't even have the materials here in Moscow."

"Where are they?"

"During the evacuation of Moscow in 1941 all the documents of the Comintern were removed and sent to remote locations. The materials for major parties were returned after the war, but because the American party was of so little interest, most of it was never brought back. As far as I know it's still there in sacks. If you like I can show you some things, but there isn't much here in Moscow."

When we were done, Firsov took me into the repository, which consisted of floor-to-ceiling metal cases. He opened one at random, took out the piece of paper on top, and handed it to me. He waited for it to sink in.

"How did you get this?" I asked. It was a flier announcing a street demonstration run off on a duplicating machine in Detroit, Michigan, in the late 1930s. "How did it get here?"—here in the basement vault of the former Central Party Archive, the former Institute of Marxism-Leninism in Moscow, guarded by the statue of V. I. Lenin downstairs and the hovering presence of his protective archivists upstairs. This immediate contact with my homeland was even more powerful than the face of the Marlboro Man on the side of the building on Kutuzovsky. This now completely meaningless event took place sixty-odd years ago in Detroit, Michigan, a city Firsov had never seen and probably knew nothing about, but which for me was the home of the Detroit Tigers, Ty Cobb, Al Kaline, the Pistons, General Motors, and Motown, not more than 275 miles from my home in Chicago. The flier was to me more of a family photo than a "document."

"But how did you get it?" I repeated.

"They sent it," was the simple reply. "They sent us everything," Frisov said with a broad smile. "They just sent it."

"They sent it?"

"*Da.*"

"But why?"

Firsov shrugged. "That's what they did."

"Come," Firsov said, "I have something in my office I would like to show you." Soon I found myself back up on the third floor standing in front of one of the doors sealed with thread and wax. Firsov gently removed the thread from its bed of paraffin and replaced it in its cylindrical holder. He inserted a long metal key and opened the door. How odd, I thought, this method of sealing your door with a thin thread when for the last seventy-five years conversations at home and at work, one's books and letters, the most private aspects of one's life and mind, were scrupulously recorded by anonymous listeners from unseen microphones, probed by invisible hands that resealed the mail, and observed by cameras too small ever to find—like the golden nail in the flea's shoe in the story by Leskov. It seemed to me that sealing the door was more a ritual than a real protection, something on the order of what La Rochefoucauld meant when he said that hypocrisy was the debt vice pays to virtue. Was it simply to note with the fig leaf of this frail thread that privacy was a hallowed right, thereby insisting upon the right in principle while not in practice? To keep alive an idea that might be restored if circumstances ever were to change?

Inside Firsov's office were piles of document folders and books. A large manual typewriter stood on the desk. Firsov asked me to sit while he went to his bookcase and took down a folder. He opened it to a page and set it before me, clearly expecting that I could read the Russian text.

"Where?" I asked, stalling for time while I tried to make out the Cyrillic and piece the words together.

He pointed to the spot on the page. I nodded, but without really understanding anything except that the passage in question contained the name Pyatnitsky. "Look closely," Jeff translated as Firsov spoke. "Do you see? Do you see?" I tried desperately to see, to pick up the thread of the words, but it eluded me.

Firsov was excited. "It proves the Comintern from the beginning, from the very beginning, was involved with the NKVD and espionage. Right here. You see?" He put his finger on the exact spot that proved his point. "From the beginning. It was always an instrument of the foreign policy of the Soviet Union. It was never simply responding to the will of the foreign parties or the masses they represented. Never. Never. Orders came from the Central Committee through foreign intelligence. It was a fascist structure. First Lenin. Then Stalin."

I could not decipher the proof right before my eyes in Firsov's office, but his energy and delight in being able to reveal this stunning document was like another secret door that had opened, a door I would one day pass through, but only later. Once Fridrikh Igorevich emigrated to the

United States, he became simply Fred, a name I never felt comfortable calling him, but which he insisted on.

"In America as well?"

Firsov grinned and shrugged. "We will find out."

"Tell Jonathan about your interview on television," Jeff urged.

Firsov shrugged. "You tell him."

"There was a television discussion of the crimes of the Soviet past, and Firsov was asked to participate as an expert on the history of the Comintern. He was going to speak about the Comintern and the terror of the 1930s. Everything was set—I was watching on the television in my apartment—Firsov was introduced, and the second his face came on screen and broadcast nationally, for some reason the electricity was cut and there was a blackout."

"But why?"

"Why? Look at Fridrikh Igorevich's face."

I looked but didn't see anything.

"He has a Russian last name—his father was Russian. But any Russian looking at his face would know he was Jewish—his mother was Jewish. They couldn't have a Jew speaking on national television about the crimes of the Soviet Union. Too dangerous, even now."

"Is this true?" I asked Firsov.

"Possibly," he said in Russian.

The shock of this immediacy returned after we had published the first volume in the Annals of Communism in 1995, *The Secret World of American Communism*, edited by Harvey Klehr, John Earl Haynes and Fridrikh Igorevich. The documents assembled for this work became that other secret door. They led onto a corridor whose end we still have not reached.

The Secret World of American Communism made headlines nationally in the United States, England, France, and Germany because it provided significant new documentation to show that the Communist Party USA was engaged in espionage on behalf of the Soviet Union. It also confirmed the testimony of Whittaker Chambers and Elizabeth Bentley about the activity of the CPUSA. Among the political left wing in the United States it caused a storm of protest because it strengthened the case against Alger Hiss and necessarily reopened discussion of Joseph McCarthy. It caused an equal fury in Moscow because much of the relevant documentation was in the form of memoranda between the NKVD and the Comintern. While these memoranda were classified as top secret in the closed KGB archive, copies were available in the Comintern files—which we had access to.

In the wake of the controversy that broke out on both sides of the world, I received a telephone call from Professor T. T. Timofeev, a member of our Russian advisory committee. Soon after we had signed the contract with Rosarkhiv, we had assembled a board of advisers—both American and Russian. Timofeev had been recommended by Rosarkhiv because he spoke English and was an expert on American affairs. Now he was on the telephone, long distance from Moscow, telling my assistant it was urgent. He explained to me in excellent but heavily accented English that he felt our project was not "balanced," and so he wished to withdraw his name from our editorial committee. I attempted to persuade him to remain, but it was no use. His decision was final. The series would not provide a balanced picture and he didn't wish to be a part of it. He was the only member of the Russian editorial board ever to withdraw.

I immediately called Klehr with this news. Klehr said he had noticed Timofeev's name on the editorial committee, but had not connected the dots. "Go back and read the section on Eugene Dennis," he said. "I'm certain that Timofeev is Dennis's son." The story is both revealing and sad. Eugene Dennis, who succeeded Earl Browder as leader of the CPUSA, was in Moscow with his wife and son not long before the Nazi invasion in 1941. They petitioned the Soviet government to allow them to return home, but were told they would have to leave their son in Moscow—perhaps as ransom. Dennis and his wife left their son when they returned to the United States and never saw him again. The son eventually became Professor T. T. Timofeev.

Most of what Klehr, Haynes, and Firsov discovered in those files consisted of bits and pieces of information scattered over some ten thousand documents, like the pieces of a massive jigsaw puzzle with only the barest distinguishing marks. Only researchers with encyclopedic knowledge of their subject could have fitted them correctly into the larger puzzle. There were no smoking guns as such, documents that could stand alone and tell the "whole" story. But there were many guns with the smell of smoke in their barrels.

Two such were telegrams dating to 1925. One of them was addressed to Armand Hammer from his father, Julius, instructing him to arrange for a transfer of $6,400 to a particular individual; the other was from Charles Ruthenberg, then head of the CPUSA, to Osip Piatnitsky, head of the Comintern's International Relations Department—the same Piatnitsky Firsov had pointed to in his office—complaining that Hammer had not yet delivered the cash, which was intended to support publication of the *Daily Worker*, and asking Piatnitsky to compel Hammer to pay up. Armand Hammer had died before our book was published in 1995, which exposed him and his father as runners for the Comintern. Shortly after publication a man who identified himself as the lawyer for Armand Hammer called my office and asked that I call him back. Fearing legal repercussions, I hesitated, but finally steeled myself to return the call. He asked if I was the fellow who had published that book on American communism. I said I was, and what he said next astounded me.

"I always knew there was something fishy about Hammer, but didn't know what it was. Thank you for clearing it up."

From Firsov's office, we wound our way back to Ploshchad Revolutsii, down crooked byways that frequently necessitated cutting into the lanes of traffic where the small Zhigulis and Ladas bore down on pedestrians, scattering them like pigeons. At the metro station hordes of people poured out in all directions. Men and women carried loaves of bread under their arms or tucked inside their coats or bulging valises; some carried vegetables or cartons of milk; one man clad only in a thin gray overcoat, without scarf or gloves or hat, dashed from the swinging doors with a desperate look on his face and two eggs in his outstretched hands, a flimsy black attaché case dangling from the crook of one arm. In the moment before he disappeared, I stared uncomprehendingly at this spectral figure cradling those eggs in his bare red hands, perhaps for someone waiting anxiously at home. The smell of gasoline and bread was in the air.

"What's this?" I asked Jeff, pointing to tables arranged around the entrance of the station. "What are they doing?" At each table, it seemed, sat the same old lady, dressed in the same heavy coat with the same scarf around her head and scrawny neck and the same determined look on her haggard face, a look from another time and place, one I knew I could never penetrate: cold, hard, devoid of expectation, fear, or hope.

"They sell what they can."

"What do you mean?" I asked, edging closer to one of the tables and glancing at the shabby merchandise—an old shoe, a box of matches, a pot for cooking, a cellophane bag of women's stockings, a packet of condoms, a grayish toothbrush. The old lady did not look up or even turn her head.

"They sell whatever they have in their houses. Anything. They're desperate."

"A used toothbrush?"

"Yeah."

"They have a space station orbiting Earth while old ladies are freezing to death, selling their toothbrushes on the streets of Moscow?"

"Yeah."

We picked our way along the icy embankments to the nearest trolley stop where the bus to Kutuzovsky Prospect and Ploshchad Pobedy would come. Jeff told me the number. I repeated it.

"Good," he said. "You remember where Mariana's apartment is?"

I nodded.

"See you tomorrow. Remember: eleven o'clock with Pikhoia. It'll be a big day."

The air had become frigid. Yellow squares were becoming visible in the apartment buildings along the avenue. The cars all had their lights on, and everything seemed to float in semi-illumination amid zones of light and dark as I stood at the curb, now no longer certain which trolleybus to take, while an endless stream of red taillights floated in the distance above our heads toward a faraway and uncertain destination. From time to time I saw a mother holding a child all bundled up against the cold in a way that seemed different from anything I'd observed in the United States, as though the littleness of the child had to be fully encased and protected in a globe of fur and softness so that only the eyes and a flick of golden hair was visible. All were held very close to the mothers' bodies, reminding me of the way father penguins protect their eggs between their feet until they hatch.

Suddenly the entire scene made me think of a Russian nesting doll; all I could see were hooded ovals bobbing up and down along the street, framed in the encompassing protection of winter furs. Ovals within ovals, accentuated by the *shapki* some wore instead of hoods, even to the shape of the child at its mother's side.

My mind wandered amid these aimless impressions as a trolleybus screeched to a stop. Barely catching sight of the sign, but believing it to be right, I allowed myself to be drawn upward into the interior through a process of pushing from behind and from side to side—completely out of my or anyone's control. I found a seat in the overheated cabin, opened my parka, and suddenly felt I was being covertly observed, sized up. An American? Was that good or bad? A child in a blue parka peered out cautiously from the depths of a great fur-lined hood. I caught her eyes for a second before she glanced away as if it hadn't been me she had been observing in the first place. No one else seemed to pay the slightest attention.

The bus pulled from the curb and started off on its route as I had expected but then suddenly took a right turn. On my way to Ploshchad Revolutsii in the morning I had noticed that Kutuzovsky splits off at a certain point. Perhaps this was it—a road parallel to the one I wanted. I waited. The bus continued on this right-hand fork. I waited. The bus didn't seem at all inclined to turn back toward Kutuzovsky. What to do? Jump up and ask the driver to stop? How? In what language, with what words? Ask somebody if it went to Ploshchad Pobedy? I couldn't remember how to say "went" in the proper grammatical form used while on a bus. Then to endure the humiliation of being a stupid American—come here to do what? And if the bus kept going and going and going and eventually disappeared into the floating slipstream of those endless red taillights I had imagined earlier of whose destination I knew nothing? And if I was unable ever to find my way out again? All of a sudden a vision of disappearing with the bus overcame me. I would disappear. No, the point was I *could* disappear. Seven thousand miles from home in a world from which my grandparents *had* disappeared eighty-five years earlier. It would be so easy never to find my way out again.

Then a thought struck me that I have returned to many times since: *Let it happen. Just let go. Let the bus go where it goes and you will go where you go and that will be what happens. That will be what happens.* At that moment, this simple, total capitulation to the situation enabled me to bring my breathing under control and to keep from making a scene, something that seemed more important than getting where I wanted to go. The last thing I could imagine was calling attention to myself and breaking through the container of invisibility in which I seemed sealed. I sat back, no longer waiting, just observing the faces of the buildings growing darker and darker as we moved slowly along. I was about to yield entirely to the sensation of dissolving into invisibility, of being swept into will-less and forgetful obscurity, when the bus turned onto a gradual leftward route that in a moment became recognizable as Kutuzovsky Prospect! How did this happen? Soon we passed an archway with a sign I could just make out in the now less than half-light: Teatr Koshek. During the day I had noted that it was draped with a banner with two cats in black silhouette. The Cat House? The Kitty-Cat Theater? The Theater of Cats? For children? What could this be? Only many years later did I learn that this is where a world-famous Russian animal trainer puts his "trained" cats on show in performances that utterly delight both children and their parents. To me, however, it was a landmark implanted in my mind without my realizing it at the time. My heart soared. Here I was. How? It seemed a miracle. Three stops later the massive Arch of Triumph, erected to commemorate Russia's victories through the ages, came into view. I went to the door as though nothing in the world had happened, and when the trolley jerked to a halt, I stepped off.

What a joy to enter the mazelike courtyard of Mariana's apartment complex, wander around the frozen children's playground at the center until I found the entrance I remembered was Mariana's. What a joy to breathe deeply the smell of Moscow as I tore open the front doorway and found the elevator past the row of mailboxes with their mangled metal doors, past the garbage heaped in a corner and the wall of cracked plaster and snide graffiti that included the word "fuk." I inhaled the smell of Moscow down to the bottom of my lungs, stepped onto the lift, and when the door clanked shut I knew I was home.

Chapter 8

Pikhoia

Rudolf Germanovich Pikhoia occupied a position of considerable eminence in 1992, having been chosen by Boris Yeltsin to head the newly established Federal Archival Service of Russia, Rosarkhiv. His offices on Ilinka Street were in a complex of buildings which, I later came to learn, also housed the Central Committee Archive and the Archive of the President.

After a protracted clearance at the guard station we were met by a very pleasant young woman who nevertheless seemed acutely self-conscious of herself or perhaps her new role—a professional role—in the new government. Her eyes set wide apart and her wide, gaping mouth in combination with the awkward way she held her arms, as if she had no idea where they were to go, gave her a kind of Tolstoyan ugliness. She walked ahead of us, peering occasionally out of the corner of her eyes at Jeff and me as though to read our reaction, like a girl on her first set of high heels, sharply conscious of those behind her. Her bleached blond hair had a slightly hard, chemical sheen. The same was true of her eye shadow and nail polish—there was something ersatz about them, like the butter or coffee people used during World War II. She led us through a labyrinthine series of corridors with high, pale oak doors on either side. Except for its façade, this building had none of the shabbiness of the Central Party Archive or GARF. The Turkish runners were clean, the walls weren't cracked and smudged, the lighting worked, the officials and archivists I passed were well dressed, and although they appeared serious, they didn't have the anxious and harried look of many I had seen at the Central Party Archive.

And yet I had difficulty reconciling this interior with the grimy, unpainted exterior of the building, which looked not unlike an abandoned warehouse in Bridgeport, or with the cramped, unkempt entryway whose only amenity was an electric shoe polisher that actually worked.

The young assistant showed us where to hang our coats and hats and pointed us to the large green upholstered chairs in the waiting room. When she smiled at us all her ugliness disappeared. A portrait of Boris Yeltsin hung on the wall above some file cabinets; various publications and brochures were laid out on a table.

"Be sure to emphasize the scholarly nature of your interest," Jeff whispered, leaning over to me. He repeated this for Nikolai, who nodded. *"Da,"* Nikolai said, *"eto vazhno."*

After about fifteen minutes, we were summoned though the large double door leading to Pikhoia's office. Jeff and I walked ahead of Nikolai and were about to go through together when Nikolai held Jeff back. I turned around.

"It's bad luck for two to cross a threshold together," Jeff whispered.

Pikhoia, who was seated at his desk in the far corner of the large office, stood up and came forward to meet us. He seemed short, dark, puffy, and out of breath, as if cross or distracted, caught in the middle of something else of much higher importance. He was cordial but seemed to wish to demonstrate his importance and wasn't sure how to do so. He resolved the dilemma by assuming an irritable manner, but then realized that this might not be appropriate. He motioned for us to sit at a long table and then sat down on the other side, opposite me. An older woman with a pad of paper and a pen took her place opposite Jeff, and a tall, sandy-haired young man, also with a small notebook, opposite Nikolai. Such ritual symmetries were an essential component of all my official meetings for many years.

"Unfortunately for us these are important times," Pikhoia began. "Not like the Irish proverb, 'I wish you to live in unimportant times.' So we have to make the best of it." He waited to see if I appreciated his irony. When I showed that I did, he continued. "We welcome you to Moscow. We are at the beginning of being between two worlds. It is a difficult time. Nobody knows what will happen." Though he began with a cliché, I could see this last sentence expressed a real anxiety, though one which he had expressed so many times to his foreign guests that the words he used no longer meant anything to him. Only much later did I think about what it might mean to live in between two worlds without guarantees, without certainties, without a map, a world very much like the one I experienced momentarily on the trolleybus as we veered to the left when I wanted to go right and didn't possess the language to make myself understood.

"Nor do we in the United States," I answered a little too quickly. "But I'm grateful for your welcome and wish to tell you what I hope Yale University Press can accomplish in partnership with the Russian archives."

Pikhoia listened politely and the older woman took notes. I spoke of the project that was not yet a project, filling in blanks on the spot, proposing topics I hadn't discussed with anyone up to then, stating and restating that the history of the Soviet Union was, in my view, the entryway into understanding the history of the world for the last seventy-five years of the twentieth century. I emphasized that for me this was not only a project of understanding Soviet history but also of understanding my experiences and those of my generation growing up in post-Sputnik America. I recounted for him what went on in my parents' living room, where I first learned the name of Alger Hiss and watched uncomprehendingly the televised McCarthy hearings of 1954. "He's a very bad man," my father said, pointing to the television, but it was unclear to me at the time whom he was referring to. "Something evil is going on in America."

I told Pikhoia about the terror that seized the United States at the time of the Kennedy assassination and the effect of *The Manchurian Candidate*. Protesting the Vietnam War at Columbia was in some way a continuation of what I had seen and heard at home in 1954 and then 1963. But all this was tied directly or indirectly to an adversary about whom I and most in my generation knew relatively little: the Soviet Union.

Never clearly seen, never understood, a mortal enemy—yet for those who fell in love with the revolution and its literature and music, not only an enemy. It seemed the inevitable reflux of everything around us. It was that which had always existed contra to us, an anti-world, and in some ways an anti-self. It formed the natural complement, the necessary antithesis that mirrored our every move and made us conscious of ourselves. I didn't say all of this, but I felt it and thought it—or at least some of it at the time—and somehow I wanted Pikhoia to know that this was more than a mere business deal to me.

Pikhoia listened, but it was clear that he was listening only for the point at which I would stop.

"We will discuss your negotiations with the Central Party Archive once you have established a preliminary agreement. It will take time, but it will be a fair process. We have to think about our options and you have to think about yours. Let's hope for a better world."

He stood up and reached out his hand.

"Do svidaniya. Vsyevo khoroshego."

He was pleasant in an unpleasant way; not personally disposed one way or another, but clearly wishing me to understand that my views were irrelevant. All of a sudden, the room seemed too big, too cavernous, like a suit two sizes too big; somehow there now seemed to be too many assistants. The desk was too far back, the ceiling too high, and the long table too long. An awkwardness set in.

What was the point?

"Let's go and have coffee," I said to Jeff and Nikolai after we had been escorted out by the affable, sandy-haired assistant who seemed on the verge of saying something, but couldn't quite bring himself to do so. "I need to sort this out."

"He gave you fifteen minutes," Nikolai said. "That's very good. That's all that mattered."

"I'm not sure he gave it, but I took it anyhow."

We were to meet at Naumov's office at two o'clock. We had plenty of time to chat and Nikolai proposed that we come to his office at RGGU, the Russian State University for the Humanities.

RGGU was established in 1991 on the foundations of the Moscow State Historical-Archival Institute. Now I understood a little better how Jeff knew Nikolai and why Nikolai had contacts throughout the archival community. Nikolai was a powerful man physically, about five feet nine or ten, with hooded but kindly blue eyes set into a very symmetrical and handsome face. He grasped my hand with the strength of a man used to physical labor—a detail that confused me since he'd been introduced as a historian. All the time I knew Nikolai, whom over time I came to call, more intimately, "Petrovich," I felt there was something unfulfilled in him, some plan or ambition he had not realized, some intention that had never come to life, but remained in a closet like an old military uniform or his wedding suit.

We often talked of his coming to the United States to visit me on my father's farm. It was located in northern Wisconsin in an area originally settled by Finnish and Swedish fishermen and loggers, but where a handful of Russians and Dutch and German farmers had also landed. One of our great friends, John Roman, a Russian immigrant, had been a remarkable fisherman. Several times every summer John Roman would come to our house, always toward evening and always unannounced, with a large packet wrapped in newspaper under an arm. After tea was set boiling on the stove and my father had poured him a shot of brandy or whiskey, he would unroll the newspaper, which inevitably contained a number of good-sized rainbow trout just caught in the Cranberry River. He boasted that he could catch any fish in any lake with "voorms," a word my brother and I repeated endlessly when hunting for bait in the red clay ditches by our house.

John could catch perch, bass, trout, salmon, northern pike, walleye, and even whitefish with his "voorms," but the most miraculous moment in his life came when he hooked what at first he took to be nothing but a log rising from the bottom, but which turned out to be an immense fish. After the authorities came to inspect the lake, they determined it was a sturgeon, where none had ever been found before; the game warden estimated that it weighed probably well over a hundred pounds. The monstrous beast nearly sank his wooden rowboat. After rising lazily to the surface, it broke water and, according to John, seemed to observe him for a second before plunging back toward the bottom dragging his little boat behind. John didn't simply cut his line; in panic, he threw everything overboard—rod, reel, worms, net—and paddled back to shore as quickly as possible.

But he used another word when he came over with his packet of rainbows on a warm summer night. He would ask for "a glass of *chai*" in a deep, mellifluous voice we loved to mimic because it seemed to hold in it a million far-flung adventures. All of this was strange: *Chai*? Tea? A glass of tea? No one drank tea out of a glass. You drank it from a cup. But John Roman drank his *chai* lovingly from a glass, without milk but with sugar only, and if it was a cube of sugar, all the better. Nikolai told me he also loved to fish and had even fished for sturgeon on the Volga. Maybe we would go sometime after all the work in the archives was over and we could retire and drink tea with a shot of brandy. I dreamed of going out for pike and trout with Nikolai up in Wisconsin, but this was not to be. He died tragically in a freak accident. While he was chopping wood at his village dacha, the ax slipped and struck him in the leg, causing a deep wound. Though the wound was treated, a blood clot developed that shot to his brain and killed him before he could get to Moscow the next day.

In his office now, surrounded by his books and archival materials, Nikolai was firmly in control. "Sit, sit," he said to Jeff and me while instructing his young female assistant to bring in additional chairs. A small samovar was on the table nearby, with cups and a small dish of sugar. It was the first samovar I had seen in Moscow, and I was ashamed of my disappointment that it was nothing but a cheap, electric imitation—nothing like the fine silver samovars on display in *Doctor Zhivago* and *Nicholas and Alexandra*. How easily simple images become fixed in the mind. *"Chai?"* Nikolai asked, as several male students in jeans entered the room to see what was up. Nikolai motioned for them to sit down in a ring around us.

"Tanya," Nikolai called out, and his young assistant came back into the office from her desk outside the door. "Pour some tea."

Without a word, Tanya came over to the samovar and poured the tea.

"What was the point of that meeting?" I asked.

Nikolai said simply, *"Vsyo v poryadke."* Everything's okay. No need to worry.

"But what was it about?"

"Nothing."

"Nothing?"

"Only to see you. To size you up. Now he has to think who he wants to do business with." Jeff translated as Nikolai spoke.

"What will get him to think well of it?"

"Where he can make the most profit for himself; where he will make the most enemies—there's one thing that controls the social world here: *znakomstvo*. Don't forget it. Everybody wants to know what he will get out of it. Who is connected to who."

"What did he see? What could he imagine he could get out of it?"

Nikolai blinked both eyes like a cat. "We will live and we will see."

Nikolai seemed happy and called out to Tanya for a plate of cookies, which she quickly produced—the same dry, almost tasteless cookies I'd had at Mariana's the night before. Jeff also was pleased.

"It's important for you to be seen with Nikolai. He's respected here. It means Nikolai's risking something also—because he believes in you. Most of the foreign businessmen have no local support for what they're doing. This is the key. Remember: build from the bottom. That's how things work here; that's what people like Pikhoia respond to, that kind of pressure." I found Nikolai's openness among these students extraordinary, but this experience would be repeated many times during my time in Russia, when the conditions were right.

Much later, I discovered Stalin's famous toast of November 7, 1937; his words put Nikolai's basic principle into a much different context.

> A great deal is said about great leaders. But a cause is never won unless the right conditions exist. *And the main thing here is the middle cadres . . . They're the ones who choose the leader, explain our positions to the masses, and ensure the success of our cause. They don't try to climb above their station; you don't even notice them. . . .* The main thing is the middle cadres. Generals can do nothing without a good officer corps. Why did we prevail over Trotsky and the rest? Trotsky, as we know, was the most popular man in our country after Lenin. Bukharin, Zinoviev, Rykov, Tomsky were all popular. We were little known, I myself, Molotov, Voroshilov, and Kalinin, then. We were field workers in Lenin's time, his colleagues. But the middle cadres supported us, explained our positions to the masses. Meanwhile Trotsky completely ignored those cadres. . . . What the victory of the cause requires is the correct conditions, and then the leaders will always be found. It is not enough merely to point out the true path. . . . *The fundamental thing* is the middle cadres. That must be noted, and it must never be forgotten that other conditions being equal, *the middle cadres decide the outcome of our cause.*

Would our strategy, then, be to create a kind of miniature Soviet-style cell, an organization that was local, familiar, knowledgeable, and able to neutralize the Trotskys who would descend on the scene, that is, those with money and prestige, but no natural organization or ability to explain "our positions to the masses"? Those Trotskys included elegant French, German, Japanese, and American commercial publishers, an English publishing giant, an Italian foundation with a deep history and longstanding Soviet ties, and various individual entrepreneurs from the United States who wished to mine the archives for their own personal interests. What I didn't see at the time but is clear now is that this organization, this "cell," was designed for a world that, nominally at least, no longer existed. But while they had broken free from the Soviet past, they had not yet entered a new world where business dealings could be conducted through established norms of negotiation, and moreover where legal contracts were binding. In the absence of these protections only a small, organized, local kind of organization could be effective. Furthermore, it was what they knew how to build. And it demonstrated in a small way how ostensibly obsolete cultural structures or expectations can replicate themselves in radically changed conditions of daily life; it demonstrated how culture persists longer than ideas or regimes. How different was the need to create our "cell," surrounded by our cadres of Nikolai's young students, from the tsaritsa's need to record that, "at 10 they told us it was 12"?

We arrived at the Central Party Archive promptly and were immediately brought upstairs to the conference room.

"We must compose a protocol to show Pikhoia," Naumov stated. "We can use one of our typewriters, but we must show something." When I suggested that it might be difficult to type an English text on a Russian typewriter, Naumov smiled mysteriously.

"It has been done."

At the end of two hours we had composed a neat two-page document outlining the scholarly mission of the project; an advisory committee—both Russian and American; and a list of six projects, divided between those of purely scholarly interest, such as the letters between Stalin and Georgi Dimitrov, and others, such as the history of the CPUSA, that would have wider interest. We determined that there would be a true collaboration among the parties: each volume would have an American and a Russian editor, and each book would be published in both English and Russian editions simultaneously. Many questions were left unanswered, but we decided to solve problems as they came up rather than try to solve everything at the outset. Once the protocol was approved by Pikhoia, we could move toward a final contract.

As we were wrapping up our discussion an elderly man entered the room wearing a heavy worsted overcoat, black galoshes, and a gray Western-style hat. He came up to Naumov and whispered something, paying no attention to my presence at the long table and apparently having no interest in the document we were preparing. He listened attentively to Naumov's response, then turned and was about to leave the room when Jeff approached him and made an introduction.

"Vladimir Pavlovich Naumov, this is Jonathan Brent from Yale University Press."

"Privet," he said, suddenly looking in my direction.

"This is Professor Naumov, Oleg's father, a great figure in the archives," Jeff whispered.

"Very happy to meet you," I said, shaking his hand. The elderly professor's hand was unlike any I had ever shaken. Vladimir Pavlovich's fingers are long and beautifully manicured, smooth and undemonstrative—quiet hands. In fact, as I got to know Vladimir Pavlovich better I began to realize that the quietness of his hands was mirrored in his eyes and mouth and in his temperament. He didn't grasp my hand; it was as if he allowed my hand to grasp itself. He had a good-natured smile, and his large eyes were animated with intelligence, and perhaps something else as well, from behind the thick lenses of his ill-fitting glasses.

"Your son is an excellent negotiator," I said hopefully, not knowing the word for "negotiator," but inventing something I thought he might understand.

I couldn't tell whether Vladimir Pavlovich heard me, or whether the word I used was correct, but he smiled and half turned to find Oleg, who immediately came up to us. He helped his father on with his coat, which he had helped him off with a minute before, and led him back to the door. It wasn't clear that he had seen me or heard my name, and I had no idea why he had appeared in the room in which we were negotiating our protocol.

After we finished, I wanted to take everyone out for an early dinner, a proposition Naumov declined, but which Jeff and Nikolai accepted. The only place nearby with decent food that anyone could think of was the Spanish Bar in the Moscow Hotel in front of the Kremlin on Manezh Square.

Today a bright new shopping center stands close by and the Hotel is being renovated. The Moscow Hotel's peculiar architectural history is revealed in its asymmetrical façade: the design originally presented to Stalin had two different options divided on the drawing paper by a fine pencil line. Stalin didn't notice the pencil line, and therefore did not recognize that two different façades were being proposed. He signed the plan in the middle of the page—right on the dividing line. Too terrified to ask which design Stalin preferred, the architect solved the problem by using both and executed the plan exactly as it was on the piece of paper Stalin had signed.

The result was a building with two façades. Despite this troubled exterior, the Spanish Bar was a hangout for foreigners, the food was relatively cheap, and the service was tolerable. A large poster of flamenco dancers appeared to be the most salient effort at establishing a Spanish motif to the decor, though one or two items of Spanish origin or flavor could be found on the menu, in particular the seafood empanada.

Various other American scholars were there when we arrived, including Norman Naimark from Stanford. I said it seemed that there were many different Moscows. Some, like Firsov, expect a fascist coup; others, mere collapse and anarchy. Still others seem hopeful that democracy could take hold.

There may be a coup, Naimark said, but it won't be fascist. A strong man will eventually come out of all of this to put the pieces back together. An oligarchy of some kind is likely. Sixteen years later, Naimark's prediction in the Spanish Bar has come to seem the most accurate of all.

Vitaly Makhlin, a Russian literary scholar who joined us, said he thought nothing could save Russia. *Dukhovnost*— spirituality—was its curse and blessing. People can think only in such abstractions and can see into the heart of existence but can't fix an elevator or a television set. It's a problem. It's the Russian problem.

After we finished, I asked whether I could pay with a credit card. The waitress was uncertain and a little panicked by the request, but after some consultation in the back room said yes. She disappeared and was followed by the manager, who wished to see my passport and visa. He took them into the back room, and for about twenty minutes worked on filling out the forms necessary to complete the transaction using American Express. Finally, he appeared, apologizing for the delay, and I signed the receipt. The month following my return from Moscow, I checked my bill to see if it had indeed been handled correctly. The transaction did not appear. Nor did it appear the month after that. Nor did it ever.

I had made arrangements to meet with Vika Sagalova, an editor at a fine Russian publishing company, and as our dinner was winding down, she appeared. I had met Vika in the United States the year before through a mutual friend at Northwestern University. When I knew I'd be coming to Moscow I got her phone number and was astonished when she picked up the telephone. Vika spoke very good English and seemed anxious to make contact again.

She looked worried and distracted standing in the doorway of the Spanish Bar, surveying the room for me. When she saw me, I could tell she was disappointed that Jeff and Nikolai were also present. I persuaded her to come in, and we went to a small table in the back under a garland of artificial vines and posters of Spanish guitars.

She did not want anything to eat, maybe just some tea. Vika told me that her daughter had recently emigrated and now lived in Chicago. She wanted to become a scholar of Spanish literature.

"My eyes have grown small from crying," Vika told me. She and her husband were fearful of the chaos and instability all around them, partly because she was Jewish, though her husband was not. Terrible stories had been in the papers recently, one about the daughter of a well-known journalist who was shoved into an elevator by two thugs. They ripped off her shirt, but instead of raping her they merely carved a Star of David on her chest, doused her in vodka, and ran off.

Vika's publishing company, one of the very best in Soviet times, had just gone bankrupt. She was a senior editor. Where would she find another job?

How many books did they publish? I asked. Vika answered that they published about thirty-five a year, mainly fine literature, a respectable if modest number. But when I asked how many employees they had, she refused to say.

"Why?"

"Because you'll make fun of me."

I assured Vika I wouldn't. She hesitated. I said, "Vika, why would I make fun of you? You're a friend and colleague."

But when she reluctantly revealed that they employed nearly 750 people, I burst out laughing.

"Vika," I said, "you deserved to go bankrupt."

"I know. Certainly, I know. You see, everything is a joke."

"No, it's not a joke, but it is absurd to have 750 people producing thirty-five books. What did they do?"

Most of the employees, Vika said, were young ladies who would arrive for work in shifts. The first shift would come in around ten in the morning. They would hang up their coats, make tea, read the newspaper, gossip, and perhaps complete some form or other, take it down the hall to another department, get it stamped, and then return to their desks, where they would finish their newspaper and have another cup of tea before going home. The second shift was very much like the first except later, and so on. By the end of the day, this enormous group of young ladies would have produced nothing of any consequence. And yet the publishing house published serious literature and works of history by such authors as Vasily Grossman, Nikolai Erdman, and Vladimir Nabokov. Vika and a handful of others did all the work. They used to print hundreds of thousands of copies, most of which would remain unsold in warehouses. Today, she complained, there is no distribution and people read less and less. "All people think about is food."

"Certainly you know. Certainly you know. Why certainly you do," she said to me, and then in another burst of desperation, "do you understand my English?"

"Yes," I said. "I understand."

"Yes, certainly you do."

She thanked me for meeting her, gave me a letter for her friend at Northwestern that I promised to post once back in the United States, and asked me to call the next time I was in Moscow. Maybe things would improve. Maybe. But she was terribly afraid—every day.

I promised that I would call, and as we were about to retrieve our coats from the elderly man who presided over the cloakroom, Vladimir Pavlovich Naumov appeared again with one or two other men. When he saw me, he held out his hand, into which I once again felt my own dissolve in the absence of pressure. He asked how long I would be in Moscow. I told him I would be leaving the next day. "What a pity," he said. "You must come again."

Chapter 9

Farewell

I would pack my bags in the morning. I had one last gift for Mariana, a small box of chocolates that I wanted to give her on my last night. I would give the kosher salami I had kept with me to Nikolai. As we sat in her small kitchen drinking tea and some more of her *labadan*, the front door opened and a large, shambling young man appeared who introduced himself as Lyonya, Mariana's son; only he introduced himself to me not as if I were an American from eight time zones away, but as if I were a cousin he had never met. He was friendly without being at all polite; he had no interest in formal questions: where are you from, what do you do, what is your business here, do you have children? Rather, he spoke in a kind of half-Russian, half-English made-up language about his work in the Orthodox Church's archives, about renovations in the apartment building, the telephone system, and whatever else seemed close at hand.

The telephone rang and he trudged off to get it in a back room. As he spoke to the person on the other end, he reappeared with a long extension cord wound around his waist and arms like a vine on a tree. After he'd made a few more turns around the room, the cord caught on the leg of a chair, and Lyonya patiently retraced his steps, bending, twisting, talking volubly to the person on the other end, somehow managing to wrap the cord around himself all over again. He spoke as he might have spoken to himself in the shower. When he was finally done, he smiled with great relish: "Djeff. Djeff. You—" he pointed to the phone and laughed. "Djeff. Oh, Djeff . . ." I couldn't tell whether Jeff had been telling him about Mariana's kolbasa or about the meeting with Pikhoia. At home in his world. Nothing strange or alien. Mariana's horse medicine, the spiderwebs in the corners of the toilet, the grease along the window, the *labadan* fermenting in the kitchen, the little stove, the knife that might have floated on water, the rice with shreds of onions and hot dogs, and the hard cookies were all elements in a world in which the meeting with Pikhoia and Mariana's *bankes* had equal value. I envied him. At home, in his home, what did it matter if something was one way or another as he wound his way around his domain, pulling the extension cord after him like a child's blanket? Circling, returning, disappearing into another room, chatting, laughing, and then exclaiming "Djeff, Djeff," and all that implied of affection, concern, irony, and warmth. Someone for whom everything is an extension of this warmth, for whom the personal and the public are wound around each other as he is in his telephone cord, and whose lack of polite conversation was simply the result of not seeing that the division between outside and inside was necessary. You're in my apartment? Fine. Who are you? No, not who—rather, *what* are you?

Later that evening I remembered I would need to pay Nikolai the next morning for his work, and for this I wished to have an envelope, the Russian word for which I only vaguely remembered. I asked Lyonya if he had a *kovyor*.

"*Kovyor?*" he asked incredulously, looking around at the floor and walls.

"*Da.*"

He pointed to the rug on the floor. "*Da,*" he repeated. "*Da, da, da . . . vot,*" he said, as if coming to the end of a hopeless line of thought. The shrug of his shoulder and the look in his eyes suggested that if I truly needed it, it was at my disposal, but why I might he couldn't guess.

"*Kovyor, da,*" I repeated.

Again he shrugged, as if to say, "take it if you need it, but don't try to explain."

When he didn't produce the envelope, however, I knew the conversation could go no further. I smiled and said good night and Lyonya did the same.

I never did obtain the envelope and in the end it didn't matter. Not until I checked my dictionary did I discover my mistake, but it was too late and I didn't have the words to explain. Lyonya never asked why I might have needed his rug.

The following morning, Jeff and Nikolai came early to Mariana's apartment. I still needed to pack and settle accounts with Mariana and Nikolai. I looked around for the dirty clothes I had shoved into a plastic bag. I couldn't find them. I opened my suitcase with the thought that I may have inadvertently placed them inside and found it already packed, my dirty clothes cleaned and folded, my pants ironed and all neatly stored. How could this have happened? Had the young doctor returned? I went out to find Mariana, who was in the kitchen boiling a pot of tea.

She indicated I should sit and put a plate of bread and butter with slices of bland cheese before me. Soon I had a cup of tea. I had no words to thank her or even to inquire if she had cleaned my clothes. I took the sum we had agreed on from my pocket, counted it out, and gave it to her. Without looking at it, she placed it on a corner of the table.

"Eto malo ili mnogo?"

And to her question of whether it was a little or a lot, I tried to say that it was what we had agreed on in advance, but I never knew whether she understood or thought it was sufficient.

Jeff came in and urged us to hurry so that I wouldn't miss my flight. Mariana followed me to my room and then stood blocking the door as Nikolai picked up my suitcase. He set it down.

"Sadityes, sadityes," Mariana ordered and everyone sat down. But when I sat on the edge of the bed she objected, indicating I had to sit on my luggage. After a minute's silence, she clapped her hands, jumped from her spot, kissed me on both cheeks, and called out, *"khorosho."* We were now free to go. I told Mariana I would come back. She asked if I could bring her a strong lock for her door, and I said I would try.

Part Two

Searching

Chapter 10

In the Labyrinth

I returned to Moscow in July to resume negotiations with RTsKhIDNI and Rosarkhiv. I spent another ten minutes with Pikhoia, explaining our intentions in what seemed to me the cavernous void of his office; but I spent several days with Oleg Naumov continuously shaping and reshaping the mutual responsibilities to be written into the eventual contract. Early on, I became persuaded that the only way to bring the negotiations to an end was to defy the advice of a hard-nosed international publishing lawyer we had engaged to help with the contract. The aggressive Madison Avenue approach he advocated called for exclusive rights and would have ensured a marginal role for our Russian partners. It also would have ensured the end of the project. Instinctively, I didn't even show Naumov the sample contract our lawyer had produced—at considerable expense to Yale—until after we had finally come to terms. When Naumov read it over, he told me flatly that if we had approached them in that manner, the deal would have been dead. All trust would have been broken.

Instead, I inclined toward a strategy I learned as a boy on my father's farm in Wisconsin. We had to lay an underground pipe from the house to our barn about three hundred yards away. The pipe from the house was two inches, but when we brought it up out of the ground at the barn, our Finnish carpenter, Olavi, reduced it to one inch. If you reduced it to one inch at the barn, I asked, why didn't you reduce it at the house? Why waste all that two-inch pipe?

"Where would you like to be choked: at the neck or at the ankle?" Olavi replied.

This simple bit of wisdom seemed appropriate to more than laying pipe. First there had to be trust and this couldn't be achieved with the restrictions imposed by our attorney. But the essential problem was deeper. Our lawyer was doing what he had to do, what he was being paid to do: to look out for *our* interests exclusively. In making the agreement with the archive we had to have a contract that safeguarded the *mutual* interest of both the press and the archive. Only then could it be successful.

Nevertheless, from a publishing standpoint the loss of pure exclusivity was worrisome. How could we ensure that the materials we intended to publish would not be used elsewhere? This was a chronic concern of Western publishers. How could we be certain that the same materials would not be sold twice? And how could I persuade the management of Yale University Press to undertake an expensive and precarious project such as this without ironclad legal safeguards?

The only safeguards we had, and still have, are the quality of the work we would commission and the alacrity with which we could accomplish it. But this was not something I could easily sell to skeptical publishing professionals and colleagues. In the end, it was John Ryden, director of the press at the time, who saw the possibilities of the project and allowed me to take it away from our Madison Avenue lawyer and work with Yale lawyers, whom I could have some chance of persuading. The slightest misstep at this point would have been fatal.

In August I got word from Nikolai that the contract had been "approved," but, as he had predicted in July, panic quickly ensued. The Russian translation of the English-language contract was single-spaced and the English was double-spaced. As a consequence, it would have to be redone, resubmitted, and reapproved. Beyond this, there was much nasty gossip in the archive world in Moscow that leaked into the press and the universities. The hard-line communists, of which there were still many, routinely denounced such deals, and the nationalist xenophobes thought it was a betrayal, another way by which the West would rape the motherland. Nikolai assured me, however, that *"vsyo normalno"*—everything would be fine. He was convinced that the new administration could withstand this pressure because of all the safeguards built into the contract and the international reputation of Yale. The contract had become more than simply a business document, he told me.

And, in fact, by October 1992 the contract was duly signed. Naumov and I immediately had the same thought: "The first thing we must do is kill all the lawyers," I said to him when we had finished the last iteration, after hundreds of drafts and false starts. When I received final signed contracts back from Moscow by express mail, all of which was handled by Nikolai, it seemed our strategy had been correct and the battle had been won. I was excited and called Naumov in Moscow. The line was silent, and then I heard his laconic reply in halting English: "We have won the battle and now the war can begin." But when he said this, I felt that he and I would be on the same side.

The wisdom of his response was brought home to me in December 1992, when I received a very strongly worded message that the contract had been voided and that I had to come to Moscow immediately to renegotiate it. Renegotiate—what? Had our Madison Avenue lawyer been right? Was Olavi and his humble two-inch pipe all wrong? Maybe trust could go only so far.

I was told categorically that if I didn't show up in Moscow in January, the contract would be nullified. Serious flaws had come to light that could be resolved only in Moscow.

I was incredulous. What had happened? I was not being invited to Moscow; I was being summoned. The contract had been approved by both Rosarkhiv and Yale's lawyers. Only the word "resolved" (*reshat*) held out some hope, suggesting that they, too, envisioned a solution.

After much unhappy discussion both at work and at home, I decided the only thing I could do was to return to Moscow and renegotiate. Everyone suspected a fraud, an underhanded tactic—bribery? Why did I think that if I went to Moscow they would reconsider? Had they received a better offer? What a fool I had been to trust in this process, and what a fool for having felt so confident as to begin notifying people and the media of the major new scholarly initiative. What a fool I would be in the eyes of everyone. What a damn fool when it all came crashing down into nothing.

I sent a terse e-mail to Nikolai asking if three days would be enough. One, he responded enigmatically, might be enough.

Was that a good thing or a bad thing? More evidence that it was futile and he didn't wish to tell me? I asked Nikolai again if coming was necessary. "Come now or don't bother coming again" was his answer.

No one, not even Olavi, could help me in this situation, and I felt torn in a way I had never thought possible. Nor could I explain to anyone what was at stake. There was nothing to show yet, no documents, no actual publications. How could I demonstrate to others how important this project was when there was nothing substantial to distinguish it from countless other academic pipe dreams that came to nothing? How could I communicate to anyone the thrill of holding that 1930s flyer from Detroit in my hand, and of *knowing* it signified that much more lay concealed in those metal boxes in Firsov's archive?

Furthermore, I had moved my family to New Haven from Chicago in October 1991, and in November 1992 we still had few friends and no relatives close by. Our eldest son was in high school, our second was not yet two, and our daughter had been born in November. "If you get on that plane, don't bother to come home," my wife said in one heated conversation.

In truth, I did not know how any of this would be resolved. There was nothing else to go on except an obscure faith in my family's ability to withstand the tensions and pressures of this time and my faith in the goodwill of my Russian colleagues to find a solution to our problems.

I did not know what these problems were, but I suspected they were connected with the fact that over the past month a permanent director, by the name of Kyrill Anderson, had been named. I assumed from his last name that Anderson was of Scandinavian descent, but I could surmise little else. The only other piece of information I received from Nikolai was that Anderson was considered a *delovoi chelovek*—a man of business sense who can get things done.

When I arrived in Moscow in January 1993—now a year after my initial trip—the orange, red, and blue ruble notes that first struck me as more like Monopoly money than currency with real value were being replaced and were trading at one thousand to the dollar. There was talk of simply lopping off a zero or two in order to avert a monetary crisis. The half-constructed building in Revolution Square I had seen the year before, draped in a protective green dust cover, with the sign of some Austrian company fixed to it, remained behind the same green veil, in the same unfinished state, like a bride abandoned at the altar. The streets were as gray and barren as ever, the people as anxious.

In September 1993, Boris Yeltsin would dissolve the Russian parliament and fighting would erupt on the streets of Moscow; on October 2 Yeltsin would shell the Russian White House (the parliament building) in order to crush his political opposition. There had been rioting around the Ostankino Tower, the major radio and television transmitting antenna. One rioter claimed there were over a thousand deaths. When a reporter told him he hadn't seen any bodies, not even at the local hospitals or morgue, the man reportedly just laughed and said, "Of course there are no bodies. How can there be bodies when the police eat them?"

When I arrived in Moscow in January, months before these events, there was much discussion of a red-brown alliance between unreconstructed communist and nationalist-fascist groups to oppose Yeltsin. The extremist journalism I had found on my first trip continued to thrive in the metro stations and sidewalk kiosks. The atmosphere was gloomy and resigned.

Outside the Central Party Archive (now the Russian Center for the Preservation and Study of Records of Modern History, RTsKhIDNI), the same colorful poster beckoned passersby to distant eastern lands; Marx, Engels, and Lenin still peered gloomily down at Bolshaya Dimitrovka Street. Nothing had changed. Inside, the same diminutive gray-haired old lady in the same grayish blue smock with white stockings rolled above her ankles stood in the corner of the drafty coatroom by the guard station staring as before at a spot in the middle of the large entryway to the archive, and as before made no effort to take my coat because, I thought, it seemed to her I simply wasn't there. The same guard cast the same bored glance at my *propusk* and waved us through with the same half-conscious look in his eyes. The same bowl of fresh violets was at Lenin's feet, the same fixed look was in his eye, and the same stagnant, sour smell filled the corridor.

I rode up to the second third floor and walked down the hall thinking I might not walk down this hall again. A pack of Winstons and the excitement of the historical moment might not be enough. In the waiting room outside the director's office, the same calendar hung on the wall and the plastic clock stood at five o'clock. But after a few moments, Oleg Naumov came out, accompanied by the new director, who shook my hand warmly.

"Well," he said, "it seems we have work to do. We might as well get to work." He spoke excellent English, but with a strong, almost guttural accent I couldn't place. Standing well over six feet tall, Kyrill Anderson is an enormous man with hands like powerful tree roots, a thick, bullish neck, and massive shoulders. He speaks with casual wit, collects pipes, Netsuke figurines, and other miniatures, and is a specialist in eighteenth- and nineteenth-century French history, taking particular pride in the archive's unmatched collection of caricatures from the time of the French Revolution.

At our first meeting, he didn't wear a suit or even a sports jacket, and didn't strike me as particularly *delovoi* in his leather vest and tie; but he also didn't strike me as the opposite. He had been abroad; he was cheerful and confident; he didn't need to impress anyone.

"Come this way," he said, waving us into the conference room that also served as Naumov's office.

Before we seated ourselves across from each other at the long table, Naumov switched on the lights. Anderson saw my reaction. "Well, you see, conservation. It's a little chilly, too," he said, "it's good for the documents. In any case, it can't be helped. It's Russia." It was chilly because they could turn on the heat only certain hours of the day.

"Well, so, here you are in Moscow," Anderson began after I had taken the seat I had occupied the year before. "I hope your trip has not been too difficult. I'm glad you have come. *We* have a problem. It is our problem, not yours, not mine. We must work together for a solution. Do you agree?"

I had never heard such words spoken in my previous negotiations in Moscow. I had never heard them in the United States either. I readily agreed.

The key problem, it appeared, was the extent to which Russian scholars and researchers could make use of the materials in the archive while we were preparing them for publication.

"We are a research institution," Anderson explained. "We can't prevent Russian scholars from having access, and we also must find a way of publishing these books in Russia."

This seemed the easiest hurdle, and I offered complete permission to publish the books in Russian. But it wasn't that simple because without money to print the books, what good was permission? We had discussed this before, but without reaching a firm decision on the matter of the subsidy that Yale would have to supply for printing, paper, and composition. It took two days to work out appropriate algorithms for access and percentages for subsidy. The Russian printing process is different from ours: the size of the printer's sheet is different, costs are assessed differently.

Why was it so different here? I was tempted on more than one occasion to ask. But I could hear Anderson's reply: "Why are *you* so different?" It had never occurred to me until now that the English meaning of a word was not *the* meaning of that word. Or if it came from a Latin root that the Latin meaning was *the* meaning. When I first came across the Russian word *rezolyutsiya*, I connected it with the English word "resolution," which is, indeed, one of its meanings in Russian. But the secondary meaning was the one I kept finding in documents; it didn't mean "resolution," but "instructions" to be appended to a decision. The word *pretenziya* presented the same situation. One of its meanings in Russian is "pretension," but it is more frequently used in the documents I have studied to mean "claim." Such semantic shifts occur across all languages, but it was not until I was face-to-face with them and annoyed at the difficulties they posed that I began to ask myself why they couldn't just make use of *our* meaning. Was it not the same problem? *Our* meaning was precisely just that: *ours.* In language there are no absolutes. Nor in publishing. Nor in many other things.

Still, I would have to explain this to John Ryden, and that was the part of all this that was most emphatically *not* our problem, but mine alone. I recognized that it was vital the books be available in Russian for Russian readers; otherwise, was it not some form of plunder? Otherwise, how would this knowledge penetrate Russian society? And without this knowledge, how could a new society begin to be constructed?

When we finished renegotiating several points of the original agreement, Kyrill suggested that I return to the archive before I left Moscow for a final conversation. I asked if he foresaw additional problems. No, he said, but it was best to be careful.

Success. I almost jumped out of my skin as Jeff, Nikolai, and I zigzagged breathlessly down the frozen streets amid the tightly bundled crowds. The sky was low and gray; as was the case the previous January, pyramids of ice, some four or five feet high, were heaped in the middle of the sidewalks. Large gaps opened in the pavement, and tin drain spouts bulged down the faces of the buildings like swollen veins. From time to time small cadres of Red Army recruits, wearing Red Army insignia, pushed aggressively through the soft mass of people. Defiant, boyish eyes glared anxiously from under the gray felt army hats with plastic, five-pointed, ruby stars fixed to the front.

Success. Had it been a test? How committed was I? How committed was Yale? To come and *not* try to bribe or cajole or force? As yet, we hadn't raised a penny for the project and I knew it would take a lot, particularly to help subsidize the Russian volumes. I told Jeff what my grandfather had said when my father announced that he would go to college—the first member of the family to do so.

"Wonderful," my grandfather said. "This is America. Everybody can go to college."

"But, Pa," my dad pleaded. "College costs money."

My grandfather laughed. "Money? Any fool can go to college with money. The *khukham* goes without money. And that's what you've got to be."

Jeff thought a moment. "Be careful with Yiddish here," he said. "A lot of people in the archive won't appreciate it. Firsov will tell you." Especially at our next meeting, Jeff cautioned. Remember, it's KGB. They'll be sizing you up.

Word did travel throughout the archive community and had reached the ever-listening ears of Lubyanka Square, and the KGB representatives I had not been able to see the year before again expressed the wish—why, I never discovered—to see me now. A General Staroshin was preparing some documents of great value, but what they were neither Jeff nor Nikolai could say. At the appointed time, we came to the basement room in a building somewhere in Moscow's center. Two men in dark suits were there before us and asked us to wait. One was tall and thin with a narrow, oval face and a sallow complexion; the other was about my height and had a wide, squarish, stocky build. The general would only be a minute. In the meantime, we could make ourselves comfortable. As we stood there the shorter of the two men approached me. His thin companion stood behind him.

"Yampolsky," he said, taking my hand, like a car salesman. Then he added gently, "You are Italian?"

"No."

"No," he repeated reflectively.

His companion now stepped forward. "Zavyalov," he said in an insouciant, flutey voice. Unlike Yampolsky's, his long, snakelike hand didn't so much grasp as enfold my own. There was dirt under the broken nails, as if he had just come out from under a car or tractor. When Zavyalov smiled, you could see the yellow teeth jutting out at odd angles. A wisp of black hair hung in a crescent moon over his forehead, and a colorless tie lay askew around his neck. He looked at me carefully with sad but scheming black eyes. I asked if he spoke English, and he answered with a sheepish grin that exposed more oddly shaped and discolored teeth, several capped with gold.

"Your mother was Spanish, then?" he wondered, picking up where Yampolsky left off.

By now I knew what they were driving at, but I didn't help him.

"But your family from Mediterranean, no?" he tried again, inclining his head to one side as if to play the violin.

"No," I said, losing patience. "One grandfather was from Kiev and the other from Lvov."

"Ah," Yampolsky breathed with satisfaction. *"Yevreisky Lvov"*—Jewish Lvov.

That settled, Zavyalov and Yampolsky retreated a few steps and back into their own thoughts to wait for their boss to appear.

Zavyalov, with his sad but scheming eyes, his crooked teeth, his sallow complexion, and the wisp of black hair on his forehead. Zavyalov, who I came to know as Sergei and would see on every visit—sometimes as a deputy director of a publishing house whose offices were in the showroom of a new automobile dealership, sometimes as a student of history at a newly formed university, sometimes as a consultant on new technologies. Over the years we had many pleasant and intense conversations that never produced a single result. Once when I arrived at his new office I noted someone else's nameplate on the desk. Sergei would appear as if from the wings of the stage on all my succeeding trips to Moscow until on one trip he did not materialize.

"Where is Zavyalov?" I asked Nikolai. *"Zavyalov propal,"* Nikolai said simply. Zavyalov had disappeared—but in the sense of having fallen off a precipice, or simply vanished, poof. *"Zavyalov propal,"* Nikolai said, and I never saw or heard from him again.

After settling the question of my origins, an older man in a gray suit with graying hair walked briskly into the anteroom. Yampolsky pulled open the door and held it as Jeff, Nikolai, and I followed the general.

We took our seats on one side; the gray-haired general sat opposite, flanked by his two advisers. It was a basement office and through the row of windows above our heads you could see the feet of people passing by on the street. After the introductions, General Staroshin stood and extended his hand across the table.

"I wish to congratulate you, *Gospodin Brent*, on the birth of your daughter."

I had communicated the fact that my daughter had been born six weeks earlier to Jeff but no one else. Confused but also pleased, I rose to take his hand. Part of me wished to know more about this man and to thank him for knowing so much about me; part of me wanted to turn around and go home. "The KGB remains all-knowing," I said, and thanked him for his good wishes. He smiled and we sat down.

After some additional preliminaries, we got to business. The KGB had many valuable documents they wished to publish. These supersecret materials would definitely interest American readers because they dealt with World War II, Stalin, and the most secret aspects of Soviet intelligence work. They would be of great importance in world history, General Staroshin said.

"May I see a list of documents?" I asked.

"No, they are too sensitive," the general answered.

"Can you provide me with a précis or a description?"

"No, unfortunately not."

"I must make a deal based on no information?"

"Unfortunately, that is the case, but I can assure you, you will not be disappointed."

"General Staroshin," I said. "I do not wish to appear disrespectful or arrogant, but Yale is a scholarly publishing company. The work we publish is reviewed and evaluated by scholars and must meet the highest standards of scholarship. I must present every project to a committee of scholars at Yale University for their approval. I'm afraid I simply can't make a deal based on these kinds of assurances. I suggest you approach a commercial publishing company in the United States, one that doesn't care what it publishes so long as it's sensational."

Obviously irritated, Staroshin leaned across the table on his elbow.

"Listen," he said, pointing a finger at me. "I want to do business with Yale University Press, and when you go back, I want you to tell your director that I know everything about Yale University Press because when I was a student I studied many books published by Yale University Press. You tell him that."

Was this a threat or another gentle reminder, like congratulating me on the birth of my daughter? Should I be concerned about the "outreach" of the organization he represented?

"I will do that," I assured the general.

"I will see about a list of documents, but I must obtain clearance. You may hear from us again."

With this he stood and left the room, followed by Zavyalov and Yampolsky, who had not said a word throughout the interview. A month or two later, I did, indeed, hear from them again, receiving by mail a twenty- or thirty-page list of documents with brief captions. I sent these materials to

William Odom, a close adviser to the project, and asked for a professional opinion. Bill, who had been the head of army intelligence and worked under Zbigniew Brzezinski in the National Security Agency during the Carter years, immediately sent me a note stating that the documents were little more than self-congratulatory, self-justifying evidence that the KGB wasn't responsible for the June 1941 Nazi invasion and the debacle of the Red Army—a question still of burning importance in Russian society.

Do you want to publish a book that serves the political agenda of the KGB? Odom asked. The actual documents will not be scrutinized or put into any kind of political or military context, and they were selected to prove one conclusion: that Stalin was wholly to blame for the disaster. Some of the documents are inherently interesting, of course, but their underlying intent was not historical; it was political. How could you trust them? The bigger question, though, is not what the list of documents contained, but what it might have left out. How could you know if it was complete? How could you know if another set of documents equally voluminous did not propose an opposite scenario? Besides, they were not even complete copies, but were probably typescript texts taken from actual documents. They had no archival location data and, therefore, could not be properly cited as sources from a Soviet archive.

I sent Odom's report to General Staroshin, who immediately replied that he considered the comment that the volume would be little more than a self-serving whitewash of the KGB to be an "insult to his uniform." He suggested another meeting in Moscow, this time with General Odom, so that he could prove the validity and importance of the materials he offered. He extended the offer to allow Odom to see them for himself.

Odom accompanied me to Moscow about six months later, and we met with General Staroshin, Zavyalov, and Yampolsky in the same basement room in the same building whose precise identity I could never learn. When we sat down, I looked again at the windows overhead. At first I saw the same legs of people passing by, but after a few moments, the legs stopped; one or two people bent down and peered in. As the meeting got under way, some unidentified young men entered the room without being announced. They casually walked around the table as if to get a good look at General Odom and then left. No one said a word.

General Staroshin produced a recent issue of the *Military History Journal*, the Ministry of Defense's leading academic journal for military historians. It contained an article by General William Odom and his picture on the back cover. Major General Vladimir Slipchenko's picture was also on the back cover and one of his articles was in the journal. They appeared to be facing off against each other. Both Odom and Slipchenko were in full military uniform.

As we settled into a discussion of the documentary collection being offered to Yale, General Staroshin passed an untitled bound book of additional materials across the table to Odom, suggesting he might find them of interest. As Bill became absorbed in these, I spoke with Yampolsky about how it might be possible to prepare the materials so that Yale could publish them. We would need analysis by Western experts, full citations, and an introductory essay setting these materials in the context of the war, Stalin's control over the security apparatus, and relations with Germany from 1939 to 1941. Yampolsky listened attentively, but indicated that he thought none of this would be acceptable. The discussion was going nowhere. Bill, however, was lost in examining what Staroshin had put in his hands. After about an hour, we thanked our hosts, Bill returned the book, and we promised to reconsider the project.

"What was that?" I asked after we were safely outside.

"They are compilations of counterintelligence cases the KGB had run over the years," Odom said. "Casebooks." They appeared to contain all the operational reports connected with each case and a brief narrative tying these reports together so that the whole story of the case would be available for training or referencing other hostile intelligence agents.

Odom told me he had never seen anything like it. Case after case with step-by-step analyses of what went wrong in a given action and what went right—at least this was his conclusion from being allowed to scan parts of one of the large volumes, possibly containing a thousand pages of case records. Odom thought it was a remarkable way to provide historical context and continuity for every intelligence service that opposed the Soviet Union.

"We never did that on our side," Bill said. "Not really. Never on that level of detail. That's why they were so good. Very good. But not always the best," he added. "Sometimes even they were confused and utterly wrong."

"Could we publish *those* books?"

"Are you kidding? They'd never allow you to have them. Never."

Fridrikh Firsov invited me to dinner at his apartment that evening. We were to discuss the diary of Georgi Dimitrov and the book project on the terror in the Comintern in the 1930s. Why was the diary so important? Very simple. It was the only diary kept by a leading member of the Soviet government who was close to Stalin; as head of the Comintern, Dimitrov met regularly with his boss. Afterward Dimitrov wrote out his conversations with Stalin, in addition to much else, in the diary. Though he was Bulgarian, he wrote the Moscow part of the diary in Russian. When he was in Germany he wrote in German, and when he returned to Bulgaria after the war he wrote in Bulgarian. Quite an interesting figure. In fact, Firsov told me, he wrote the opening section in German while handcuffed in prison, studying the language.

Where did he keep it when he came to Moscow? I asked. In a safe. Wasn't he taking quite a risk?

"Not at all," Firsov said. "The only one who had a key to the safe, except for Dimitrov, was Stalin."

"And Stalin read it?"

"Every day."

A chasm seemed to open up. "Every day?"

"Maybe every other day."

"So why did he do this?"

"It's how the system worked."

Georgi Dimitrov, a Bulgarian communist and hero of the Reichstag fire trial of 1933, worked and lived in Moscow until the end of the war, at which time he returned to his native Bulgaria, where he eventually became premier of the new Bulgarian People's Republic. Stalin was recuperating from the war effort in Sochi at the time of Dimitrov's departure from Moscow in 1945. He included his letter of farewell to Stalin in his diary.

Dear Comrade Stalin,

Departing for Bulgaria in connection with the deputies' elections, I would like to express to you my most profound gratitude for the opportunity accorded to me for many years to work under your direct leadership and to learn so much from you, and also for the confidence that you have placed in me.

Naturally I will in [*sic*] future continue to make every effort to justify your confidence. But I beg you to provide me the opportunity in [*sic*] future to avail myself of your valuable advice, which is exceptionally valuable.

From the bottom of my heart I wish you good health and long life, for the benefit of the great Soviet homeland and toilers the world over.

Your ever devoted,
G. D.
3 October 1945

There are several interesting things about this letter, but the first is that he sent it on October 3, a full month before inscribing it into his diary on November 3, 1945. Why the wait? This would be one entry Stalin would not read. Did he not dare to include it until he received Stalin's response to ensure it was acceptable to the master? Such formalities—birthday greetings, who might be asked to accompany Stalin to the train station before a trip, whose names appeared in lists from time to time published in the newspapers as marked for assassination by "enemies of the state"—all this was of no small importance to Stalin, the *Vozhd*. Dimitrov's servile devotion did not end with his closing words. The moment Stalin showed displeasure, in 1947, with Tito and Dimitrov's "treaty of unlimited duration" between Yugoslavia and Bulgaria, Dimitrov reproduced the letter he wrote to Tito, dated August 13, 1947, in his diary.

To Walter [Tito]:

Concerning the message of our Great Friend [Stalin], we should admit that we were carried away in the matter of the agreement. To correct this committed mistake, it is necessary, to my mind, to annul this act and, when more favorable times come, and after consultations with our Soviet friends, to sign the treaty and make it public.

Ivan [Dimitrov]

Nor did his devotion end here. Though Stalin no longer read Dimitrov's diary, Dimitrov continued to make entries in it *as though Stalin did*. Subsequent to this letter, on January 24, 1948, Stalin sent Dimitrov a letter protesting remarks Dimitrov had made at a press conference in Romania.

We consider it our duty to bring to your attention the fact that the part of your statement at the press conference in Romania . . . concerning the federation or confederation of people's democracies, including Greece, Poland, Czechoslovakia, etc., is viewed by the Moscow friends as harmful, causing detriment to the countries of the new democracy and facilitating the struggle of the Anglo-Americans against these countries.

It is hard to figure out what could have made you make such rash and injudicious statements at the press conference.

24 January 1948

Druzhkov [Stalin]
Dimitrov immediately responded:

To Druzhkov [Stalin]:

I confirm the receipt of your telegram. I am grateful to you for your remarks. I shall draw the proper conclusions.

Ivanov [Dimitrov]

Dimitrov clearly received these communications from Stalin in encoded form, hence "Druzhkov" and "Ivanov" and locutions such as "Moscow friends." Nevertheless, he instantly inserted them into his diary. He remained the faithful servant to the end, recording his master's displeasure and rebukes as if to prove to himself—or to others who might come after—the slavish loyalty that his thoughtless behavior in negotiating with Tito appeared to jeopardize. Stalin was present to Dimitrov without being present.

Dimitrov returned to Moscow in 1949 for medical treatments and died in Barvikha Sanatorium on July 2, 1949, under what many thought at the time were suspicious circumstances. To this day, no one knows whether Stalin had Dimitrov medically assassinated. This would have been by no means out of the question. Much new documentation suggests that this is precisely the fate Stalin engineered for his other trusted servant, Andrei Zhdanov, head of the Leningrad Party and Politburo member, in August 1948. There is no doubt that Dimitrov and Zhdanov, like Yezhov before them, would have gone to their deaths with Stalin's name on their lips.

Firsov had read the diary because a microfilm copy was in the Comintern collection in Moscow, but the original remained with Dimitrov's son, Boyko, in Sofia, Bulgaria. If we were to publish the diary, Firsov would need to check the microfilm against the original to see whether anything had been omitted or added. However, Firsov explained, there was another complication. Dimitrov's granddaughter lived in Moscow. The daughter of Dimitrov's adopted daughter, whose real father was a famous Chinese communist who died in the 1930s, was not on good terms with Boyko, her uncle, and was, by all accounts, not easy to deal with. However, according to Russian law we would need to obtain her permission as well as that of Dimitrov's son before we could publish this work.

We must do two things, Firsov advised. The first was to arrange to meet the granddaughter in Moscow. The second was to arrange to meet Boyko in Sofia. Would I do this? Publication of the diary was contingent on agreement with the family, not with the archive, so I decided both to go to Sofia and meet the granddaughter. Firsov thought he might be able to find her, and he knew how to reach Boyko, who spoke good English.

The following day I received a message through Jeff that we must meet in a particular metro station, second car from the end, on a particular track, at 2:00 P.M. exactly. Do not be late. She would find us. Firsov would join us, but didn't wish to be immediately present at our meeting because he thought it might frighten her. Only if need be would he join us from where he would be stationed.

Jeff and I went to the correct position on the metro platform and waited. When she didn't show up, Jeff whispered that he thought we were being observed. Eventually, a slender, nervous-looking man in his midthirties or early forties approached. You must be the American publisher? he asked in staccato English.

I said I was. What did we want? Why? His client could sign nothing. Why did we bother her? He was her lawyer and would look everything over very carefully. We could be sure of that. As he was speaking, an attractive, slender Asian-looking or rather Eurasian woman in her early thirties came toward me from behind a column. She said nothing. When I extended my hand, she pulled back behind her lawyer. He resumed his interrogations. What did we wish to publish this for? Who were we? What was Yale University Press? He would read the contract over carefully, but was certain there would be much to negotiate. Do not, he warned, try to be in touch with his client again. He took the contract and left. This was the daughter of Dimitrov's daughter. Her thin frame swayed nervously as we spoke. I never heard from either of them again.

The daughter herself had died some years previously, and there was speculation, I learned, of family intrigue, possible mental instability, and foul play. But the details were murky and Firsov insisted that I not pursue the matter further. However, this made all the more urgent the trip to Sofia to meet Dimitrov's son, who had also held an important post in the former Communist government of Bulgaria. Firsov would call that evening.

The next day, I spoke directly with Boyko on the telephone. He would be delighted to meet me. He already had many ideas about publishing the diary. He spoke English well. I would get on the first flight from Moscow to Sofia, and he would meet me at the airport with a copy of *The Economist* under his arm.

At the airport the next day I asked the guard at passport control whether I would need a visa to enter Bulgaria. No, certainly not, was the answer. Why? Russia and Bulgaria are fraternal countries, very friendly. There would be no need. And to reenter Russia? Of course not. Russia and Bulgaria are on the best terms with each other. Why would I need a visa to come back?

I boarded my Aeroflot flight to Sofia at ten thirty in the morning. I would touch down around one o'clock and return with Boyko to his house, where we would have lunch and discuss publishing the diary. I would stay overnight in a hotel and leave the next day. Beside me in the plane was a Russian man who spoke a bit of English. Jokingly, I mentioned that my travel agent had said that Aeroflot was a very good airline except that you didn't know when you'd go up or where you'd come down. My new friend, who described himself as a *biznes* man, did not enjoy the joke.

"No," he said. "Russian plane is strong," and he made two fists. "Strong. Like Russian woman."

We passed the rest of the flight discussing Russian history and literature. I revealed that my grandfathers had both come from Russia and that my family name was originally Brodsky, not Brent. He invited me to call him the next time I was in Moscow, and I would come to his dacha and enjoy his *banya* and meet his friends. The flight was smooth and uneventful. At about one o'clock, as the plane was about to hit the tarmac and we were preparing to say good-bye, a voice came over the loudspeaker. I looked out the window at what seemed like a familiar landscape.

"What did she say?" I asked, unable to make out the crackling, rapid-fire announcement over the intercom.

My friend looked perplexed and said there must be some mistake.

"What did she say?" I asked again.

"Due to technical difficulties, we have returned to Sheremetyevo Airport," he said. "But this is not possible."

As we exited the plane, with the urgent promptings of the crew, we were surrounded by fire trucks, ambulances, and police. My first thought was, *No. This is a joke. We're really in Sofia. It just looks like Moscow.* But my friend's ashen face told the story.

"Please," he said, taking my arm. "Please, come with me." He led me and two utterly dazed young Chinese students, who stood near us and knew no Russian or English and clearly had little concept of what was going on, to the airport café; there he entertained us with caviar, vodka, black bread, and hard-boiled eggs for five or six hours until a replacement plane could be obtained from Alma-Ata. When I offered to help pay for our feast, he flatly refused.

By 10:00 P.M., I was at Sofia Airport. It was dark and I could only vaguely make out the mountain range that formed a ring around us. I had no hope of seeing anybody with a copy of *The Economist* under his arm, but there he was on the other side of the customs line. He spotted me instantly.

"We were very worried," Boyko began. "But it's really quite normal. You must get used to it if you are to be in this part of the world for very long." He spoke English with hardly a trace of an accent. He had been in the sector of the Bulgarian government responsible for foreign trade. He took me straight to the hotel. Tomorrow we would talk in earnest. He would take me to Dimitrov's tomb and I could see for myself how disgraceful and ungrateful the people were toward Dimitrov, who had given his life to save them. At one point, he even feared that the tomb would be desecrated, so late one night they removed the body and reburied it without ceremony in a public cemetery.

The hotel appeared empty, but there was someone at the front desk and Boyko guided me up to my room. He would call in the morning. The most striking feature of the hotel room was not the paper-thin walls and the paper-thin blanket and the paper-thin mattress, and the sliver of soap in its silky wrapper on the washbasin, but rather that in place of the mint one might have found on one's pillow in an

American hotel, there was a cellophane packet containing a single condom.

The following day, we easily came to terms, and Boyko assured me that he could take responsibility for his niece's signature and guarantee that the contract would be fulfilled. He took me to see Dimitrov's tomb, now entirely defaced with rude graffiti, dishonoring the memory of this hero of the Reichstag trial in Leipzig in which he outwitted Goebbels and upheld the honor of workers and peasants worldwide. When he returned to Moscow, he was greeted by Stalin as one of the great figures of the communist movement. As leader of Bulgaria after the war, Dimitrov did not impose the harsh retaliatory measures of his Moscow mentor against bourgeois enemies.

"The advantage of the Soviet form," Stalin advised in December 1948, "is that it solves the problems quickly—by shedding blood; but you [Dimitrov] can do without it because the capitalists in your country surrendered immediately. In other words, you were lucky, and we are responsible for your luck, as we readily admit."

Where there is a man, there is a problem. Where there is no man, there is no problem: this was Stalin's favorite personnel management rule-of-thumb. And yet he called Dimitrov "lucky." Stalin's self-awareness is astounding: his *self-conscious* understanding of his personal responsibility, duty, and historical role raises him into a category considerably above the mere butchers and sadists who often performed his dirty work, a category often reserved for tragic heroes. After Stalin's sober admonishments, Dimitrov writes,

We stayed till morning. Stalin was very lively and cheerful. He was treating his guests. He played some records, told us jokes, and even danced.

The December 1948 date of this meeting coincides with the onset of Stalin's final period, when his mind returned to the purges of the 1930s through which he achieved absolute power. In January 1948, he had assassinated the world-acclaimed actor and director of the Moscow Yiddish Theater, Solomon Mikhoels, whose work on Stalin's behalf in 1943 earned him the highest honors his homeland could bestow, but who now represented a link to the incipient state of Israel and the United States. New documentation strongly suggests that in August 1948 Stalin had engineered the demise of Andrei Zhdanov; Zhdanov had been a favored colleague whose son had even married Stalin's daughter, but by 1948 he had fallen out of favor, as had Politburo members Vyacheslav Molotov, Anastas Mikoyan, and Kliment Voroshilov, among others. The liquidation of the Jewish Anti-Fascist Committee in 1952 would coincide with the execution of top leaders of the Leningrad party; and the anticosmopolitan, anti-Semitic campaign would soon boil to a crisis. By 1950 Stalin would begin plotting a nuclear confrontation with the United States.

I asked again at Sofia Airport whether I needed a visa to reenter Russia and received the same response as before. I returned to Sheremetyevo without incident, but was immediately stopped at passport control and led into one of the closed rooms into which I had seen the Asian merchants disappear on my first trip. The cracked green walls of the office were bare except for a portrait of a Lenin, under which I sat silently for several minutes awaiting my fate. Soon the severe young guard returned and brought me upstairs to an immigration agent, who demanded to see my visa and passport.

I explained in my inadequate Russian that I was told I didn't need a reentry visa. He shrugged. How could I have been so misinformed? I wanted to know. He had no idea but it wasn't his concern. The law was the law. The situation was simple. I would have to get on another flight to Sofia, buy a visa, and return to Moscow.

This is a joke, I said. I simply refuse. There is no way I will ever get on another Aeroflot plane to Sofia. I would rather go to jail. Do you want to put me in jail over something as stupid as this? I'm an American citizen. I'll make a terrible fuss about this nonsense. The poor man could understand little of what I was saying and suggested that I find the representative of Balkan Airlines in the airport who spoke English and might be able to help. Good luck.

I went off by myself into the maze of Sheremetyevo's offices, knocking on any door behind which it seemed someone might be found. By happy accident, I turned a corner and came upon the office for Balkan Airlines. The representative was at his desk and seemed glad to have the opportunity to speak English. He was cordial and bemused. Instead of a portrait of Lenin, his walls were decorated with colorful posters of Bulgaria. One showed Sofia surrounded by the magnificent Vitosha Mountains, which I had only glimpsed the day before.

"I was told I didn't need a visa when I left yesterday," I complained.

"Yes, of course," he said. "But this is Russia, and unfortunately, here it is always today."

We returned through a series of interconnected hallways to the immigration agent. My Bulgarian friend spoke to him privately for a moment, and together they devised a solution: I would purchase my visa right here in Moscow for $150 from the agent, who quickly filled out the necessary forms. However, another $100 was necessary as a down payment on the hotel where I would need to be booked. I explained that I was living in a private apartment and didn't need a hotel. It didn't matter. The law was the law. Go to the hotel, explain the situation, and they'll give you back your $100. It's a mere formality, he assured me. I knew it wasn't.

Nikolai and my new translator, Olga Varshaver, were still waiting downstairs, unable to get information from any source and frantic at the thought that I had somehow disappeared in the bowels of Sheremetyevo. We drove to the hotel. I explained my situation as best I could to the young women behind the counter at the reception desk. At first they were stony and indifferent, but when I used the word *koshmar*—the Russian word for "nightmare"—to describe my experience they looked at each other and burst out laughing. They took down my telephone number and assured me I would be notified the minute my $100 was received from the immigration office at Sheremetyevo.

The next day I met Anderson and Naumov in the archive for our final meeting, as Anderson had suggested.

"We have solved all but one major problem," Anderson said at last.

"What?" I asked.

"Well, you see, it is a wonderful contract," Anderson said after a moment in which my heart sank.

"But it seems," he continued, "that it was signed by the wrong person."

"What?" I said again in disbelief. It was signed by Naumov and approved by Rosarkhiv.

"Well, so, you see. But Mr. Naumov is no longer the head of the archive." With that and with Oleg sitting beside him, he drew a line through Naumov's name and signed his own above it.

"There," Anderson declared, with an ironic glint in his eye, "now it is correct. Now, we have a contract." He held it by a corner in the tips of his massive forefinger and thumb, as a cat might hold up a mouse for inspection by its master. So much work had gone into it, so much anxiety—so many new things I had to negotiate and renegotiate, think and rethink, and here it was now finally "correct."

"Congratulations," Anderson said. "This is a fine contract. But remember one thing, if I might say so. If I don't want to work with you, it's nothing but a piece of paper."

Façade of RGASPI from Archive brochure.

Brochure for the Moscow Circus: "My Old Circus, My Love."

Poster: "Let's Fulfill the Plan of the Great Work." (Klutsis G. (1895–1938): "Let's fulfill the plan of great work." Moscow, Leningrad 1930. From "Constructivism in Soviet poster. Golden Collection—Moscow: 'Kontakt-Kultura,' 2006.")

ЗНАКОМЫЙ НЕЗНАКОМЕЦЪ.

Illustration of the "familiar stranger"—the International Jew, produced
in "Pamyat'," No. 3, 1992, page 11.

Photograph of the royal family in "Pamyat'," No. 3, 1992, under the headline: "Judgment of the people or ritual murder?"

Front page of *Russkoe Voskressenie*, No. 8/16.

Photos from *Narodnoe Delo*, No. 2 (3), p. 4. An anti-Semitic, nationalist newspaper of the early 1990s. In the white triangle over the Jew's eye are the words: "Washington. London. Paris." Behind the Jew are gallows.

Большевики повели борьбу за созыв III съезда партии. В августе 1904 года в Швейцарии под руководством Ленина происходило совещание 22 большевиков. Это совещание приняло ~~написанное Лениным~~ обращение «К партии», которое стало для большевиков программой борьбы за созыв III съезда. На трех областных конференциях Комитетов большинства (южной, кавказской и северной) было избрано Бюро Комитетов большинства, которое повело практическую подготовку к новому съезду партии.

4 января 1905 года вышел первый номер большевистской газеты «Вперед», ~~которая продолжила линию старой «Искры», готовила рабочий класс к революционным боям.~~

КРАТКИЕ ВЫВОДЫ

В период 1901—1904 годов на основе роста революционного рабочего движения растут и крепнут марксистские социал-демократические организации в России. В упорной принципиальной борьбе с экономистами побеждает революционная линия ленинской «Искры», ~~побеждает ленинский план организации пролетарской партии,~~ преодолеваются идейный разброд и «кустарничество».

«Искра» связывает между собой разрозненные социал-демократические кружки и группы и подготовляет II съезд партии. На II съезде в 1903 году образовалась Российская социал-демократическая рабочая партия, принимается программа, устав партии, создаются центральные руководящие органы партии.

В борьбе, происходившей на II съезде за окончательную победу искровского направления, внутри РСДРП появляются фракции, ~~(группы)~~ большевиков и меньшевиков.

Главные разногласия развертываются по организационным вопросам.

Меньшевики ...

Накануне первой русской революции большевики и меньшевики выступают как ...

¹ История ВКП(б).

Street scene along Kutuzovsky Prospekt, January 1998.

Inside the office of N. G. Tomilina, director of RGANI (formerly the Archive of the Central Committee). Note the map of the world in the background with the U.S.S.R outlined over my head. Nikolai Petrovich Yakovlev stands front left. N. G. Tomilina and the author are in the center flanked by archival workers.

Stalin's marginal notes on his copy of *The Proletarian Revolution and the Renegade Kautsky*.

From *Piggy Foxy and the Sword of Revolution*, p. 198, drawing by
V. I.Mezhlauk, entitled, *At the dead end* [February, 1937], depicting
"Bukharin's school" and the figures of Kamenev and Piatakov.

Front and back of box of chocolates on sale at Sheremetevo airport, Moscow, as of 2008.

Chapter 11

Turmoil, Misdirection, Fear

After the euphoria of 1991 and 1992, harsh realities began to set in. The hotel behind its green veil that I had wondered about in January 1992 was still unfinished in 1993. Deals behind closed doors were being made, but with whom? To what end? Even as the bones of the Romanov family were being restored to their rightful place in Russian history, Russian history seemed to have undergone another catastrophic displacement, and this displacement, like the opening of fault lines during an earthquake, allowed many volcanic pressures to burst upward.

On the front page of *Pamyat* (issue No. 3–1992), the newspaper of a prominent xenophobic, anti-Semitic, nationalist group of the same name, was a reproduction of a 1913 photograph of Tsar Nicholas II with his wife and children gathered around him. The children are beautiful. Empress Alexandra sits slightly lower than her beloved Nicky, with the tsarevich in his sailor suit at her feet, while the legendary Anastasia, by no means the loveliest of the five daughters, stands at her father's arm. It is an image of family harmony, dynastic strength, and appropriately restrained imperial power. The expression of the autocrat is benign, and the expression of his wife is properly subdued.

"The Verdict of the People or Ritual Murder?" reads the headline at the top of the page. Between the headline and the photo is the following caption:

The national-patriotic front "Pamyat" considers it its sacred, Christian duty to inform its fellow-countrymen in detail of all the monstrous truth of the evil act performed against out great sovereign Emperor and his family.

Below this caption is an article explaining that in 1917 the Bolshevik Party was composed largely of Germans and Jews, with very few actual Russians. Therefore, the death of the royal family might have been the product of a so-called ritual murder allegedly performed by Jews before Passover. The fact that the family was executed in July and Passover usually takes place in April apparently had no bearing on this theory.

Was this headline merely the obsession of an extremist, nationalistic, cryptofascist group? Pamyat's emblem is the traditional two-headed eagle with a "Russian" (left-facing) swastika emblazoned in its center. Two years later, as Yale University Press was preparing the Tsaritsa's 1918 diary, the head of the Russian Orthodox Church in Boston asked to meet with Robert Massie at Yale University's Beinecke Library in order to discuss the case of the murder of the tsar and his family and to inspect the remarkable collection of Romanov materials at Yale. I had invited Massie to write the introduction to the diary and he, in turn, suggested I attend the meeting.

In a room in the basement of the Beinecke Library, at Yale University, in 1995, the head of the church delegation mentioned that the church was now in the process of considering the canonization of the royal family. I asked how it was proceeding. "Slowly," was the answer. When I asked why, the reply astounded Massie more than me.

The church father said that the exact cause of death had to be ascertained. And therefore the church had to determine whether their deaths occurred as a result of (1) a legal decision made by the new government, (2) the action of an angry or unorganized mob, (3) the action of a rogue element within the government, or (4) a ritual murder.

I asked what he meant by ritual murder. He said a ritual murder was performed by Jews who would kill a Gentile child and take its blood to make matzoh for Passover. The man in charge of the execution of the royal family, Jakov Yurovsky, was a Jew.

In the end, this charge of ritual murder was quietly forgotten, yet by the mid-1990s, the trickle of such extremist and atavistic ideas became difficult to control. All of a sudden there were many trickles: some were nationalistic or fascistic; some were mafia style; some were the work of "oligarchs," or old-fashioned communists, or religious fanatics. No civil institutions were capable of controlling them. In the words of the head of one of the state archives, "The best thing for Russia right now is for nothing to happen."

The political extremism of groups like Pamyat was fueled by the downward spiral of the Russian economy, the lack of jobs, and the directionless political and social leadership. Almost daily in certain nationalistic newspapers one read of the crisis in the Russian "soul." The word "democracy" ceased to have much meaning when a professor's salary was no more than $100 per month and inflation was out of control. Instead of a *demokratiya* (democracy), many people now spoke of living in a *dermokratiya* (a shitocracy).

Nikto ne pomozhet Rossii krome nas ("nobody can help Russia except ourselves") was a sentiment in wide circulation. Though these pleas for national introspection often reflected the Russian penchant for what Vitaly Makhlin at the Spanish Bar had called excessive *dukhovnost*, or spirituality, it expressed a genuine need to find a new collective identity amid the ruins of the former Soviet empire. Unlike in Eastern Europe, where the collapse of the Soviet Union was greeted by the majority of the populations as liberation, here it was a sign of moral and political failure and extreme national vulnerability.

The newspaper *Russkii Vestnik*, which identified itself as the "only general national newspaper in Russia," produced a short pamphlet in 1993 entitled *Puti Russkogo vozrozhdeniya* (the way of Russian rebirth). It concluded:

> The only possibility of escaping further deterioration of the situation [in Russia], chaos and the ruin of Russia as a state, and the Russian people as a spiritual and ethnic whole is the immediate return of the country to the path of its natural, orderly, original development.

Russkii Vestnik's hope was that all the positive aspects of Russian life—both before and after the revolution—could be harnessed together in this effort. Many other journals took more extreme approaches, and there was much public speculation about whether Russia would become a fascist state. In many restaurants at this time the theme music of *The Godfather* could be heard over the loudspeakers, while unrestrained gangsterism, looting of public resources, and wholesale government corruption swept the country.

When a new tax policy was announced, one government official said to me: "Surely the tax idea is pure cheating by the government. The government would be helped much more if it would pay people what they were owed instead of collecting taxes like the Sheriff of Sherwood Forest."

Nikolai remarked, "For every one hundred rubles, ninety-five are taken in taxes. Of course no one wants to pay them. Andrei Kozyrev [appointed foreign minister by Yeltsin in 1992] has made Russia look like a rag on which the West can wipe its feet. Anarchy is Russia's biggest problem."

In the mid-1990s, the Russian government was collecting less than 20 percent of the taxes owed it. No government can call itself a government of the people under those circumstances. But what would it be a government of?

This was the situation in 1994 when I received a call from Jeff while I was in Moscow informing me that Professor Vladimir Pavlovich Naumov, Oleg Naumov's father, wished to know whether I would be willing to meet with the head of the Central Committee Archive to discuss a project of potentially great interest. Would I be available? I had not seen or heard from Vladimir Naumov since our brief encounter at the Spanish Bar two years previously. What spurred this sudden desire to see me? Something to do with the Kirov assassination of 1934, Jeff said. Professor Naumov believes that he can prove Stalin's connection.

Over the years I had heard rumors—of special access to KGB and presidential archives, long-standing relations with the organs of power during the Brezhnev period, and an ability to enter almost any door in Moscow. Some had said they would never work with Vladimir Pavlovich Naumov. Others revered him. I was eager to meet him.

The Central Committee Archive is located in the same office complex as Rosarkhiv. Nikolai, Olga Varshaver, and I were led down a different set of corridors, a winding maze of passages and doorways, until we came out in the archive's reading room. It was a magnificent room with a high ceiling and beautifully decorated walls. On the wall opposite where we entered large portraits of Marx and Lenin hung from the ceiling. Glass cases along one wall provided space to exhibit books, documents, or announcements. On each of the neatly arranged writing desks stood an emerald green glass-shaded bank lamp. Later, the director told me that the reading room had actually been a nineteenth-century bank.

As we passed through the reading room I was struck by its decorum and simple elegance and by the care with which it was maintained amid the deteriorating conditions on the street. Finally we were brought to a large room at the end of a hallway. I looked about but couldn't see Vladimir Pavlovich. Instead, Nataliya Georgievna Tomilina, the director of the Central Committee Archive, greeted me with both warmth and curiosity. The lady who had shepherded us through the building compound to this room quietly took her place at the far end of the table where others of the staff were seated. The table was set with numerous plates of every kind of delicacy: smoked chicken, blini, caviar, pickles, cheeses of different sorts, mushrooms, apples, brown bread, sausages, and sliced meats. Behind the teacups were glasses for water and vodka.

I was directed to a seat next to Natalyia Georgievna, which I took as a sign that this would not be a formal negotiation, and as we exchanged some words about my visit to Moscow and the nature of the work of the archive, the door opened and Vladimir Pavlovich quietly entered.

"Professor Naumov," Tomilina said. "This is Jonathan Brent."

"Znayu," was his response—"I know," as he smiled and reached out his hand. He took the open seat next to me.

"Professor Naumov is an honored researcher in our archive," Tomilina continued. "We hold his advice in high regard, and he suggested we be in touch with you to see whether there might be an opportunity for mutual collaboration and understanding." Nataliya Georgievna spoke warmly of the work of their archive, the depths of its holdings, and their desire to welcome researchers and scholars from around the world. I felt immediately at ease. Her manner was official, yet thoughtful and friendly, enormously compassionate, yet in every way professionally meticulous. Olga translated, and before I could respond, Naumov stood up with a glass of vodka in his hand.

"We have invited Jonathan Brent here today because over the last few years he has shown himself to be a reliable partner with the Russian archives. He has respect for scholarship. He is honest. He pays people directly for the work they do. Yale is a publishing company with a worldwide reputation, and the value of our archives will be increased by our association with Yale University Press. But everybody knows this already. What I want to say may surprise Jonathan, but I don't wish him to be made uncomfortable. Jonathan believes that he is Yale's representative to the Russian archives, but I wish to say to you that he is our representative to Yale."

The shot of vodka that followed Naumov's toast reached my head and stomach simultaneously with an impact that seemed to lift me off the ground. What was this mission into the archives all about?

The personal and the public seemed turned inside out—like a ribbon twisted in the center and tied at both ends. Was there an alternative life I had been working my way toward that I was only dimly aware of? The life that would have been mine had my grandparents stayed in Zhitomir and Lvov and if my father hadn't changed the family name from Brodsky to Brent? And yet, had they remained, I would most likely never have been born in the wake of the Civil War, the terror of the 1930s, the Holocaust of the 1940s, and the postwar decimation of Jewish culture in the Soviet Union. They had left; I had come back. It hadn't occurred to me in quite this way before. Now this seemed the central fact of what I was doing in Russia, and Naumov had somehow divined it.

But how? *I* was the Russian archives' representative to Yale? How had Professor Naumov grasped so readily the silent, interior dialogue I had not even acknowledged to myself? How had he unlocked *that* door? Particularly since I hadn't laid eyes on him in the two years following our last encounter in the Spanish Bar? Who was this good-natured, knowing, cautious man whose manner, it seemed to me, resembled that of the snow leopard I had once read about who sees without being seen?

The Kirov assassination of December 1934 is widely understood to have ignited the events leading to the Great Terror of 1936–1938, yet the official record of arrests and executions released in the 1990s shows another story. In 1921, at the conclusion of the civil war, over 200,000 people were arrested, 76,820 for counterrevolutionary crimes; in 1928, at the beginning of collectivization, 112,803 were arrested, 72,186 for counterrevolutionary crimes; but then as collectivization got fully under way and Stalin's grip on power was finally consolidated, the numbers go steadily up:

162,726 in 1929
331,544 in 1930
479,065 in 1931
505,256 in 1933; 283,029 for counterrevolutionary
    crimes

Not until 1937 do the arrests exceed these heights: 936,750 arrested, 779,056 for counterrevolutionary crimes, of which 353,074 were shot, generally after trials that lasted no more than twenty minutes. The process of the terror was by no means the result of a single order from above or a single event from below. It engulfed the country and had a slow, steady gestation. Kirov's assassination did not ignite the Great Terror, but was another significant factor in its composition.

The bloodletting that Stalin advised Dimitrov to forgo in 1948 was not trained solely on the unrepentant kulak peasants, the bourgeoisie, or the capitalists; nor was it directed solely at magnates, religious fanatics, or outspoken political enemies.

In fact, the Great Terror of 1936–1938 was directed mostly against loyal party members and ordinary Soviet citizens, against members of the Comintern struggling for a socialist revolution in Germany, Italy, and Poland, and against Stalin's closest colleagues: Bukharin, Zinoviev, and Kamenev, among others.

In 1948, Stalin gave Dimitrov the advice a statesman might have offered a junior partner—calm, reasoned, cautious, judicious. Undoubtedly, he knew that Dimitrov would write this advice down in his diary and that years later it would become a source by which Stalin's legacy would be judged. Twelve years previoiusly the ruthless cruelty of his regime inspired Akhmatova to wonder who was human and who a beast.

Had Stalin grown into a statesman over those years? Had he engineered the terror or fallen into it against his will? By manipulating the Kirov assassination to precipitate a crisis, did he then find a way of legitimizing the Soviet regime and his seizure of total power? Was he merely following the wisdom of Bukharin, one of his victims, who wrote that the purge was a "great and bold" political idea by which the leadership would bring "about a *full guarantee* for itself"?

The mystery of Kirov's assassination lay at the heart of these questions and became for the Soviet Union what Kennedy's assassination became for the United States: an enigma not to be solved. Several separate inquiries were conducted throughout the Soviet period, but each proved something different or proved nothing at all. Each had its own political agenda. The Kirov Assassination is a signal instance of a historical fact converted into a political weapon. Perhaps our inquiry could finally disclose the truth.

The Great Terror has been explained as the outcome of mass paranoia; the will of a single, irrational, or even insane leader; or a process of gradual sociopolitical deterioration brought about by factionalism and oppositional interest groups competing for power. It seems to have had no single cause, but descended like Camus' plague. To this day, we still do not understand precisely what Stalin's terror was aimed at eliminating or why the innocent and the ordinary were swept up along with those who had legitimate claims to power. The history of the Great Terror is therefore fundamentally different from that of most other state-sponsored mass murders or genocidal actions of the twentieth century. Trotskyists? So-called "wreckers"—those accused of purposefully trying to impair Soviet industry, agriculture or bureaucracy? No thinking person *could* have believed that all 936,750 people arrested in 1937 were Trotskyists or wreckers. Did Stalin truly believe Bukharin was in league with Trotsky? Such a delusion would negate the principle upon which Stalin could be viewed as a rational actor, as his advice to Dimitrov in 1948 and much other evidence suggests he was.

During the terror, there is little evidence that Stalin or his closest colleagues ever suffered from such delusions or fully believed the objective charges they brought against those they persecuted. Often they didn't even know the names of their victims. Regional party heads were given quotas of arrests to fill, and they filled them. The mystique of the terror is that many, if not most, of those engaged in it, like Yezhov, believed that what they were doing was right, but not necessarily for the reasons articulated in the decrees or public proclamations.

In some way, still not fully understood, what happened in those terror-filled years is connected with the Stalinist state's ambition to encompass and control everything within it. It has the power to be, as Stalin put it, the "engineer of human souls." The theoretical basis for this power can be found in many writings of Lenin and others, but Nikolai Bukharin's 1921 treatise entitled *Historical Materialism: A System of Sociology* is particularly important because it connects the nature of this state with the nature of man:

> Furthermore, if we examine each individual in his development, we shall find that at bottom he is filled with the influences of his environment, as the skin of a sausage is filled with sausage-meat. Man "is trained" in the family, in the street, in the school. He speaks a language which is the product of social evolution; he thinks thoughts that have been devised by a whole series of preceding generations; he is surrounded by other persons with all their modes of life; he has before his eyes an entire system of life, which influences him second by second. Like a sponge he constantly absorbs new impressions. And thus he is "formed" as an individual. Each individual at bottom is filled with a social content. The individual himself is a collection of concentrated social influences, united in a small unit.

The party, which ruled the state, was responsible for shaping this "content." Stalinism did not undertake a *de*-humanizing of man in the modern age, but rather the *re*-humanizing of man, the redefinition of his essence, not the destruction of it, because this "essence" did not exist. The person is nothing but a skin stuffed with the historically conditioned "facts" of his life. It is a mistake to think that only Dr. Vasilenko, or the nameless "savages" and "Stone Age" people of the gulag, described by Vyshinsky, were turned into nonpersons in this system. The endpoint of Bukharin's logic is that everyone is a nonperson. No one is exempt. Inwardness and all that comes with it of selfhood, consciousness and conscience were nothing but the illusions of a long history of Western metaphysics. What remains after the illusions of the bourgeois sausage, such as "life, liberty and the pursuit of happiness," universal justice, or truth are scraped away? Power alone and its terror, a fury that in Lenin's words can express itself and "therefore must" in an inward-turning whirlwind of self-destruction. The physical destruction of individuals had been long preceded by their philosophical negation.

Unknown to myself, I had been scrutinized during my visits to Moscow, assessed, perhaps tested in ways I had not understood; and now before me was Vladimir Naumov, this elderly, soft-spoken gentleman whose voice wound a thread of irony through all he said, and whose playful eyes seemed always ready to acknowledge any detail of life. One of his favorite locutions after I came to know him better was, *"Yest takoi anekdot"*—"There is such a story, . . ." after which would follow a parable, a witticism, a folktale, or an amusing anecdote about a colleague or friend. Vladimir Pavlovich cannot walk down a street in Moscow without stopping to pass the time with an elderly woman, stockings rolled up to her knees, back bent, sweeping the street with a long-handled twig broom, or a glum shopkeeper standing before his storefront, or an idle policeman or university student. I have seen him tease information like a census taker from taxi drivers and waitresses about their work, their political views, and their personal circumstances. For him the material construction of his world is both endlessly fascinating and something that always seems to take him a little by surprise. He occupies himself with it as little as possible. His interest is exclusively with knowledge of what lies behind the visible circumstances in motivation, world view, and what he calls "mentality." He is not an idealist; he is simply convinced that what you see with your eye is only the smallest part of what might be there.

Naumov had been a child during the height of the terror, little more than ten when Kirov was assassinated. He survived and rose to an eminent position during the Gorbachev regime, as the leading researcher for the Presidential Commission for the Rehabilitation of Repressed Persons under the general chairmanship of Alexander Yakovlev.

As we sat at the long table in the Central Committee Archive proposing toast after toast, each evoking another detail in the picture of our mutual interests and divergent backgrounds, the initial shock of suddenly recognizing myself to be *their* representative to Yale wore off and I thought to ask why the mystery of the Kirov assassination was so important to Naumov. His eyes sparkled behind their thick lenses.

"In this murder," he replied, "we will see how the system worked, but we must go deeply into the KGB archive for this."

"Will we get to the bottom of the KGB?"

"Of course," he answered, his eyes widening behind his glasses. "But the KGB has many bottoms."

After our meeting concluded, I left with Olga, who lived in the same building as Mariana and had translated *The Wizard of Oz* into Russian. Dusk had set in and we decided to walk back to the apartment. Though the air was chilly it was not cold, and as we strolled along Tverskaya, Olga noticed lights flashing above our heads, indicating a cabaret.

"This is where I would go for an afterschool treat on my way home as a child," she said. "Shall we go up and see what's there now?"

"Do you want dinner?"

"No. I'd just like to see what it has become."

We went up a dark entryway toward an unpainted, metal door, where a burly young man in a dark suit sat on a wooden stool. He waved us in but stopped me as I was about to enter. He held up both hands, spreading his fingers.

"Ten dollars?"

He nodded.

"For me?" I pointed to myself.

He shook his head, then put up both hands again. I gave him twenty. Satisfied, he let us pass. We were seated on bar stools at a small round table. A "waitress," with no pretensions of wishing to serve us, set a beer and a thin, dried piece of brownish meat in front of us on an otherwise empty plate. The "menu" described the piece of meat as a *kotleta*, but it was nearly impossible to pierce with the fork or cut with the dull knife and could not be swallowed under any circumstances. $20 for this? I set it aside and stared gloomily at the unlit, empty stage. In a moment a floor show began. A pretty young woman stepped out dressed like the Russian version of Little Bo Peep in a floor-length white dress and bonnet and twirling a white parasol over her shoulder. She had lost her sheep, and in a moment, while dancing to an ever faster American disco beat, she lost her dress as well. When not a single article of clothing remained, her male sheep came bucking and baaing up to her on all fours from the wings of the stage. She flipped her parasol over her shoulder and ran off. She was stunningly beautiful and seemed out of synch with the overheated, pounding rhythms of the disco music. The naked beauty of her body was no longer an object of desire but something that turned desire back on itself and brought it to an abrupt end. She was obviously a trained dancer, but the mechanical purity of her gestures and movements said: *This is not me. Do not think that this is me. I am not here.* Her performance was graceful, but lacked grace, as though she were awkwardly aware of having gone over a line, while lacking the power to stop.

"How is this possible?" I asked.

"Everything changes. I came here as a girl for a glass of milk, and now look at what has become of the milkmaid," Olga said.

"She's very good, though."

"At first she looked familiar, but I thought it was impossible. Then I realized—she lives on the floor below me in my building. She trained professionally for the ballet.

She's a very nice girl. I know her mother quite well. Every student can recite Pushkin by heart in this shitty country, but there are no jobs, there is no future here." Olga's voice rose threateningly. "To survive you have to become a stone. How will I ever speak to her again?"

The next time I came to Moscow, the cabaret was gone.

Chapter 12

"Farewell, Dead Men"

Before I left for Moscow in 1993, Carol Avins, then at Northwestern University, proposed that Yale publish the hitherto untranslated 1920 diary of Isaac Babel, which had just appeared for the first time in a Russian edition. Though incomplete, this work provided incomparable insight into the background of Babel's masterpiece *Red Cavalry* and demonstrated unequivocally Babel's profound sympathies for the Jews the Red Cavalry encountered on its savage path through the Ukraine and eastern Poland. One could find the originals for many of his characters in it. One could find, perhaps, his original voice. It was an essential text and a masterpiece in its own right.

Through Vika Sagalova, whom I had met the year before, I could arrange to meet with the remnant of Babel's Moscow family—his widow, daughter, and grandson—and with luck sign a contract for this precious work in which he describes Zhitomir, the city my grandfather had left fifteen years before Babel arrived. In Zhitomir, Babel meets "a little Jew, a philosopher," in the Jew's curiosity shop. "Unimaginable shop," Babel writes. "—Dickens, brooms and golden slippers. His philosophy—they all say they're fighting for justice and they all loot." Babel drinks the philosopher's "sweet, anemic tea," feels he's "beginning to get [his teeth] into life," but concludes with the valediction, "Farewell, dead men." The dead men were the ones who stayed, the ones who thought things could go on as they had for centuries, who wanted to preserve a heritage, but unknowingly facilitated its extermination.

From Zhitomir, Babel and Budyonny's cavalry go west and here Babel discovers "the ineradicable cruelty of human beings." The destitution of the people and their semibarbarism is incomprehensible. "I am exasperated—can't get over my indignation, the filth, the apathy, the hopelessness of Russian life are unbearable, revolution will have some effect here." The revolution for Babel and many others was a way out of this hopelessness and mindless cruelty, but not because of the anachronistic "sweet, anemic tea" of his Jewish curiosity dealer; rather, because of the truth of Lenin's vision.

But what good is this vision in the face of the reality he witnesses all around him? "A terrible truth—all the soldiers have syphilis. . . . The scourge of the soldiery. Russia's scourge. It's terrifying. They eat crushed crystal, drink either carbolic acid or a solution of ground glass. All our fighting men—velvet caps, rape, forelocks, battles, revolution and syphilis. All Galicia is infected. . . . Slavs—the manure of history?" he asks.

In Dubno, the devastation wrought by the retreating Poles is almost unbearable to witness.

Now everybody's trembling again, and again the endless self-abasement, and hatred of the Poles, who pluck their beards. The husband—will there be freedom to trade, to buy a bit of something and sell it straight off, not to profiteer. I say there will be, everything's changing for the better—my usual system—miraculous things are happening in Russia—express trains, free food for children, theaters, the International. They listen with delight and disbelief. I think—you'll have your diamond studded sky, everything and everyone will be turned upside-down and inside out for the umpteenth time, and feel sorry for them.

By now the "express trains, free food for children, theaters . . . [the] diamond studded sky" was little more than empty propaganda, which Babel mouthed out of pity, not conviction. Yet his observations provide background for Stalin's enthusiastic assurances to Gorky, that Russia would become "a first-rate country with the biggest technically equipped industrial and agricultural production. Socialism is invincible. There's not going to be any more '*beggarly*' Russia. That's over! There's going to be a mighty and plentiful *vanguard* Russia."

Then come the ruined synagogues.

Everything destroyed . . . everything is fleshless, bloodless, to a grotesque degree, you have to have the soul of a Jew to sense what it means. But what does the soul consist of? Can it be that ours is the century in which they perish?

The dreams of "express trains, free food for children, theaters, the International"—the reality of the "manure of history," the crushed crystal the Cossacks drink for their syphilis, the rape, the pillage, the "ineradicable cruelty of human beings" collide in this doomed, forgotten, upside-down, Chagallesque world.

In Radziwillow during the fight for Brody, Babel bivouacs in a cottage occupied by an old man and a young girl. They serve him "splendid sour milk. . . . Tea with milk." But when his companion goes out to find sugar, machine-gun fire erupts and they flee in panic. "What I feel worst about in this whole business," Babel writes, "is the tea I was deprived of, feel so bad that it seems strange to me. I think about this all night, and hate war."

The tea he was deprived of and the perishing of an entire people are spoken of in almost a single breath. It was not the works of Pushkin, Tolstoy, and Dostoevsky thrown overboard by the revolution or the monuments of Michelangelo and the symphonies of Beethoven flung into the dustbin by a new aesthetics that Babel mourned. It was that little humanizing cup of tea with milk—a typically Western, not Russian, way of drinking it—like the three centimeters of the tsarevich's knee. It was the end of a civilization in which that cup of tea was possible. In 1920, Babel had already reached the *tupik*, or dead end, depicted in the 1937 cartoon of the "Bukharin School."

I met with Antonina Pirozhkova, Babel's widow, and with Babel's grandson, Andrei, in their Moscow apartment. She is still quite beautiful, with her silver hair drawn back and fine hands. We quickly agreed on terms for publication of the diary. I would meet Antonina Pirozhkova several times thereafter both in Moscow and in the United States, where she now resides. It was through her that I came to know more about Babel's life.

"Perhaps you would like to see Babel's KGB dossier," Vladimir Pavlovich suggested after I told him of my interest. He could arrange it, but I would need the permission of the family. Antonina graciously signed the necessary letter and a day was set for my visit to the Lubyanka reading room. By now my reading Russian was nearly fluent and I felt confident I could read through the entire file in a few hours. To my joy, the KGB agreed to photocopy the entire dossier for me to study at my leisure. What I found in Delo 419, Archive P-1252, marked with Isaac Babel's name, I read in an afternoon, but it has never left me over these fifteen years.

The tall, well-dressed middle-aged woman who brought me the file wore her hair in a complicated 1950s fashion. Her purple eye makeup had the same metallic sheen I had noted in the young woman who had led us to Pikhoia's office. She didn't smile or indicate that she was in any way pleased to be helpful, but her manner suggested that she also wouldn't stand in the way. She brought the file out and pointed me to a small wooden desk in the unheated, brown-walled reading room. After setting the file before me, she returned to her glassed-in observation area at the entrance of the room. When I took out my laptop computer in order to take notes, she came rushing back and ordered me in no uncertain terms to put it away or risk having it confiscated and my privileges revoked.

Chapter 13

The Secret Death of Isaac Babel

On May 15, 1939, according to Antonina Pirozhkova in her memoir, but on May 16, 1939, according to the records of the NKVD, Isaac Emmanuelovich Babel was arrested in his dacha on the outskirts of Moscow in the writers' colony of Peredelkino. The state had built this modest but comfortable dacha for Babel some years earlier. He was so pleased with it he called it affectionately his "villa," and Babel often secluded himself there to work, leaving his wife and daughter behind in Moscow, somewhat as he had left his first wife and daughter behind in Paris in the 1920s.

The outlines of this story have now been told several times—by Antonina herself in her memoir and by Vitaly Shentalinsky in *Arrested Voices*—yet much of importance has either been omitted or missed in both these accounts. Antonina was awakened by NKVD agents at five o'clock in the morning and told to lead them to her husband, which she did. She then accompanied Babel back to Moscow in the NKVD sedan and took leave of him for the last time outside the gates of Lubyanka Prison. The file states that "no complaint" was made by the family concerning the search.

"They didn't let me finish," Babel said to her just before they took him behind those gates. Then he added, more quietly, "Tell André," by which Antonina understood him to mean André Malraux, with whom he had become acquainted during his trips to Paris and Malraux's famous visit to Moscow in 1934. Babel had always been intrigued by the West. He knew French fluently and had composed his first early stories in French after the style of Maupassant. At the age of twenty-six, when he wrote his 1920 diary, he records his first premonition of what the West is like in his conversation with an American airman shot down by the Red Army:

> Frank Mosher. An American airman. . . . Asks me anxiously whether he's committed a crime, fighting against Soviet Russia. Our cause is strong. Ah, but all at once—the smell of Europe, its cafés, civilization, power, ancient culture, so many thoughts, I watch him, can't take my eyes off him.

In 1920 the West is an intoxicating enemy; in 1939, the West is Babel's only hope.

Vitaly Shentalinsky, who had obtained access to Babel's NKVD file, attempted to tell the story of what happened to Babel on the other side of the gates of Lubyanka. But his 1993 account of Babel's arrest, trial, and execution doesn't convey the deeply perturbing ambiguities of this event for Babel personally, nor is it entirely accurate. Shentalinsky states that Babel was arrested because he was denounced by Nikolai Yezhov, the recently arrested head of the NKVD with whose wife Babel had an affair in the early Thirties. Shentalinsky writes that Babel's confession, addressed to Beria, who had become head of the NKVD following Yezhov, was written "probably at the instigation of the interrogators." In other words, that it was a coerced confession that did not express Babel's real views. Shentalinsky also writes that Babel "no longer believed that he would survive," without explaining why, if he thought he wouldn't survive, he felt compelled to write the penitent confession? Moreover, Shentalinsky never asks why Babel was arrested in May 1939 or what purpose his arrest might have served except that it was part of the general madness of the system; he notes that "Babel retained no hope for himself but was tormented by the fate of others," yet he does not account for the fact that Babel never retracted his testimony about two Soviet writers, Ehrenburg and Yuri Olesha.

Babel's arrest, torture, trial, and execution, documented in the NKVD dossier, provides a case study of what Vladimir Naumov said to me about the Kirov assassination—that it shows how the system worked, what the meaning of it was both to Babel and to those into whose hands he had fallen. It is not enough to say that the Soviet system was "mad," or that it was "a monstrous anomaly," as Robert Conquest states in the introduction to *Arrested Voices*. Even after the publication of Shentalinsky's book the story of Babel's real death was not told.

Babel's NKVD file makes it possible to tell this story despite the many questions that remain: Who, for instance, is the anonymous informant of a damning 1937 denunciation? Where are the manuscripts and other personal effects confiscated by the NKVD during their search of Babel's dacha? Was Babel telling the truth when he said he had almost finished a new novel? Why did he not retract all of his denunciations of others? The picture presented in the dossier is neither heroic nor edifying.

Coming at the very end of the last wave of the Great Terror of the 1930s, but just two and a half months before Stalin signed the nonagression pact with Hitler, in August 1939, Babel's arrest and execution was an irreplaceable loss for Soviet and world literature; yet it is doubtful that he would ever have written another great work if his life had been spared.

By May 1939, Babel had gone through a long period in which he had published very little, and though he begs the court at the end to allow him to finish a novel he is working on, little suggests that this novel could have "torn the veil of existence with laughter," as his earlier stories had done. By the end of his imprisonment and considerably in advance of his execution, the Isaac Babel whom Lionel Trilling had written about in his famous introduction to *Red Cavalry*, the writer of "intensity, irony, and ambiguousness," had ceased to exist.

Born in Odessa in 1894, two years after his great Polish-Jewish contemporary Bruno Schulz, and about ten years after Kafka, Babel was in the vanguard of Jewish creativity in the twentieth century. With Schulz and Kafka, he wished to face the catastrophic changes of the modern period without destroying the specifically Jewish sensibility that defined his genius. Unable to plunder and loot like his Red Cavalry comrades, Babel ruefully admits, "I'll never be a real Budyonny man." He never loses his deep sense of himself as a Jew, while at the same time wishing to evade it. "I like talking with my own kind," he writes. He asks a Red Army man for bread: "I don't have anything to do with Jews," is the reply. "I'm an outsider in long trousers," Babel reflects. "I don't belong, I'm all alone." And of the Cossack: "Many-layered: looting, reckless, daring professionalism, revolutionary spirit, bestial cruelty. We are the vanguard, but of what?" And later: "I must look deeply into the soul of the fighting man, I am trying to, but it's all horrible, wild beasts with principles."

To Babel modernity was the "whirlwind" of revolution, with its promise of modernization and the "smell" of Europe, its "cafés, civilization, power, ancient culture" that he found in the borderlands of Poland. Unlike many of his compatriots, he bypasses Yiddish, in which he was fluent, to compose his great work in Russian. He wishes to be a Russian, not a Jewish, writer. He identifies with the great Russian culture and the revolution. Even as he is "exasperated" with the "hopelessness" of Russian life, he believes that the revolution "will have some effect here." He feels at peace with the "sweet, anemic tea" of his Dickensian curiosity dealer, but leaves him with the thought: "Good-bye, dead men." Divided and alone, driven to be a great writer in the great world, Babel made "silence" an ironic mask through which he could preserve the balance of his dual identities.

After his arrest, his silence became complete. As is widely known, the NKVD confiscated fifteen folders of manuscripts from Babel's Moscow apartment and nine folders of manuscripts from his dacha. Among these were one nearly finished novel, a screenplay, a book about Gorky, and numerous stories. After 1940, the publication of Babel's works was banned until his rehabilitation in 1954; but from 1954 to 1990 his works were virtually unobtainable by the majority of the Russian population and his memory was almost completely expunged from "official" Soviet literature.

The work of obliteration, however, went deeper than the suppression of his books. Babel's NKVD dossier tells the story not simply of the bureaucratic procedures used to arrest, convict, and execute a great writer; it demonstrates how the system attacked his essence—his consciousness and self-identity. In the end, officially, Isaac Babel no longer existed as Isaac Babel and never had.

With wholly unintended irony, the proceedings of his trial commence with his judge, V. V. Ulrich, confirming the identity of the defendant, which, according to the charges brought against him, the confessions extracted from him, and the judgment made upon him, had long ago ceased to exist. The dossier is a record of Babel's duel with his own nonexistence in border regions of absurdity and madness that are like a shadow of his first great conflict in the borderlands of western Ukraine. But now the fight is not with White Guard Russians or Poles, but with the "logic" of Stalin's interrogators. By 1939 the fury of the revolution has given way to bureaucratic protocols, official memoranda, file numbers, provisions of the criminal code, and preprinted forms of a vast administration of terror. It is a duel Babel can't win.

The *Red Cavalry* story "Argamak" concludes with Babel's narrator reflecting on his quarrel with a Cossack horseman. "And how was I to blame?" Lyutov wearily asks himself. The squadron commander answers the unspoken question, "I see you . . . I see the whole of you. You're trying to live without enemies. That's all you think about, not having enemies." By 1939, Babel's enemies had closed in on him. After his arrest, his interrogator demands to know whether Babel acknowledges his guilt. Babel hesitates, he acknowledges his guilt, he retracts it, qualifies it. The investigation pushes on. Babel makes the fantastic confession that he was the leader of an anti-Soviet organization among writers, setting as his goal the undermining of "the existing structure of the country, and in addition the preparation of terroristic acts against the leadership of the government." Babel admitted that since 1934 he had been a French and an Austrian spy, a fabrication that at first seems to have little relevance to the international situation of May 1939, but may in fact have been closely linked to it. Babel asks to be allowed to repent. Repentance was not an option.

A month later Babel issues a partial denial. Three months later at the so-called trial, he categorically denies all of the charges—though not every admission he had made during interrogation—stating that never in his life did he "undertake a single action against the Soviet Union" and in his confession he slandered himself. No doubt this is true. But it is beside the point. As M. D. Ryumin, an MGB interrogator, once told a hapless victim, "The question of your guilt is decided by the fact of your arrest, and I do not wish to hear any kind of conversation about this."

In his retraction, Babel stated that all the individuals he cited as accomplices (most of whom were already dead) were entirely innocent of the charges he made against them. However, in the list of individuals Babel cleared, he omitted the name of Ilya Ehrenburg. What he had said about Ehrenburg's activities in France in the early 1930s provoked sufficient attention from the NKVD that the next day an order was transmitted by the interrogator to review Ehrenburg's file. Was this an act of spite at the end of a long, uneasy friendship? Had Ehrenburg in fact been guilty of some activities of which Babel had knowledge? That Ehrenburg was not arrested then or later as a result of Babel's charges against him proves in reverse precisely what Ryumin said: his innocence was decided by the fact that he was not arrested. Denunciations against Isaac Babel began accumulating as early as 1934 and included statements from a fellow writer, Boris Pilnyak, who was arrested in 1937 and never heard from again. Shentalinsky asserted that Babel's arrest was instigated by Nikolai Yezhov's vengeful confession, taking, as Shentalinsky puts it, "revenge both on his wife and her former lover."

However, the full transcript of Yezhov's confession relating to Babel, while indicating Yezhov's suspicions of their affair, and his suspicions that they *might* be involved in something more serious, provides no substantive details whatever to support a case that Babel and Yezhov's wife were involved in espionage. Yezhov's testimony is, if anything, an honest portrayal of what, in his own words, he "observed" between Babel and his wife. It seemed suspicious, but among all the other denunciations of Babel, it provides, in fact, the least for the NKVD to go on. Because this testimony has been the subject of much debate about Isaac Babel's arrest, I will quote in full the relevant passages from May 11, 1939.

Yezhov: There was a special friendship between Ye.S. Yezhova [his wife] and Babel. . . . Further, I suspicioned, in truth, on the basis only of my personal observation that this could not have come about without an espionage tie between my wife and Babel.

Question: On the basis of what facts do you declare this?

Yezhov: I know from the words of my wife that she became acquainted with Babel, around 1925. She always maintained that there was no sort of intimate tie with Babel. The connection was limited by her wish to support her acquaintance with talented, contemporary writers. At her invitation, Babel was several times at our house, where I naturally met him.

I observed that in the mutual relationship with my wife Babel displayed something demanding and vulgar. I saw that my wife was simply rather afraid [of him]. I understood that what was going on did not have to do with the literary interests of my wife but was something more serious. I ruled out an intimate relationship on the grounds that Babel would hardly demonstrate such vulgarity toward my wife knowing the position in society I occupied. To my questions to my wife whether she did not have the same relations with Babel as with [Mikhail] Koltsov [with whom she also had an affair and who was arrested in 1938], she became quiet or weakly protested. I always supposed that with this indefinite answer she simply wanted to hide her espionage connection with

Babel from me, apparently from the desire not to let me into the multiplicity of channels of this type of connection.

At this point in the interrogation, Yezhov appears definitely to accuse Babel of being a spy, and this is where Shentalinsky ends his account. However, Yezhov's interrogator isn't satisfied with the ambiguity of Yezhov's statement and seeks further detail, which Yezhov's response fails to provide.

Question: What you have said thus far about Babel is not a sufficient basis for the suspicion that he was an English spy. Did you slander Babel?

Yezhov: I do not slander Babel. Yezhova [his wife] never said that her connection with Babel had to do with English intelligence. In the present case, I express only a supposition, based on observation of the character of the mutual relationship between my wife and the writer Babel.

A "supposition" is hardly a denunciation and the interrogator drops the subject. What is most important here is not whether Yezhov implicates Babel or not, but that the interrogator pressures him to denounce Babel as an *English* spy. Why English? The relevance of the international situation now becomes clearer. Were Babel to be a German spy—something much more likely to have been the case because Babel had contacts in Germany, while he had no known contacts in England—suspicions might be raised about the advisability of the impending Hitler-Stalin Pact. If this is so, then clearly both Yezhov's and Babel's testimony was being read by more than just their NKVD interrogators. If this was so, then the *political* nature of these arrests suddenly becomes clear. One of the uses of these confessions and interrogations was to advance Stalin's foreign policy by *proving* through these confessions and interrogations the validity of his intentions—in this case to sign a nonaggression pact with Hitler.

Yezhov, however, does not comply, and even the interrogator could not find in Yezhov's comments sufficient grounds to accuse Babel.

Yezhov is clear: his statements represent nothing more than supposition. Furthermore, Yezhov was not protecting his wife, who had committed suicide in December 1938 for uncertain reasons. Mikhail Koltsov, mentioned in Yezhov's interrogation, was also shot in 1940 and was also accused of being an English spy.

The NKVD interrogated Babel closely on this point and even had procured a confession from the former husband of Yezhova, Alexei Gladun, former director of the Kharkov Instrument Plant, who was fired and imprisoned for his failure to fulfill his goals for the Five-Year Plan. On May 22, 1939, six days *after* Babel's arrest, Gladun "confesses" that his wife (referred to in the interrogation as Khayutina, her maiden name), who had divorced him to marry Yezhov, was an English spy.

Question: Did Rosengolts [another "terrorist"] know that Khayutina was an English spy?

Answer: Of course he knew. Of this I personally informed him and told Rosengolts that Khayutina was close to Yezhov, and that through her it would be easier for us to get assistance by fulfilling the plan to recruit Yezhov into our espionage work. Rosengolts expressed satisfaction about the possibility of recruiting Yezhov in our espionage work in the service of English intelligence.

The case would be simple: Yezhov's wife was an English spy; she recruited Yezhov, and Yezhov protected Babel. Unfortunately, Yezhov did not cooperate and the English espionage angle had to be quietly dropped in the Babel case. In his sentence, Yezhov was accused of abetting several different intelligence services; in addition, he was accused of having murdered his wife. What is evident in the way the case against Babel progressed is that the NKVD was *constructing* it, step by step. Trying first one approach, then another, never stating a goal, but clearly linking the interrogation to the international situation. Babel was no longer an individual; he had become a cogwheel in a larger machine. His fate was not personal.

Babel's particular actions or thoughts were irrelevant to how this machine operated. Babel stood for something that the NKVD, with Stalin's direction, was manipulating, putting into a context, making internally coherent, and connecting to a multiplicity of other such cases. Determining what kind of spy he was—English, German, French, or Austrian—was clearly part of the process.

If the arrest of Babel was connected to the impending pact with Hitler, Stalin may have wished to send a clear message to his German adversary, and to his own security services and Politburo at the same time, that he, too, knew how to deal with the Jews by arresting the most famous Soviet Jewish writer of his day—and furthermore that this Jewish writer was in league with their common enemy—either the English or the French, who had both infuriated Stalin in the spring of 1939 with their failure to conclude a security agreement with the Soviet Union. Babel asked Antonina Pirozhkova to tell André Malraux of his fate, but it now appears that he was arrested precisely because of his European celebrity, the very thing Babel imagined might have saved him.

Neither Stalin's personal anti-Semitism nor Babel's own actions were the operative factors. Ilya Ehrenburg was Jewish, but he was not arrested. Babel "confessed" that Ehrenburg had recruited him into espionage on behalf of the French and never retracted this part of his confession, stating at one point in his May 1939 interrogation that "Malraux named only Ehrenburg to me as the basic channel for the transmission of espionage information." Ehrenburg, who was never arrested, was another such cogwheel. Why would he have been protected and Babel not? Babel had ceased writing or at any rate publishing. His silence was clear evidence that he could not overcome his antipathy for the Soviet leadership. Ehrenburg published prolifically. He would do whatever the state needed. And even after Stalin's death he continued to perform the necessary service when he wrote, "Stalin lives."

In the machine of the Stalinist state, Babel, Ehrenburg, and even Yezhov were tiny gears. In Babel's "Statement to the People's Commissar of Internal Affairs of the USSR, 11

September 1939," we can see just how these gears meshed to produce a result that would have been highly satisfactory to the Soviet power structure. It is a statement of inexpressible sorrow—of which Babel had a premonition in 1920 when he confided in his diary: "Why can't I get over my sadness? Because I'm far from home, because we are destroyers, because we move like a whirlwind, like a stream of lava, hated by everyone, life shatters. I am at a huge, never-ending service for the dead." The service for the dead concluded with his own self-conscious self-extermination. As with Akhmatova in *Requiem*, he no longer was who he was.

> The revolution opened for me the path of creativity, the path of happiness and useful work. My individualism, false literary views, the influence of Trotskyists to which I succumbed at the very beginning of my literary work—all this forced me to swerve from this path. With every year, my writings became more unnecessary and hostile to the Soviet reader, but I considered myself to be right, and not the Soviet reader. From this ruinous rupture, the very source of my creativity dried up; I made attempts to liberate myself from the captivity of this blind, self-absorbed limitation. But these attempts proved to be meager and weak. My liberation came only in prison.

> In the months of my imprisonment, more has become clear and understandable to me than, perhaps, in all my previous life. With horrible clarity, the mistakes and crimes of my life pass before me—the decay and rot

surrounding me among the Trotskyists for the most part. With all my being, I feel that these people are not only enemies and traitors to the Soviet nation, but also in their point of view is something that contradicts everything in which true poetry consists: simplicity, clarity, cheerfulness, physical and moral health. This point of view expresses itself in cheap skepticism, in the foppishness of professional lack of faith, in a squeamish enervation and decadence evident even in the first years of the revolution, and moreover in an undiscerning personal life in which the very dirtiest debauchery is raised up into a principle. In my present isolation, with new eyes, I have witnessed a Soviet country which is, in utter truth, inexpressibly beautiful, and is all the more tormenting in view of the vileness of my past life. . . .

Citizen People's Commissar [Beria]. Seized only by the wish of purification and redemption, and not caring for the consequences, I speak of my crimes. I wish to give an account also of another side of my existence in my literary work which has for so long passed torment-edly, concealed from the outside world, but which, with disruptions, has steadily continued. I ask you, Citizen People's Commissar, to allow me to put a selection of my manuscripts in order. These consist of drafts of sketches about collectivization and kolkhozes in the Ukraine, material for a book about Gorky, drafts of several tens of stories, a half-finished play, and a finished variant of a screenplay. These manuscripts—the result of eight years of work, I have envisioned finishing for publication this year. I ask you also to allow me to prepare a plan for a book in belletristic form about the path my life has taken which in many respects is typical of the path taken by others leading to a fall, to crimes against our socialist country.

With tormenting and merciless brilliance all this passes before me; with pain I feel, as if it were the returning inspiration and strength of my youth, a thirst for work burning in me, the thirst to redeem myself, to brand my life as incorrect and criminally squandered.

I. Babel

This confession was addressed to the People's Commissar of Internal Affairs and dated November 11, 1939. Confessing to his "incorrect and criminally squandered" life, Babel echoes his own prophetic words from the 1934 International Writers Congress in Moscow, in which he concluded his lengthy address with the following ironic quip:

With Gorky I would like to say that . . . everything is given to us by the party and the government and only one thing is taken away: [the freedom] to write badly.

Comrades, we must not conceal that this is a very important right and it is not a small thing to take it away [*laughter*]. It is a privilege of which we make considerable use.

So, comrades, at this writers' congress let us pledge to give up this privilege, and then God help us. However, since there is no God, we must help ourselves [*applause*].

The freedom to write badly, the freedom to speak badly, the freedom to think badly is a freedom without which only God can save us and without God the terror of the 1930s descended.

Poland, through which Babel could smell the intoxicating culture of the West, had ceased to exist in the fall of 1939, and so did Isaac Babel, the writer, some four months before Isaac Babel, the man, was shot.

Had he been given clemency and allowed to live, Babel would not have been Babel. Lionel Trilling's comment, that "no event in the history of Soviet culture is more significant than the career, or, rather the end of the career of Isaac Babel," takes on in this context an entirely different, and appropriately Babelian, irony. His death saved him from the shameful fate of being "correct."

Babel was no hero. Nor was he entirely free of the charges brought against him by the NKVD. He consorted with Trotskyists and had been introduced to Trotsky by his friend and editor, Alexander Konstantin Voronsky, who, after Gorky, was perhaps the most powerful literary editor of avant-garde writing in Russia in the 1920s. All testimonies from friends and from Antonina Pirozhkova herself document Babel's disillusionment with the regime, his scorn for the political show trials of Bukharin, Zinoviev, and Kamenev, and his despair over the fate of his friends in the military. But there is no evidence whatever to suggest that he was in any way what the NKVD compelled him to confess: "the leader of an anti-Soviet organization among writers" whose ambition was to perform terrorist acts against the Soviet government and its leaders.

Like nearly all such proceedings, the interrogation and confession of Isaac Babel were never made known publicly during the Soviet period. It was for internal consumption by the government. The public acknowledgment of guilt was clearly not at issue. Internal acknowledgment was. If Isaac Babel admitted his guilt; if the great director Vsevolod Meyerhold and armies of others admitted theirs, the government could legitimate itself *in its own eyes*. It is now known that confessions such as Babel's were circulated within the Politburo. Stalin kept a set of such confessions in his dacha.

The purges served the purpose of not simply eliminating real or imagined enemies; it served the more existential need of the system continually to reassert its legitimacy in the absence of true popular support. Rather than demonstrating the internal strength of the system, the purges proved how vulnerable it felt itself to be.

The essential rightness of Stalin's methods and the wisdom of his leadership would be bolstered and supported precisely because Isaac Babel admitted he had led an "incorrect and criminally squandered" life. If Babel said this, how could anyone disagree? Furthermore, by building a case (though in Babel's instance only half successfully concerning English and French intelligence and quite pointedly *not* building a case that he was a German spy), Stalin was continuing to build a case against England

and France within his own Politburo, a case that was essential to make in advance of the nonaggression pact with Germany.

Stalin's "machine like no other," to quote the opening of Kafka's *In the Penal Colony*, had not gone berserk. Quite the contrary. The fact that the general public did not read the fake confessions or even know the charges brought against so many of Stalin's victims was evidence that the machine was working perfectly. Like a work of art, it served no purpose but itself.

Unlike Babel, Alexander Voronsky, his friend and editor, quite clearly did harbor political ambitions. Unlike Babel, he did not give the government what it wanted. A friend of Lunacharsky and Trotsky, Voronsky was the editor of *Red Virgin Soil* and published all the major new Soviet writing, including Babel's first stories. He was removed as editor of *Red Virgin Soil* in 1927 for ideological reasons, but met with Stalin himself at the beginning of 1929 to discuss the state of Soviet literature. Voronsky's daughter relates that their conversation raised the question of starting a new journal with a military-political focus. Voronsky agreed to run it, but insisted on complete freedom to edit it as he saw fit. Stalin refused. That was the end of the conversation. Voronsky was sent into exile and was arrested a second time on February 1, 1937. On June 10, 1937, he was shot for anti-Soviet agitation and participation in an anti-Soviet organization. Babel remained in touch with him after his exile and, contrary to what he told the court, he went to visit Voronsky on at least one documented occasion.

Once Trotsky was banished from the Soviet Union in 1929, Voronsky's days were numbered.

Because he was so closely linked to Babel, I wished to find out what happened to Voronsky. Had he, too, denounced Babel? What compelled him to persist in a path that would clearly doom him? Vladimir Pavlovich suggested I go through the same channels as before if I wished to read his NKVD dossier, but how to get permission from a relative? What relative? His wife had been arrested with him. How could anyone have survived?

Olga Varshaver was able to make inquiries through her network of colleagues from the old Writers' Union and discovered that the granddaughter of Alexander Voronsky lived in obscurity on the outskirts of Moscow in a small apartment.

"It's fitting," Olga pointed out, that she lived on Vladimirka, at the limit of the outer ring on the outskirts of the city. In prerevolutionary times, this was the road political prisoners would take on their way to Siberia.

The granddaughter of Alexander Voronsky had been born in Kolyma, the most notorious region in the gulag system. It is estimated that it contained over nine hundred thousand prisoners, of which some five hundred thousand died, either by shooting or starvation. The writer Varlam Shalamov, a political prisoner consigned to Kolyma, was at work on the side of a mountain that had been cleared of brush and stumps by the new American tractors sent through lend-lease.

The mountain had been laid bare and transformed into a gigantic stage for a camp mystery play.

A grave, a mass prisoner grave, a stone pit stuffed full with undecaying corpses of 1938 was sliding down the side of the hill, revealing the secret of Kolyma.

In Kolyma, bodies are not given over to earth, but to stone. . . . All of our loved ones who died in Kolyma, all those who were shot, beaten to death, sucked dry by starvation, can still be recognized even after tens of years. There were no gas furnaces in Kolyma. The corpses wait in stone, in the permafrost. . . .

These graves, enormous stone pits, were filled to the brim with corpses. The bodies had not decayed; they were just bare skeletons over which stretched dirty, scratched skin bitten all over by lice.

Upon his execution, Voronsky's daughter was arrested and sentenced to eight years in the gulag and eventually was transported to this barren region of "undecaying corpses." After her sentence, she was released and got married, not knowing that her mother had already died. During the period of Khrushchev's "thaw," what was left of the family returned to Moscow.

It is August 1995 and the heavy, overheated air of Moscow does not move. Nikolai's car smells of grease and gasoline. We drive far out along the outer ring to Vladimirka through what has become a new phenomenon: the *probka*, or cork, the term for a traffic jam. With horns blaring in the heat and cars spread over the roadway in complete disregard of conventional traffic lanes, each nosing into unoccupied spaces, cutting each other off and creating a mass blockage, Nikolai tells me that something barely visible is happening to the people: they are becoming much more aggressive.

But when I ask how this aggressiveness is demonstrated, he can't easily say. It's in small things, the way they walk down the street, cut in front of you, push others away, as if fighting for air.

We arrive at one of several typically rundown warrens of moderately tall high-rise buildings with pale blue pockmarked crumbling façades, rusted metal front doors, and broken steel grates over the windows on the lowest stories. The courtyard is littered with twisted steel cables, broken glass, what appears to be an abandoned Pobyeda raised on blocks. Stray dogs sleep in the shadows along the sidewalk, which is overgrown with weeds and cracked by winter heaving, forcing people to pick their way around raised islands of displaced concrete. After circling several times, unable to find the correct entrance, with much discussion between Olga and Nikolai, we seem to come upon it by accident. The buzzer works. She is expecting us. The apartment building reminds me of housing projects in Chicago. Something inside has been torn apart as if by a wild beast. The lift doesn't work and we must walk up several flights. The fishy smell of garbage chokes the stairway.

We go to the end of the hallway, as instructed. When we knock, the door is almost immediately opened by a woman who appears to be in her late forties. There is something fragile and meek in the awkward way she holds her body, welcoming us to her apartment, but not quite wanting to see us at the same time, averting her glance as we shake hands, but attentive to our every movement. She doesn't grasp my hand, but allows hers to be grasped, as if to say, *Don't look at me. I'm not anybody worth looking at, and my hand is not worth holding.* As if she were only the maid and feared that at any moment the real owner of the apartment would appear, and she would have to withdraw into another room. Silence settles around us as we follow her down the hall. She has light brown hair and wears a neat, plain dress.

She shares the apartment, but with whom I don't know, and the doors at the other end of the hallway are closed as we enter. The smell of cooking grease is in the air. She opens a door and we step into her room—her bedroom, her library, her living room. It is bare, except that in the center is a small writing desk with chairs. Surrounding us from floor to ceiling on all four walls are thousands of books. Not everything can fit on the shelves and many are stacked in neat piles all around. The books are shelved in double rows.

My heart breaks when she puts her card on the table for me to take: "Tatiana Isaeva. Editorial Assistant" for what seemed to be a publication—*Vozvrashchenie (Return)*. Assistant? For what? To whom? What texts or languages could these be? I cannot imagine this painfully modest, inoffensive, quiet person consulting with anything or anybody except ghosts of the past in voiceless tongues. The air in the room is stifling. One could be drawn back and back and back into the whispering shadows, down into a murky world of memory and pain. I begin to feel dizzy. I present her my card and mention Isaac Babel. She nods.

"Your grandfather was very important for him and many other writers," I say, breaking the silence. The living energy of the room seems about to swirl down into that silence like water down a drain. Only the sound of my own voice blocks it. Only it counters the invisible heaviness, filled with voices I can't understand, that seems to be growing over us with the midafternoon shadows. She nods again.

"Do you have any objection to my reading your grandfather's NKVD dossier to learn more of what became of him?"

She shakes her head and quietly replies. No, she has no objection, but wishes me to know that most everything I will read in the file is lies. She tells me that she was born in Magadan. Life was very difficult. Now things are better. Would I care to see a book of stories her mother, Voronsky's daughter, wrote? It is a very sad book, but I might find it interesting because in the preface it speaks of Voronsky too. It's about life in the camps. I take the little paperback she offers. It is printed on flimsy paper in which the process of oxidation and foxing has already begun; on some pages the print is heavy and on others, words or phrases seem about to disappear, like the sound of Tatiana's voice. It smells of Moscow. I have it before me now as I write this, remembering the shy, almost unbearably quiet and diminutive presence of this last link to one of the great literary figures of the revolution whose photograph I see for the first time. It is the photo taken at the time of his arrest in 1937. His hair is gray and his steely expression is grim. He was fifty-three, but appears much older. He can see the future as if in a mirror.

Tatiana has carried on what her mother began—a quiet but tireless campaign to restore Voronsky to his rightful place in Russian literature. Her efforts have met with some success. A fine study was published in 1989 by Galina Belaya with the suggestive title *Don Kikhoty 20-kh godov* (Don Quixote of the twentieth century), and in 1991 a biography of Voronsky was published in Russian. A volume of his important writings has appeared in English, translated by Frederick Choate, from a small socialist publisher in Michigan.

I couldn't wait to leave, to breathe fresh air, to feel the sunlight. Tatiana signed the letter I needed for the KGB archive, and the next day I returned to the reading room. The same lady with metallic purple eye shadow and the elaborate hairdo brought out Voronsky's file. He was an old Bolshevik, a true believer since the 1905 revolution. The file was thick with denunciations and interrogations.

Like the others, Voronsky was given the chance to make a statement before sentencing. Babel begged only for the opportunity to finish his work. Yezhov went to his grave with Stalin's name on his lips. Voronsky had a different message for his judges. He stood up and declared that as they had judged him, history would judge them. They, not he or those he supported, had betrayed the revolution. His words were powerful, direct, uncompromising, and clear. He had denounced no one; he retracted nothing. The speech lasted only a few minutes. No one attempted to stop him. It was faithfully recorded by the court stenographer and preserved. The next day he was shot and all trace of Alexander Voronsky vanished for over twenty years. The gears continued to whir.

Chapter 14

Raoul Wallenberg

Around this time I happened to read an account in the *New York Times* of an organization called ARC that was searching for information about Raoul Wallenberg, who is credited with saving the lives of as many as one hundred thousand Hungarian Jews in 1944, but who disappeared without a trace after a famous meeting with the Soviets in January 1945. The article mentioned a man by the name of Boris Yuzhin, a former KGB officer and American double agent. Yuzhin was one of the Soviet spies denounced by Robert Hanssen, the FBI agent who in 2001 pled guilty to working for the KGB. Yuzhin was arrested in Moscow in 1985 and sentenced to fifteen years in prison, but he was released by Boris Yeltsin in 1992. The other KGB double agents denounced by Hanssen were shot. Yuzhin was lucky.

Now he resided in California and had devoted himself to searching for prisoners of war who disappeared in Siberia in the 1940s and assisting efforts to ascertain what happened to Wallenberg. Many theories abounded at the time. Some researchers believed that he had died of a heart attack or had been shot while still in Moscow in 1947. Others insisted that he was still alive and claimed to be able to provide eyewitness accounts by fellow inmates who had seen him recently in one or another arctic camp. The mystery of Wallenberg's disappearance was deepened because no one knew why he was arrested or what the basis of the Soviets' action against him was. No government documents have been produced to support any of the theories. Wallenberg was a great hero who simply vanished into the nothingness of Soviet bureaucracy.

I called Yuzhin and told him that I would shortly be going to Moscow and would very much like to pursue any leads he could offer. He gave me the name and telephone number of someone in Moscow who speaks English.

"Say nothing. Only my name," he instructed. "Ask about the Kutuzov file."

Soon after arriving in Moscow, I did as I was told.

After a long silence, the man on the other end of the line said firmly in English, "Never say that name in Moscow again, certainly not over the telephone." Nevertheless, he agreed to meet in a restaurant nearby his office. He had a story to tell me.

Olga and Nikolai were unhappy about this meeting. Why get in touch with these people? they asked. I'm doing nothing wrong, as far as I know, only searching for information, I insisted. Maybe so, Nikolai said, but it's never good to meet with these people. Once you meet with them, they know who you are. They never forget.

Around midday, Nikolai, Olga, and I go to the basement restaurant the KGB officer had specified. It is cool and dark and there are no other people. We go to a table in the back. In a minute a man dressed in a suit and tie comes in, pauses at the doorway, and scans the room. In the glare of the light from the street, it is difficult to see him, but he spots us and quickly approaches. I stand up and introduce myself.

"Very well," he says, "what do you wish to know?"

"I was told about the Kutuzov file. Does it exist?"

"The Kutuzov file is real."

"What is it?"

He told the following story. After the revolution, a young man who happened to be a distant relative of Prince Mikhail Kutuzov, the hero of the War of 1812 and Tolstoy's *War and Peace*, was stopped by the Bolsheviks at the border as he was attempting to flee the country. Rather than be shot, he, like many others, agreed to become an informant for the Cheka, the forerunner of the KGB. He went to Paris, where he informed on Russian émigré circles, many of whom were old friends and acquaintances. In 1944 he was posted to Budapest. An affable, cultured and witty man, he quickly made friends with Wallenberg. He worked in the hospital that somewhat improbably took care of Soviet prisoners of war. Wallenberg liked him. He reported everything Wallenberg said and did back to Moscow in what became known as The Kutuzov File.

"Where is the file?"

"It used to be in the KGB archive. One day it disappeared."

"And now?"

"I don't know. Nobody knows. Maybe they sold it to the Swedes. Maybe it was destroyed."

"Did you read it?"

"No."

"What is its value?"

"It tells the story of Wallenberg in Budapest. It shows why they had to execute Wallenberg."

"Had to?"

"They had no other options."

"But you never read it?"

"No."

According to KGB General Pavel Sudoplatov, Wallenberg was executed by lethal injection, in 1947, while still in custody in Moscow. Kutuzov's existence and his relationship with Wallenberg were independently confirmed for me by a man, still living in Budapest, who told me that as a boy he had worked for Wallenberg and remembers a charming Russian man who often came around to Wallenberg's residence. But his name wasn't Kutuzov, Mr. Forgascne told me. His name was Tolstoy. Apparently, this was the name Kutuzov used in Budapest. In fact, Kutuzov's family had married into the Tolstoy lineage. In him the general and the novelist merged; his one great work, the Kutuzov File, dissolved into the same silence that enveloped Babel's confiscated manuscripts.

Chapter 15

Erofeev's Widow

To my great joy I discovered that the widow of the novelist Venedikt Erofeev lived in Moscow and enjoyed company. I had published, or rather republished, an English-language translation of *Moscow to the End of the Line* while still at Northwestern University Press, and I was eager to find out if there were more works by Erofeev that I might be able to publish at Yale. Without question, Erofeev ranks with the greatest writers of the second half of the twentieth century. The subtly self-reflexive narrative of his great novel, its comic pathos in combination with its brutal, psychological realism, make it one of the most profound investigations of modernity produced in any literature of the world. Unlike much facile postmodern writing, Erofeev's novel provides no easy or formulaic exits from the problem of transcendence, no cheap solutions to the lostness and the radical displacements of consciousness in the modern world.

"It's nothing," I said to myself. "Nothing. There's a pharmacy, see? And over there, that creep in the brown jacket scraping the sidewalk. You see that too? So calm down. Everything is going along as it should. If you want to

> turn left, Venichka, turn left, I'm not forcing you to do
> anything. If you want to turn right, turn right."

Everything is going along as it should, Erofeev's hero tells himself. If you want to turn right, turn right; if you want to turn left, turn left. What it comes down to for Erofeev is how to connect this freedom with "the creep in the brown jacket scraping the sidewalk." If you can't connect it, you have no idea what freedom is. *Moscow to the End of the Line* is his one great novel. I wanted to find another.

His widow, Galina, lived in a high-rise much like Tatiana's. She was heavyset, energetic, boisterous, high-spirited, with short brown hair cut straight across her forehead. Delighted that someone from the United States had come to pay homage to her husband's memory, she had invited friends to join us for lunch. She seemed always in motion around the table, always talking, always taking someone by the arm, or placing something before you. She had prepared an assortment of wonderful things to eat as we discussed Venedikt. I told her I thought he was often badly misunderstood and suffered from a fate similar to Henry Miller's—that of being a writer known largely for his transgressions—but whose interests were much deeper. Many consider Erofeev to be little more than a writer about drunkenness, but that isn't at all the truth, I said. He uses drunkenness and alcohol to blast through artificiality, through art itself, as Miller uses sex, so that he can enter a different imaginative space. In the end, though, Miller remains a realist struggling against the superficiality of American values and society. Erofeev is different. His imaginative conception pierces deeper into existence than

Miller's; he depicts the fate of the spirit, which wanders like a drunken bum in an uncomprehending world. She was happy with this, but didn't care for the comparison with Miller. In his will Erofeev wrote that the price of his novel should never be more than a liter of vodka, a custom that was strictly observed until the Soviet Union itself reached the end of the line.

"Let me tell you a story about Erofeev that will show you what kind of man he really was," she said. People from the extremist organization Pamyat wanted Erofeev to address their annual meeting a year or two before he died. At the time, he was confined to a wheelchair and could speak only through a box in his throat because of his throat cancer. For the most part Pamyat's political outlook was nationalist, xenophobic, and anti-Semitic. They wanted to claim the great Erofeev as one of their own and thought from hints in some of his writing that he shared their political views about the need to create a purely Russian literature.

Erofeev continually put them off, Galina said. But one day a delegation simply showed up at the apartment. He refused them, but another delegation came and this time he agreed. The day of the great event arrived, and Galina wheeled him out onto the stage before the packed auditorium. Every seat was taken and people stood in the aisles to hear what Erofeev would say. Journalists were there to take down every word.

But Erofeev says nothing. He just sits in his wheelchair and looks at the crowd. The crowd becomes nervous. What's going on? When will he speak? They start to squirm and shuffle their feet. Some begin to clap. Erofeev remains silent.

Galina looked at me, wide-eyed. She had no idea what was going to happen. "Nobody did."

Finally, Erofeev makes a sign with his hand and the hall quiets down. He lowers the microphone to the box in his throat.

"Thank you for inviting me," he whispers haltingly through the box. "I am deeply moved because now I know you truly love me for myself and my writing. Nothing else explains this great crowd because . . ." He paused a long time, Galina said, before finishing his sentence. "Because otherwise, in fact, we have absolutely nothing in common." That was it. Everyone was stunned.

Terrified the audience would kill him, Galina ran out and whisked Erofeev away before anyone could react.

On my next trip to Moscow, I wished to see Galina again, but was told that she had fallen to her death cleaning the windows of her apartment while standing on the outside ledge without a safety belt.

Chapter 16

Vsyo Normalno

In 1998 Russia was a country on the verge of coming apart—economically, socially, militarily, politically. When I arrived in late August, the streets of Moscow seemed to combine entropy with anger, hopelessness with barely concealed resentment. Nikolai had become the president of the Kendo Society of Moscow. He was a master of this Japanese art of stylized nonviolent violence. He complained again that people had become much more aggressive. In what way? I asked, but again his answer was vague: in general, in the way they do things, in the way they drive, in the way they push at street corners, the way they talk to you at the shops, the way they walk down the street. As we made our way through Revolution Square, two young recruits wearing Russian army uniforms came up to us and spoke in hushed but fervent whispers to Nikolai, after which he reached into his pocket and gave them some rubles.

"What did they want?"

"They are hungry and begging for bread."

"Begging for bread?"

"Look at what has become of the army that defeated Hitler," Nikolai said, unable to hide his emotion. "Begging for bread on street corners in Moscow."

Nikolai told me he would do everything in his power to keep his son out of the army. The beatings and brutality meted out to ordinary Russian recruits in the Russian military is staggering, according to Anna Politkovskaya in *Putin's Russia*.

> You can decide for yourself whether you would like to live in a country where your taxes sustain such [an army]. How you would feel when your sons turned 18 and were conscripted as "human resources." How satisfied you would be with an Army from which soldiers deserted in droves every week, sometimes whole squads or entire companies at a time. What would you think of an Army in which, in a single year, 2002, a battalion, more than 500 men, had been killed not fighting a war but from beatings? In which the officers stole everything from the 10-ruble notes sent to privates by their parents to entire tank columns? Where officers are united in hatred of soldiers' parents because every so often, when the circumstances are just too disgraceful, outraged mothers protest at the murder of their sons and demand retribution.

Politkovskaya, a human rights activist and journalist, was murdered in Moscow on October 7, 2006. Her murder remains unsolved. Many suspect the KGB; many suspect rogue elements in the military; some suspect Vladimir Putin himself.

In late 1998, I asked Vladimir Naumov whether he thought the people might take collective action against the government to address the situation. In response, he told me the following joke making the rounds in Moscow.

Three Jews are walking down the street. One asks his friend, "Do you own a dacha?" His friend replies, "Of course." They ask the third, who confesses that he's too poor to own a dacha. "Listen," they say, "we'll put our money together and buy you one." Three Georgians are walking together, and the first asks the second, "Do you own a car?" "Of course," is the reply, "a very nice one." The third, however, doesn't have a car, so they put their money up to buy him one. Two Russians are walking along, and the first asks the second, "Have you ever been in prison, my friend?" "Of course," his companion replies. "And Misha, has he ever been in prison?" The second thinks for a second and says, "Why, no, he hasn't." So the first says, "Then let's find a way of putting him there."

"This is the way Russians help each other," Naumov commented. After a moment, he added, "It's the end of the regime, the end of democratization in our country."

Naumov introduced me to Alexander N. Yakovlev, former ambassador to Canada and an architect of perestroika during the Gorbachev years. Dr. Yakovlev, who was in his seventies when I first met him, founded the International Democracy Foundation; his mission before his death in 2005 was to publish as many documents from the Soviet period as possible. He was also the head of the Rehabilitation Commission, of which Naumov was leading researcher.

When I first met Yakovlev in his Moscow office, I was struck by his gray hair swept neatly back and the jagged lines of thought that converged on his forehead like a geological pattern. He limped from a World War II injury and possessed penetrating eyes. Having studied at Columbia University in

1958 and served as Soviet ambassador to Canada, he spoke excellent English, but often pretended to understand less than he did. His manner was both cordial and distant, and his tone of voice turned easily to irony, deflecting familiarity. On my present visit to discuss possible collaborative ideas he was particularly distracted and gloomy.

"There's nothing to be happy about," he said.

I asked whether it was possible to gauge the loyalty of the people to the government by how small a proportion of the taxes the government was actually able to collect? No, he bridled, it wasn't a matter of loyalty.

"If my foundation had a kopek, I wouldn't pay it to the government either," he said. "Why should I pay them 80 percent of the income of the foundation? Why? For their corruption and incompetence? No." He paused to make sure I understood. "I am a true Russian patriot. I believe in my country. I would give my life for my country, but I wouldn't give the crooks in the Kremlin a ruble." Loyalty to Yakovlev could only be to his country, not the government. I had asked him a question he simply could not logically answer.

He said that he thought the growing number of openly anti-Semitic, fascistic newspapers, some with moderately large circulations, was a good barometer of the growing drift backward to totalitarian forms of thinking. "Totalitarianism in the West," he said, "is always accompanied by the hatred of Jews." In Russia, the Jew remains the outsider, the symbol of Western liberalism—despite the fact that so many were in the Bolshevik Party in 1917, despite the fact that Lenin, Trotsky, Zinoviev, Kamenev, Kaganovich, and scores of other leaders were either Jewish or part Jewish or, in the case of Molotov, Andreev, Dimitrov, and Voroshilov, had Jewish wives. Even Nikolai Yezhov, head of the NKVD. Even Stalin's daughter's first husband was a Jew.

When I offered Yakovlev a copy of a new Yale book, *Socialist Realist Painting*, as a gift, he merely scoffed, saying tartly, "There is not now and never has been any socialist realist art. It's a contradiction in terms—it was not socialist and it wasn't art."

Before his death Yakovlev had great plans for an international cold war journal. He wanted desperately to spread information and knowledge as a means of combating the wave of extremist thinking threatening to engulf Russia and the West. Though in 1998 he hadn't given up hope, he was clearly a man searching for a way out of the intellectual, political, and spiritual collapse of his world, the *tupik* in which he found himself. In the end, he said quite simply, "What can you do when you have no money?"

I asked whether he might be interested in commissioning a textbook on Soviet history using the documents Yale University Press and his foundation have published.

"It's not possible," Naumov broke in. To write a textbook, he explained, meant to have some kind of unifying narrative with an underlying conception. A point of view. No one, he insisted, would undertake such a daunting and dangerous task at the present time. To offer a unified interpretation of the Soviet period meant, first, that you wished to know the truth, and second, that you had the courage to tell it.

"Many think enough documents have been published," Naumov continued. "The history of that time is still not being taught in many Russian high schools and universities. No one dares. It will take a generation. If not more."

Yakovlev nodded in agreement.

By mid-August 1998, the ruble was trading at 7,000 to the dollar. This represented approximately a 40 percent decline in purchasing power for the average Russian since the previous January. At one point the ruble had gone down to 12,000 to the dollar and near panic ensued. Outside the major cities there was simply no money at all and people were bartering potatoes and other household goods to get by. Many people in government and out were predicting civil collapse.

Although there was no visible sign of panic along Kutuzovsky Prospect, long lines had formed before the currency exchanges dotting the boulevard, with men and women holding paper bags full of rubles hoping to exchange them for dollars before the ruble disappeared altogether from sight.

While all around them the picture of the world was changing and it must have seemed that the ground was disappearing under their feet, the images above them on billboards projected a new life, clashing terribly with what was before their eyes. Advertisements for a new cellular telephone company had sprung up along the avenues. Its slogan, in English, was "Be Happy." On practically every block one could see an advertisement declaring *Otvetny udar*—the answering blow—with a picture of a gold-plated 1930s socialist realist man and woman, arms thrust forward in true revolutionary style. In the 1930s they would have been brandishing the red flag of Soviet revolution and power;

now, they held up a package of Zolotaya cigarettes against the backdrop of the New York City skyline. This would be the answering blow, struck against American domination of the tobacco market, the new revolution being sold the Muscovites as they raced to cash in their rubles.

The shop windows were packed with expensive foreign products: Sport Siti ("Sport City") displayed Reebok, Kettler, Speedo, Adidas, BH Fitness, and Bauer products at 20 percent off. A Xerox Copy Document Center showed off the latest technological improvements. "Clothes for the home and relaxation" could be found in a shop window filled with stylish black-and-white undergarments for men and women. In a shop with the name "Men's and Women's Clothing," Dior, Wolf, Lejany, and Alessandra Traini labels invited you inside to feel on your skin what the future would be. An eyeglass store displayed Yves Saint Laurent, Valentino, Tiffany, Oliver, and Longines eyewear. Next door was a window for the Dizain Tsentr ("Design Center") dominated by a photograph of a clean, well-lit, modish, all-white room. In the background was a heap of art books; on top, an album of the acclaimed Italian designer Walter Albini, no doubt chosen for its color and his name. In the foreground an attractive blonde, hair cut short, sat cross-legged on a white sofa, wearing black bobby socks and no shoes. She covers her pretty face with a hand as if she'd just heard a delicious joke, a piece of hilarious gossip, or fantastic news about the novel she'd just written. The white telephone receiver is facedown on the sofa, as if to say, "Hold on! I'll just be a sec." Beside her is her portable typewriter with a sheet of paper not yet ripped from the platen, and at her feet the open telephone book. That last detail is the giveaway: There are no telephone books in Russia. This shop window did not advertise a sofa or a design; it advertised a dream. No Russian walking past would ever curl up on such a sofa, answer such a telephone, or laugh at such a joke. This is a sofa in a room in a city that does not exist, at least not in 1998.

The dream goes on, like the famous dream that flits from house to house at the end of Bulgakov's *White Guard*, except now it goes from billboard to billboard and from shop window to shop window. "I love you" says one that offers neither a product nor a provenance, but only the dreamy Slavic face of the New Russian woman with hypnotic turquoise eyes. "He eats so much!" reads another depicting the kind of well-appointed kitchen that one might expect to find inhabited by this surreal face of love; instead, a very "real" Russian wife holds a large copper saucepan over the head of her jovial, fat, large-nosed husband seated at the table preparing himself to be served.

Another shop window displays the holy triptych of this New Russian kitchen: three adjacent panels depicting a shiny new dishwasher, a stainless steel sink, and a wood-paneled work space overhung with a bright armory of copper pots and pans. *Heaven is around the corner*, these advertisements say, no different than in the United States, saturated with the material abundance that capitalism affords. *Get there, get there, get there* is the unconscious, unspoken command. *Get to the promised land of the white sofa, the short blond hair and the black bobby socks, the dishwasher, the answering blow. Make yourself new and wholesome and attractive. Acquire objects of pleasure and fantasy. Feel it on your skin.*

The billboard announcing the New Russian *Vogue* provides the vital nexus: *"V Rossii nakonyet,"* the caption reads. In Russia at last—the long wait is over, like the advent of Orthodoxy or St. Cyril's alphabet. Two beautiful models face each other at right angles so that their ample busts appear just to touch—a loaded visual pun implying a joyous tête-à-tete, a meeting of minds and bodies passionately, perhaps subversively, desired. One of the models is American, blond, full face, smiling out at the viewer with perfect white teeth; the other, in profile, is a silky brunette with high Slavic features. Red Square and St. Basil's Cathedral shimmer behind them like an enchanted vision. Their tight-fitting shirts and open, expectant smiles proclaim the new day in which East meets West. The titillating point of contact is engorged with money, fashion, sex, and fantasy, while the stolid power of the Kremlin and the mystical power of St. Basil's float helplessly in the background. Nothing can stop this. It was meant to be. The old politics and the old religion be damned! This is the new Hegelian moment. The end of history will come at the point of their embrace—at last.

Not far from the New Russian *Vogue* is an overhead billboard advertising elite apartments at $1,900 per square meter (today such apartments would sell for at least three times as much), while underneath it at the curb a bearded man sits with the watchful face of a Chekhov coachman and a stray dog peers from a nearby alleyway, unaware that the headline in the leading financial paper, *Kommersant*, was the simple word *Obval*—"Collapse."

The faces of many buildings, recently restored to the dreamy cream colors beloved by Moscow's grandees of centuries past—mild pinks, yellows, blues, and greens of a softness and delicacy almost unimaginable, as in the portraits by Borovikovsky, Rokotov, and Levitsky that hang in the Tretyakov Gallery—soften the harsh space around them, but do not mitigate the sense of crisis. The composure of the people along Kutuzovsky is impressive. Only the picture of a man and a woman feverishly counting out rubles from a large shopping bag before a currency exchange expresses the tension everyone feels.

Olga Varshaver and I take a bus to meet with the head of one of the largest of the state archives, also the most prosperous. A tall, visibly drunk young man with greasy hair approaches from several seats away.

"Vat iz freedom?" he asks in heavily accented English, leaning uncomfortably close to my face. I feel as if I'm looking at a broken mirror. There is a dark red cut above his right temple, a freshly healed wound over his smashed nose—the bridge of his nose is flattened as if by a hammer. His eyes are dull and glassy. His clothing seems too small for his lanky frame.

"What is freedom?"

"*Da.*"

He waits. His breath stinks. I say nothing.

"A graveyard," Olga answers.

"*Nyet, nyet,*" he waves away the facile cynicism.

"Some people think freedom is doing what you like," I offer lamely. "Others think freedom is self-control." He waits as if expecting something more. But I switch gears.

"What is freedom in Russia?"

"To love vooman, many vooman," he says.

"To love or to use?" Olga asks in English.

"Shto?"

"To love or to use?"

"Love many, many vooman—to khoom and vat?"

"So freedom is doing as you like. . . . Is that freedom for you in Russia?"

"In Russia," he says, "freedom—*govno*."

"Govno?"

"Sheet," he says emphatically. "Freedom—sheet. You understand me, brother?" He holds out a grimy hand and I clasp it.

After our business meeting in the archive, the director sat down on the edge of his desk, clasped his large hands in his lap, and smiled boyishly. "Jonathan," he said, "it can't get worse." And then a kind of black rage took hold of him. His voice rose. "Jonathan, I need money. I have no money. What will I do? What? I have no money." He paused, stared at the floor. Then, as if to reassure himself, and speaking more to himself than to me, he said, "I'll survive somehow. We'll all survive somehow. We did it before. There'll be a black market. Let them close the country. Let them make it thirty kopeks to the dollar. We did it before. We'll do it again!"

I came back to my apartment, now no longer Mariana's, in a building located within the complex where Brezhnev and Andropov once lived—an apartment building for the *nomenklatura* where in years past government limousines might have been seen in the courtyard rather than the run-down Zhigulis and Ladas of 1998 parked along the curb and sidewalk. The elderly widow from whom I rented stayed with her daughter while I was in Moscow.

Since my last visit the previous January, the building's entryway had been repainted; the elevator, which had not worked, had been repaired; and a new front door had been installed with a functioning coded entry system. The small two-room apartment had a new front door with strong brass locks, but otherwise was unchanged. Even the newspapers piled in the corner by the door were the same as those I had idly leafed through back in January. No new ones, yet none discarded either.

Little of substance had changed inside this modest apartment over those eight months of economic and political turmoil on the street below, despite the advent of Russian *Vogue*, despite the crash of the ruble, despite the answering blow. The world of *this* apartment in *this* world was defined by the tables whose uneven legs required the slightest calculation as to where and how to place a cup of tea; chairs against whose backs you could not rest your full weight, beds with the abiding smell of mold, a sink whose faucet swung instantly to the side to spray the floor if tapped too hard, a stove whose burners remained a mystery, twig brooms in the corner, mirrors hung on the nub of a screw that would crash down if touched the wrong way, a bathtub with its plastic shower curtain hung on a single strand of wire that reached only halfway across.

At a touch the aged suction cup for the soap holder loses its grip, the dish towel shreds, the hot-water knob comes off in your hand, the bathroom mirror swings wildly to the side as in a horror movie. All of these fragile, half-broken, or breaking things had lasted longer than the power of the Kremlin to stabilize the ruble, than the strength of the Soviet army. The power of this weakness is almost indestructible.

It was August and I arrived home sweaty and in need of a bath. No hot water. No hot water anywhere in my section of Moscow. I had been told this was part of a municipal plan to "fix" the aged pipes beneath the city and that it would be restored the following day. Whether this was simply another Gogolian canard or a cover for sheer incompetence was impossible to know. No one I spoke to among my acquaintances could be certain. By two in the morning, still unable to sleep and still without hot water, I resolved to have a bath. I had used the old four-burner gas range for nothing more than tea, but I resolved to use it now to boil my bathwater.

When I lit one of the larger burners, flames shot up six inches and I realized I had to use the smaller ones up front or risk burning down the kitchen. Not able to take a bath in a teapot of water, I found a large aluminum pot, filled it from the sink, and placed it on the stove. It never boiled, but it warmed up. I took it to the bathtub and poured it in. I went back for another. When I returned to the bathtub the water was gone—it had disappeared through a tiny crack in the plastic plug. After an hour of boiling, carrying, plugging, I managed to immerse myself in about four inches of warm water. The next evening, the hot water ran like a fountain.

While Audis, Porsches, Volvos, Mercedes-Benzes, and gigantic Wagoneers roll down the immense boulevards at high speed, displacing the diminutive Moskviches and

Zhigulis; and "Miss Bust," "Pussycats for Purrfection," and other "butterflies of the night" promise universal delights in the English-language newspapers; while restaurants in the heart of downtown Moscow assure their patrons of "pleasant and safe surroundings" in which to enjoy their meal, the new Russia is still searching for its identity. To most, like my friend Nikolai, the city has become mean, aggressive, and threatening. One feels a constant, if sleepy, danger. Not long ago, to celebrate its 850th birthday, a large sign appeared in the city center: "To Moscow!" it read. "Let us keep it clean and orderly as befits a capital." Underneath a *dvornik* from the nineteenth century in a blue cap and soft black boots has set about cheerfully performing this directive with a twig broom and wooden dustpan in hand. Among the litter and stink of the Moscow streets, shiny silver- and golden-globed Orthodox churches that had been boarded up not long before have suddenly sprung back to life.

I have about twenty minutes to kill before meeting Nikolai for lunch and I sit on a public bench beside a fountain in the center of Moscow, cooling myself. I notice a school bus packed with children drive past on the circular drive around the fountain. The kids—perhaps ten years old—have mischievous, happy expressions on their faces. For some reason the bus comes round again and I look more closely at the children in the windows. Each has his middle finger plastered up against the window; they are ecstatic to see my astonishment.

Nikolai and I go to a stylish restaurant in the city center. There are two of us, but we are brought only one menu; when we ask for a second, the waitress says they are temporarily out of them despite the fact that the restaurant is nearly empty. The menu is elaborate, with many foreign dishes and a wine list. One listing is for lamb cooked with fried *baklazhan*—eggplant. On the opposite side, the English translation is given as lamb with fried *aborigines*—a failed attempt at aubergines. Half the items on the menu are not available. We settle on soup and a particularly delicious Russian specialty, *sudak*, what they call "pike-perch" or walleye pike. The next day both Nikolai and I are sick. I tell him that it must have been the soup—it wasn't hot enough. No, Nikolai says, it was our fault. We didn't drink vodka.

Nearby my apartment is one of the grandest accomplishments of Mayor Yuri Luzhkov (Moscow's equivalent of Chicago's Mayor Daley): the construction of a magnificent mall on a bridge over the Moscow River. It has an exceptionally fine atrium filled with expensive foreign shops, slow-moving escalators, and moving walkways. After an afternoon with Naumov studying documents, we decide to explore it and arrive at Vensky Dvor ("Viennese Court"). Here we are served perfectly prepared smoked salmon on toast with cucumbers, horseradish, and baby tomatoes presented with a sprig of fresh parsley and accompanied by whole-grain rolls and Austrian butter. The white china plates sparkle, the weighty forks and knives are spotless, and the immaculate linen tablecloth is crisp. My healthy Jack Daniel's with ice is followed by a precisely brewed cappuccino sweetened with *suiker* from Holland.

The Vensky Dvor arches over the Moscow River and is decorated with the motif of a ship—open, light, with porthole-shaped windows, sailing above Moscow, or rather, one has the feeling, around it. You can sit in a deck chair and watch the excursion boats on the river and the cars streaming around the Russian White House and beyond, in strangulating loops, toward the Kremlin. I mentioned to Nikolai that I thought the notion of a ship flying over Moscow was particularly apt—Chagallesque.

"Of course," he said, "because it is a ship going nowhere."

More security guards wearing MVD badges were stationed throughout the building with cellphones and walkie-talkies than there were customers. *They will come and we will be ready for them*, their curious, idle looks in my direction said. But above the dining area was an innovation I had not seen in any fine restaurant anywhere else in the world: a closed-circuit television camera trained not on the people entering through the doorway but on the patrons enjoying themselves at the tables.

I pointed this out to Vladimir Pavlovich, who merely shrugged and made a hissing sound. I asked whether he thought my telephone was bugged.

"Of course."

"But why?"

"Just to let you know they're still listening."

"But to what?"

"They don't know yet. Maybe they'll know in a year or two."

"There is nothing for us to believe in," Nikolai said, "except these ships that go nowhere and old ways of thinking. We're all pagans, but we really don't have even that." A new generation of "candle holders" attend the Orthodox Church without inner conviction but hoping to get some,

Nikolai said. They sing, they hold the candles, but they know almost nothing of the religion. In the meantime, old habits have not disappeared. The old government is not dead; it is only sleeping.

Nikolai himself has made several trips to Japan to study kendo; it has given him something to hold onto internally. It is neither a religion nor a philosophy. It is a way of life.

"To succeed you must release yourself from your own ego. You must see the sword coming down on you and move to save yourself, rather than become preoccupied with your fear of the sword and what it may do if it strikes. You must become free of inner preoccupations. You must learn detachment. That is your one freedom. Thereby you can see what is the case." You can free yourself from your own desires, wishes, fears. What is the case is what is necessary and what is necessary is what was summed up in the word Nikolai invariably used to describe his state of affairs: *normalno*. How are things? I would ask. *"Vsyo normalno"* would be the invariable reply. I asked once what precisely he meant by this term: It is everything that is necessarily the case, as if to say, "Everything is the way it should be."

Only in retrospect, after Nikolai's horrible death from an ax he didn't see coming down on his own leg from his own hand, reflecting on that shining moment at Vensky Dvor, at the doorstep to Putin's new regime, under the watchful lens of the security camera, while hunting documents on Kirov's assassination with Vladimir Pavlovich Naumov, do I begin to have any sense of what Nikolai meant. *Vsyo normalno*—Everything is *normalno*.

Chapter 17

Vergil

That evening Naumov called asking if I could come to his apartment the following day to discuss our projects further—he had something special he would like to mention.

The metal door to Naumov's building is painted a solid gray and has the look and feel of a bank vault. His grandson opened it for Olga and me after we buzzed up. It is a spacious apartment, packed floor to ceiling with books, journals, and manuscripts. Open any cabinet door along the hallway and instead of plates or cutlery, you will find stacks of document folders, books, newspapers, and more manuscripts.

Pictures of Naumov's children and grandchildren are on every wall, and on the floors are beautiful old Turkish rugs. It was late afternoon, the lights to the apartment were not on, and shadows began to accumulate around Naumov's small desk in the corner of his living room, where he sat surrounded with papers and stacks of documents. A relatively new Panasonic television with a sixteen-inch screen stood across from his desk in a cleared space. My eye followed the electrical wire to where it plugged into a white plastic wall socket that looked as if it dated from the 1940s.

When we arrived, Naumov had been engaged in cutting photocopies of documents out of oversized sheets of copy paper. After our greeting, he sat down at his desk and resumed this task while discussing the current state of the country. Once he finished cutting out each page, he would take the leftover strips of paper, arrange them carefully into piles of equal length and width, bind them with oversized, Soviet-era paperclips, and then store them away in his desk drawer for future note-taking.

We talked for several hours, and our conversation drifted back and forth between his work in the archives and the notion that the country could be understood only by taking a full account of the "mentality" of the people. Buildings, cars, cell phones, expensive clothes were one thing; but the mentality of the people would determine Russia's future. It was deeper than anything to be seen on the street or on the billboards. The people, Naumov was convinced, would wait. They were exhausted, not ready for further political upheavals. Things would stay the same. There was no alternative. Not yet.

Had I ever heard of something called the doctors' plot? he wanted to know. Vaguely, I admitted. It was the plot against the Jewish doctors, if I remembered, whom Stalin accused of murdering Kremlin leaders. Naumov nodded.

"There is some new information," Naumov added.

"That proves the doctors' innocence?"

He shook his head.

"That proves they were guilty?"

He shook his head again.

"No, no," he said dismissively. "Much more complicated. It is a very dark story."

"Then write about it. Write a full account for my series at Yale."

"No, I can't. I might be accused of being anti-Semitic—which I'm not. I need somebody who can write about these things correctly."

"Who?"

"You."

"But I know nothing about it. I hardly know the first thing about Soviet history."

"You know more than you think you know. I'll teach you the rest. We'll work together. I will show you some documents. Come on the weekend to my dacha."

On Saturday, the ruble was not being traded and the city had a chance to catch its breath. It was a beautiful day, with alternate cooling rain and bright midsummer sun. Tall groves of black-green birch trees and towering pines shimmered as we drove past. Along the way to Naumov's dacha, about forty minutes outside Moscow, are numerous roadside stands run largely by people from the Caucasus, I am told, who have been coming for millennia to sell their sweet, oblong whitish melons (*uzbek dinya*), watermelons, cherries, bananas, pistachios, and vegetables.

Before me stretches a long day of pleasure, of eating, drinking, discussing—politics, Soviet personalities, intriguing or confusing new documents—and admiring the beauties of the Russian countryside that come practically to the door of Naumov's modest dacha. I had never seen a house in the United States, except one occupied by a lumberjack near my father's farm in Wisconsin, that was so completely embedded in the forest. There was no lawn, no formal flower garden, no circular driveway or shaping of the natural world around the dacha. The house was not overrun by nature; it was in some kind of dialogue with it. The Naumovs' dacha was not unique. This absence of human intervention seemed to reflect a specifically Russian sensitivity to natural beauty. The conscious (or perhaps only semiconscious) withholding of the will to shape the natural world seemed to me quite at variance with the dominating imperatives of Soviet ideology. Here, the world of human force and power could not intrude.

Oleg Naumov has rebuilt the house, laid new floors, repaired the toilet, put up beautiful pinewood paneling, and reconstructed the upstairs study from which his father can look out into the forest on one side and survey the work of some of his New Russian neighbors on the other. These neighbors are busily constructing dachas of their own, clearing the land of brush and using Swiss architects, Swiss builders, and Swiss materials imported in sealed containers from Switzerland.

"New Russians," Naumov mutters dryly, pointing across the row of trees separating the properties. He tells the following joke in Russian.

A New Russian is driving his brand-new Mercedes down the highway and comes upon a friend, also a New Russian, stopped along the shoulder. The hood of his friend's new Mercedes is up. He stops his car. "What's the trouble?" he asks. "The damned car is no good," his friend says. "Look at it. Now I'll have to buy a new one." "But what's the matter with it?" the first man asks. "The damned thing is out of gas."

Before eating we hunt mushrooms beneath the birch and pine trees along the sides of the house. Oleg, my interpreter Olga (who, I discover, was in high school with him), and Naumov's wife, Valentina Ivanovna, wander with eyes down seeking out these prizes from the forest floor. Having taken her finds into the house, Valentina Ivanovna now stands at the corner of the porch and declares loudly, so that I will surely understand, "Here is something that absolutely cannot be found in America!" She points to a bright, lithium-red mushroom under a tall spruce; beside it like a twin was another that glowed orange as a harvest moon. Quite beautiful. Quite deadly. *Mukhmor*, they are called here: "fly killers."

Valentina Ivanovna is a large woman with a sturdy frame; for the past two years, she has suffered from a weakened heart and takes frequent naps. Yet she had worked alone all day in the kitchen. The table included chicken cutlets fried in egg batter, brown bread, eggplant stuffed with soft cheese and various seasonings, braised potatoes, pear tomatoes, and cucumbers, along with some kind of pressed meat served with horseradish. Then she brought out her favorite dish: homemade pizza with sausage, mushrooms, onions, and red peppers.

"What language shall we speak?" she asks with mock seriousness, while standing at the head of the table. "English, Russian, French, German?"

"Jonathan understands but doesn't speak Russian well," Olga explains.

Valentina Ivanovna ponders the situation.

"Then we will speak Japanese," she says brightly. "Who will go first?"

No one responds.

"Then I will," she says. "Yap, yap, yap, yap, yap, yap, yap."

We drink many toasts, consuming first the bottle of Glenfiddich I had brought and then two-thirds of a bottle of Chivas Regal. Other bottles on the table remained: red and white juices, Georgian wine, and special vodka. These we would get to in due course. There was no reason to rush.

Naumov brought out a folder and placed a document in my hand. By now I could read Russian well enough to know instantly that this was a copy of testimony given to Lavrenti Beria, dated March 27, 1953, by Semyon Ignatiev, the former head of the MGB (the KGB of the time), concerning the arrest and torture of the doctors in 1952. According to Ignatiev's testimony, Stalin directed him to give all the confessions and testimony to Stalin himself, bypassing the Central Committee. He instructed Ignatiev not to modify the materials in any way because, as Stalin put it, "we ourselves will be able to determine what is true and what is not true, what is important and what is not important." Stalin himself would determine the truth.

What made the document particularly vivid was Ignatiev's account of Stalin's orders to torture the prisoners to extract the confessions. He threatened Ignatiev personally and the entire MGB if they didn't produce the necessary confessions. "You work like waiters in white gloves. If you want to be Chekists, take off your gloves. Chekist work—this is for peasants and not for barons," Stalin said, ordering the MGB to beat the doctors "with death blows."

"Has anyone ever seen this document?"

Naumov shook his head.

"Is there more?"

He smiled. "Much more nobody has ever seen, including a report on Stalin's death that raises suspicions."

"Can we use this?"

"Why not?"

But what was the import of these materials? How would they substantially alter the basic picture that the Jewish doctors were innocent and Stalin was guilty of a cruel fraud?

"Nobody was innocent in that system," Naumov said. "Nobody. The judges and the damned were all implicated. A good man can't exist in a bad society. That is what we have to show. How everything was connected. It is not enough to say, 'Stalin was guilty,' or 'The doctors were innocent.' Our job is harder. It is not about politics or morality. It is about how people lived."

He asked me to come upstairs to admire the study that Oleg had built for him. The sky was still light over the dense forest.

"I have nothing but documents here, but to understand history," he told me, "you have to overcome the documents. By themselves, documents will never be enough. In fact very little was written down." The documentation on the Katyn massacre is unique because it was here that Stalin miscalculated, thinking that since Poland had been wiped out and would never rise again to be a state, it was not dangerous to save the documents authorizing the murder of the Polish officers. It is also important to see that Stalin, Beria, and the rest didn't begin with the clear intention of executing the Polish officers. The documents make that very plain. But once they saw that the Poles would never alter their political views or give up their hatred of the Soviet

Union, they decided they had no option but to shoot them. Inveterate enemies of the state had to be shot. What the documents do not show is *why* they felt they had no option. Why was this decision the inevitable result of the freedom their ideology provided?

In general, Naumov told me, Stalin often communicated his intentions in "half-words," hints and casual remarks. Sometimes he would say the opposite of what he meant and leave it to subordinates to decide his intention. For instance, after a Politburo meeting in which it was debated whether a man should be arrested, Stalin as a rule would not sign a decree or arrest warrant. Instead, he would say something like, "It's a pity. X was such a good man." The others would know what he meant and act accordingly. If you did not know, if you couldn't anticipate his meaning, you would not survive long. That is why the existing documents are so precious, but also insufficient.

Soon we are called down for shashlik that Oleg has prepared in his outdoor grill, which has been burning all afternoon. There is plenty of light still in the sky, but the air has gotten thin and chill. On the table is an enormous platter of this savory delicacy, which we eat until we're stuffed. There are more toasts. Oleg makes a toast to his home, to the place where there is stability, love, sacrifice for others, and continuity. Valentina Ivanovna brings out a plate of fresh cucumbers with the stems left on. She left them on, she says, because they are so beautiful. *"Oy, kak eto pakhnyet!"* she exclaims as she slices one, closing her eyes—"how wonderful it smells!" She hands one half to me and another to Vladimir Pavlovich.

At the end of the meal she takes out the enormous whitish yellow melon I had bought from one of the roadside stands. She leaves it in the center of the table for several minutes so that everyone can admire its heft and breathe its aroma.

"Do you think it's good?" she asks, taking it into her lap, and with a large kitchen knife cuts it into wedges. Carefully removing the rind and disposing of the plentiful seeds in a separate dish, she distributes the melon, which Oleg samples at her direction as he might wine. When it is found to be sweet, everyone is allowed to eat.

When we are through with the melon, the elder Naumov stands and raises his glass. The most important outcome of our project, he says, was the trust and friendship it has produced that is not simply professional. I second this. I wanted to believe this and want to believe this still. Trust and friendship are all the more precious in light of the world of lies, paranoia, suspicion, and cruelty amply attested in the documents of a world that existed not so long ago. They are all that will remain once that ship in Mayor Lushkov's mall finally comes unmoored and sails over Moscow.

Chapter 18

Yezhov's Office

Vladimir Pavlovich had prepared the way for me to work in the Russian Federal Security Service archive—the FSB; formerly, the KGB—on the dossier of Isaac Babel, but one day he asked whether I might possibly be interested in meeting the head of the FSB archive to discuss a possible collaboration. Would it be possible to work there with integrity, without falsification, with real historical objectivity? I asked.

Why not? was Naumov's reply. The FSB is different now, he said. The heads have all changed. They, too, are interested in unearthing the past. They, too, are interested in a new Russia. Then he said something for which I was not prepared: "They would like to meet you."

It seemed to me I had nothing to lose, and Naumov and I discussed the kinds of projects we would like to work on and what might be acceptable to the archive. Highest on the list was a volume on government suppression of the arts from the revolution to Stalin's death. How did this happen? What did the artists themselves, Gorky foremost among them, actually think about Stalin? Did they collaborate in their own demise, Babel's irony notwithstanding? Whether directly with a bullet to the head or indirectly through madness and destitution, or silence, the following partial list of repressed writers, artists, and scholars—some famous, some not—is worthy of reflection. It is taken from the volume Yale Press eventually published on this subject.

Anna Akhmatova, poet, expelled from the Writers' Union, 1946

Leopold Averbakh, literary critic, shot 1937

Isaac Babel, writer, shot 1940

David Bergelson, writer, shot 1952

Alexander Blok, died from lack of medical treatment in 1920

Andrei Bubnov, commissar for education, shot 1938

Mikhail Bulgakov, censored, unable to leave the country or publish (1891–1940)

Sergei Dinamov, literary scholar, shot 1939

Robert Eideman, Latvian poet, shot 1937

Itzik Fefer, Soviet poet, shot 1952

Aleksandr Gavronsky, film director, repressed 1956

Yakov Golosovker, philologist and translator, in gulag 1936–1942

D. D. Golovin, opera soloist, repressed

Maxim Gorky, died 1936 under mysterious circumstances; many still suspect he was poisoned by Stalin

Ivan Gronsky, party and literary functionary, repressed in 1937 but survived

Nikolai Gumilyov, poet, Anna Akhmatova's first husband, shot 1921

Aleksandr Isbakh, novelist, repressed but survived

Ivan Kataev, writer, colleague of Voronsky in *Pereval* group, shot 1939

Vladimir Kirshon, playwright, shot 1938

Nikolai Kliuev, poet, shot 1937

Sergei Klychkov, writer, shot 1937

Mikhail Koltsov, writer, friend of Babel and Ehrenburg, shot 1940

Boris Kornilov, poet, shot 1938

Pyotr Kriuchkov, Gorky's secretary, shot 1938

Georgy Kuklin, writer, shot 1939

Lev Kvitko, poet, shot 1952

G. Lelevich, poet, shot 1937

Fedor Levin, critic, accused of "cosmopolitanism" in the late 1940s

A Lezhnev, critic in *Pereval* group, shot 1938

Ivan Luppol, literary scholar, repressed in 1943

Ivan Makariev, secretary of RAPP, the proletarian writers, union, in gulag 1937–1955

Leonid Maliugin, playwright, accused of cosmopolitanism in late 1940s

Osip Mandelshtam, poet, arrested in 1938 and died in gulag

Perets Markish, poet, shot 1952

Vladimir Mayakovsky, poet, committed suicide in 1930; Stalin pronounced him "the best and most talented poet of the Soviet era"

Dmitry Maznin, poet, shot 1938

Pavel Medvedev, literary scholar of Bakhtin circle, shot 1938

Vsevolod Meyerhold, theater director, shot 1940

Solomon Mikhoels, actor, director of Moscow Yiddish Theater, assassinated on Stalin's orders in 1948

Ivan Mikitenko, Ukrainian writer, shot 1937

Vladimir Narbut, poet, shot 1944

Isaak Nusinov, literary scholar, repressed 1950

Yuri Olesha, writer, attacked repeatedly in the 1930s, fell silent and died in 1960

Pyotr Oreshin, poet, shot 1938

Boris Pilnyak, writer, shot 1937

Valerian Pravdukhin, writer, shot 1939

Nikolay Punin, art historian, writer and husband of Akhmatova, died in the gulag in 1953

Aleksei Selivanovsky, literary critic, shot 1938

Mikhail Semenko, poet, shot 1937

Dmitry Shostakovich, composer, attacked viciously but survived

Lev Sosnovsky, journalist, shot 1937

Boris Tal, journalist, shot 1938

Aleksandr Tarasov-Rodionov, writer, shot 1937

Marina Tsvetaeva, poet, committed suicide, 1941

Illarion Vardin, critic, shot 1943

Pavel Vasiliev, poet, shot 1937

Artem Vesely, writer, shot 1939

Aleksandr Voronsky, critic, founder of *Pereval*, shot 1937

Bruno Yasensky, poet, shot 1941

Paolo Yashvili, poet, shot 1937

Sergei Yesenin, poet, committed suicide in 1925; his poems were banned throughout the Stalin and Khrushchev years

Yevgeny Zamyatin, writer, forced into exile 1931
Nikolai Zarudin, writer, member of *Pereval*, shot 1937
Vladimir Zazubrin, journalist, shot 1938
Mikhail Zoshchenko, writer, expelled from Writers' Union
   with Akhmatova in 1946

This list provides only a meager outline of what happened to the literary and artistic community from 1917 to Stalin's death in 1953. During this period, some twelve hundred writers were repressed in one form or another. The list does not include figures such as Boris Pasternak or Ilya Ehrenburg, who were intimidated but never arrested; or Lydia Chukovskaya, who was arrested in 1926 but not sent to the gulag, because she protested against some practices in an otherwise approved youth organization, but not as a writer; or Aleksandr Solzhenitsyn and Varlam Shalamov, who were not originally arrested for their writing. Shalamov was arrested for his political activities, and Solzhenitsyn because while serving in the army he had written a letter critical of Stalin.

Lubyanka is a large, yellow-brick building that could easily be mistaken for an Italian-style palazzo: it was built in 1898 by a Russian grandee in neobaroque style, and was for a time the home of the All-Russia Insurance Company. After the revolution, it provided the Soviet regime with a different kind of insurance. Before it stretches a wide square that would have been pleasant and spacious when first constructed, but today is bordered by a parking lot, while along another side is the largest children's store in Russia, "Children's World." A clock centered at the top of the building's façade overlooks Lubyanka Square. As we approached, Naumov told me that it was the tallest building in Moscow because, he joked, you could see Siberia from its basement.

Naumov and I entered through the front door and were instantly escorted up three flights of stairs by a young man who shook my hand firmly and looked me directly in the eye. We entered a long hallway lined with numerous office doors and were directed into a spacious conference room. A handsome, energetic-looking man in a well-cut, Western-style blue business suit with a monogram on the breast pocket, entered, shook my hand firmly, presented his business card, and in excellent English introduced himself as the head of public relations for the FSB. He was pleased I could visit to discuss such an important publishing initiative as Professor Naumov had described. They would try to be helpful. If needed I could be directly in touch with him in the future.

A few minutes later three other men came in dressed in the drab gray business suits I had come to associate with official business in Moscow—the head of the archive, a prominent historian, and an archivist. They went to the opposite side of the table without formal introductions. I took a seat at the table with the public relations officer on one side, my translator Olga next to me, my escort through the building beside her, and then Naumov. My hosts on the other side did not seem nearly as pleased to see me as the head of public relations. This was the first and the only business meeting I conducted in Moscow in which members of the organization with which I was negotiating sat on my side of the table.

Perhaps sensing the awkwardness of the arrangement after we all took our seats, Naumov began by describing me and my business in Moscow. This also was uncharacteristic. In all past meetings the head of the archive would extend a greeting in more or less formal language to which I would respond. In truth, I wasn't even certain which of the two men in gray suits was the director.

Naumov spoke of my background and personal interest in Isaac Babel, my steady work in the Central Party Archive, my commitment to publish a book on Kirov, and the reputation of Yale University Press both in Russia and around the world.

When he finished, there was silence. I waited for a cue from Naumov, but he didn't turn his head or gesture. I waited. Finally, the director of the archive smiled weakly. We now sat, he wanted me to know, in the office once occupied by Nikolai Yezhov. He pointed across the room to a wide bar I hadn't noticed when I came in. That, he said, is where Yezhov would entertain his comrades.

"Does it still operate?" I asked.

"Konyechno," he said. Of course.

And Beria? I asked.

Beria was here as well. It is a famous office.

It all seemed musty, old, receding gradually into forgetful anonymity. It had the feel more of an ancient schoolroom than the office where the fates of millions had been decided. The pale green walls and parquet floor bore no trace of anything that had been said or done in it—all that had been thought or felt. It seemed wrapped in silence and packed away in the attic of a distant past.

The older man, who was introduced as the FSB historian, asked what I might wish to collaborate on. Perhaps we can try one project, he said, and see how it goes. I mentioned my interest in the fate of Soviet writers.

"Such an old subject," he said, waving it away. A thick growth on one cheek resembled the nub of a small branch that had been broken off, while smaller growths on his nose and forehead looked like the swollen eyes of a potato. "You can't think of anything else?"

"It is an old subject," I said, "but you must forgive the ignorance of the West. We simply don't know how this happened, or even what happened to so many of your great writers and artists. This would be the one book I would wish to work on with you."

"You would not work with us on it, but we might work on it."

Naumov intervened, saying that I meant this only figuratively as a joint publication to be undertaken together. The head of the archive leaned over and whispered something to the historian.

We had been talking for over an hour, and it seemed as if this conversation might continue a while yet, so I pushed my chair from the table and excused myself to go to the men's room I'd seen down the hall. But as I rose and headed for the door, my escort from before rushed up to me.

"I myself will accompany you," he said, almost breathless.

"But it's right outside," I said in Russian. "There's no need."

He smiled, took me by the elbow and we left the room. At the door to the men's room, he told me he would wait, and when I came out he was standing at the entrance as if to prevent others from entering while I had been inside.

The meeting did not extend nearly as far into the afternoon as I had thought it might; in fact, after some further discussion of the kinds of materials I might like to see in this volume, the director said that they would consider what they could do. The historian shook his massive, brambly head and whispered something to the director.

"We will do this," the director said. "You will not hear from us again directly, but we will be in touch with you through an intermediary at the right time."

That was all. I never heard from them again, but about two years later, as though this meeting had never happened, Alexander Yakovlev asked me whether I might be interested in publishing a book on the repression of Soviet writers from material in the KGB. It was indeed the book I had envisioned, a priceless collection of primary documents—letters, directives, transcripts, memoranda from 1917 to 1953—in which one can read of the slow, agonizing progress of the cannibalization of Soviet society, the cultural counterpart to what Babel had witnessed in the Ukraine in the early 1930s.

Among the many documents in this volume is the transcript of a conversation between Sergei Eisenstein, Stalin, A. A. Zhdanov, and Vyacheslav Molotov concerning the second part of Eisenstein's film *Ivan the Terrible*. The meeting took place on February 26, 1947, at the height of the Zhdanovshchina—the postwar repressions during which Akhmatova and Zoshchenko were both expelled from the Writers' Union. Eisenstein and N. K. Cherkasov (the actor who portrayed both Aleksandr Nevsky and

Ivan the Terrible) were ushered into Stalin's office at 10:00 A.M.

At the far end of the office were Stalin, Molotov, and Zhdanov.

We come in, greet everyone, sit down at the table. . . .

Stalin: What are you thinking of doing with the picture? . . . Have you studied history?

Eisenstein: More or less. . . .

Stalin: More or less? I know a thing or two about history, too. You've shown the Oprichnina [the tsar's personal army] improperly. The Oprichnina was the royal army. Unlike a feudal army, which could turn its banners around at any moment and leave the war, a regular army was formed, a progressive army. You have the *oprichniki* looking like the Ku Klux Klan. Eisenstein said that they wore white hoods, whereas ours wore black ones.

Molotov: That doesn't constitute a difference in principle.

Stalin: The tsar comes out in your film as indecisive, like Hamlet. Everyone suggests to him what should be done, but he can't make a decision himself. . . . Tsar Ivan was a great and wise ruler, and if he is compared with Louis XI (have you read about Louis XI, who prepared absolutism for Louis XIV?), then Ivan the Terrible and Louis are worlds apart. Ivan the Terrible's wisdom consisted in the fact that he insisted on a national point of view and wouldn't allow foreigners into his country, fencing the country off from the penetration of foreign influence.... Ivan the Terrible's remarkable enterprise was the fact that he was the first to introduce a state monopoly on foreign trade. Ivan the Terrible was the first to introduce it; Lenin was the second.

Zhdanov: Eisenstein's Ivan the Terrible came out looking like a neurasthenic.

Molotov: In general, the stress was put on psychologism, on the excessive emphasis of inner psychological contradictions and personal sufferings.

Stalin: You need to show historical figures correctly in their style. So, for instance, in the first part, it's wrong that Ivan the Terrible spent so long kissing his wife. In those days that wasn't allowed. . . . Ivan the Terrible was very cruel. You can show that he was cruel, but you have to show why it was essential to be cruel. . . .

Cherkassov: I'm sure the remake will succeed.

Stalin: May God grant you a new year every day.
(He laughs.)

Eisenstein: We're saying that in the first part several moments succeeded, and that gives us confidence that we can do the second part, too.

Stalin: We're not talking about what succeeded and was good, right now we're only talking about the shortcomings.

Eisenstein asks where there are going to be any other special instructions regarding the picture.

Stalin: I'm not giving you instructions. I'm expressing a viewer's remarks. Historical images have to be depicted truthfully.

Stalin was a reader of history, he knew "a thing or two" about it. But he also knew about Hamlet, the Ku Klux Klan, and the aesthetic requirements for depicting historical truth. "Historical images have to be depicted truthfully," he cautioned. Stalin had suffered a temporarily debilitating physical illness after World War II and by 1947 he was beginning to put into place stratagems, such as the doctors' plot, for regaining full control of the Soviet leadership, which had necessarily passed to other hands during his illness. He was sixty-nine. He had suffered from hypertension and had possibly experienced a stroke. He had six years left to live. In providing his views to Eisenstein Stalin was perhaps also expressing his understanding of how he, Stalin, would eventually wish to be depicted.

"You can show that he was cruel, but you have to show why it was essential to be cruel," he said.

However, there is a difference. Ivan the Terrible's cruelty was to a great extent personalized. It was *his*. Stalin's cruelty was never his own. It was the state's. Stalin explains this distinction further in the conversation with Eisenstein:

> **Stalin.** One of Ivan the Terrible's mistakes was that he didn't finish off the five major feudal families. If he had wiped out these five boyar families, then there never would have been a Time of Troubles. But Ivan the Terrible would execute someone and then spend a long time repenting and praying. God hindered him in this matter. . . . He should have been even more decisive.

Ivan the Terrible had a conscience. "God hindered him in this matter." Stalin's cruelty had nothing to do with personal conscience; he worked against God. The unrestrained ideology of the state enabled him to do this. Ivan the Terrible was a powerful individual, but Stalin was more than an individual. Or less. In some important sense, Stalin had no personal will. He, too, was a nonperson.

Chapter 19

The Personal Archive of Josef Stalin

As he was leaving government service at the beginning of the Yeltsin period, Alexander Yakovlev, who had been so important to Yeltsin's predecessor, Mikhail Gorbachev, in developing the policies and principles of glasnost and perestroika, rendered a service Yeltsin never forgot. At a particularly tense moment of civil unrest in the early 1990s, during which the capacious square outside Lubyanka was filled with a mob of angry protesters, Alexander Yakovlev was called in as the only man who might be able to reason with all sides. He allayed the mob and developed an entente between Yeltsin and the KGB that remained intact through the end of Yeltsin's regime. For this remarkable service, as well as for his service to Gorbachev, Yeltsin asked Yakovlev what he could give him as a gesture of the nation's gratitude.

Yakovlev asked for one privilege: the right to publish documents from what is called in Russia the *lichny fond Stalina*—the personal archive of Stalin. Granted in the early 1990s, the right to publish these materials was not as simple as it might first have seemed. Having the right and having the materials themselves are two different things, and it was not until the beginning of the new century that these extraordinary documents would actually begin to be made available to researchers. Not until 2002 did Vladimir Pavlovich ask me to come see Yakovlev to discuss Yale's interest in publishing them; and it was not until the autumn of 2003 that Yakovlev felt certain that a coordinated publication strategy was possible.

As I took my seat in his study at the foundation in October 2003, ready to discuss the Stalin archive, Alexander Nikolaevich seemed preoccupied with other matters. "You cannot compromise with the revanchists" were the first words out of his mouth, and instead of the Stalin archive, Yakovlev wanted to talk about the mood in Russia, the inept leadership of the United States, and the generally dismal picture of the world situation. We spoke half in Russian, half in English; occasionally my translator needed to clarify a point.

Only after his assistant had brought in tea did Yakovlev seem to remember the reason for my visit. "Now let's return to our own lambs," he said, signaling that it was time to consider our common interest in preparing eight or ten volumes for publication from this remarkable holding. Publishing the Stalin archive would be his legacy, his protest against the criminality of the Soviet past and a warning to its present leaders.

Culled from a vast number of documents, the first volume of more than nine hundred pages will chronicle Stalin's seizure of power through his cooptation and manipulation of the security services from 1928 to 1953. It will explain why the system, founded by Lenin, inevitably and unavoidably implanted *strakh*—fear—as the ruling element in the psychology of the Soviet people.

Fear.

Lydia Chukovskaya evoked the experience of this fear in her short novel *Sofia Petrovna*, which she wrote in 1938–1939. *Sofia Petrovna* was not published in Russia until 1988.

> [Sofia Petrovna] was now afraid of everyone and everything. She was afraid of the janitor, who looked at her indifferently yet at the same time severely. She was afraid of the house manager, who had stopped nodding hello to her. (She was no longer the apartment representative; the wife of the accountant had been elected to replace her.) She was mortally afraid of the wife of the accountant. She was afraid of Valya. She was afraid to walk by the publishing house. Returning home after her fruitless attempts to find work, she was afraid to look at the table in her room: perhaps a summons from the police would be lying there? Perhaps they were already summoning her to the police station to take her passport away and send her into exile? She was afraid of every ring of the bell: perhaps they'd come to confiscate all her belongings.

Discharged from her job as typist in a state publishing house, Sofia Petrovna is "afraid of everyone and everything," just as Bukharin predicted when he wrote Stalin that "*everlasting* distrust" would result from the general purge and that this provided the government with a "*full guarantee* for itself." When the government arrests her son, Sofia believes at first that it has made a mistake; she believes that her government protects its people and wants truth and justice; she believes that her son will eventually be set free. Her slow discovery that the government does not want truth or justice, that her son will not be set free, and that his arrest may not have been justified, but also was not an accident eventually drives her mad.

In the last scene of the novel, Sofia takes out her son's last letter, in which he writes, "Investigator Ershov beat me and trampled me." She sits at the window, "thinking of nothing." Eventually, she burns the letter and stamps on it just as Akhmatova in *Requiem* "must smash [her] memories to bits, / Must turn [her] heart to stone all through."

Fear, distrust, and oppression do not produce resistance or even the desire for revenge. In Sofia Petrovna it produced madness. In Solzhenitsyn's Ivan Denisovich, it produced forgetfulness and indifference.

> For a little while Shukhov [Ivan Denisovich] forgot all his grievances, forgot that his sentence was long, that the day was long, that once again there would be no Sunday. . . .

> Shukhov stared at the ceiling and said nothing. He no longer knew whether he wanted to be free or not.

What does freedom mean when, as the director of the state archive said, he had "no money"? It is easy in the West to get carried away with slogans about democracy and advertising sophisms about the freedom to rise above the crowd, make the right choice, be all you can be, realize life to its fullest. In a world drenched with material goods and built on assumptions about the nature of "normal" life that seventy-five years ago would have been thought presumptuous at best, few in the American middle class must face the realization that the price of a decent bottle of wine may be nearly half one's monthly salary.

Yakovlev believed that *strakh* remains barely under the surface in the lives of most Russians today, perhaps in all but the youngest generation, whose only fears may be economic. Though hated by the revanchists, who would like to see a return to the old system, his publishing project is supported by Putin. Can fear be eliminated by knowledge? This was Yakovlev's goal. But how do you attain knowledge? Will documents be enough? I asked. Not at all, Yakovlev insisted. But without the information provided in the documents, knowledge of the past is impossible, and without this knowledge the Russian people will not be able to understand the effects of unconstrained state power. They will not understand why they need a country ruled by law—that economic prosperity and stability is not enough.

But Yakovlev had another goal in addition to smashing the prestige and authority of the Bolshevik legacy. He wished to provide the basis for a moral awakening of his country. In conversation, Yakovlev always returned to the fact that Russia was never fully desovietized. There was no Nuremberg trial, no general accounting, no public reconciliation between victims and victimizers, no restoration of property or adequate compensation to the many millions whose lives were permanently damaged or destroyed by Stalin's "utopia." Instead the country drifted, like Solzhenitsyn's Shukhov, into indifference and forgetfulness, hardly knowing whether it wanted freedom or not—hardly remembering freedom at all.

However, just beneath this apparent sleepiness remains the memory of great victories, the global projection of Soviet power, and a bruised self-image. A return to closedness from openness, to secrecy and conspiracy from legality, are, in Yakovlev's view, inevitable. Stability and prosperity will address the economic fears of the younger generation, but without legality the young will inevitably return to the dangers of their past. When Lenin ordered the looting of the churches and cathedrals, the patriarch protested that this was illegal. The revolution swept such juridical niceties away because proletarian justice was different from bourgeois justice. Yakovlev wished to reclaim an ideal of universal justice common to every class and ethnic group.

His greatest fear was that Putin governs only with the indulgence of forces greater than himself and that nobody really knows who is running the country or in what direction it is being guided by these unseen forces. He cited a comment about Putin made in 2003 by a political adviser to the presidential chief of staff, Gleb Pavlovsky, who said precisely this. Yakovlev pointed out that it was a statement Pavlovsky could not have made without someone else's permission. But permission from whom? Was it a provocation? A warning? Putin's dismissal of his prime minister at about the same time was seen by some observers as a victory for the security forces over reformers. Restoring the personnel and the prestige of the security forces has been a key priority. One fact unnoticed by the foreign press, Yakovlev told me, is significant: the FSB has taken over the border guards from the MVD—a small but highly important move in Yakovlev's opinion, something like the security camera trained on the diners at Vensky Dvor. Without knowledge of where these little moves will lead, they will define the direction of the country, and by then it will be impossible to alter.

We may think of Stalinism as something that happened long ago. No, Yakovlev insisted, the structures remain the same: secrecy, illegitimacy, conspiracy, concentration of power in the hands of the few, violence as a legitimate exercise of political power—as the only legitimating political and social factor—a class society based on the premise of doing away with classes, corruption that comes not from breaking laws but from the absence of laws.

But do you really think Putin wishes to become another Stalin? I asked.

No, Yakovlev said instantly. That's not the point. The point is that between now and then the belief in violence has changed to an understanding that violence must be disguised in various ways, but that in the end it is only violence or the threat of violence that can create stability and prosperity that will be little more than new Potemkin villages for a society that doesn't wish to see beyond appearances. His dream of a liberal democracy was precisely to lead Russia away from the model of a society ruled by violence.

Yakovlev emphasized that Russia couldn't go back to its communist past. That was over. But the structures of power Stalin established have never disappeared. They are rooted in social, political, and psychological traditions and habits. And because they are habitual they are all the more dangerous—because they are invisible and normal. Open up the Stalin archives and we can get at this root, expose it, and maybe it will die. That was his hope.

After my conversation with Yakovlev, I strolled down the Arbat near the hotel where I have been staying for the past few years at Vladimir Pavlovich's recommendation. It puts me closer to the center and gives me, he believed, better protection. My hotel has good security and clean rooms and is relatively inexpensive. The Arbat is Moscow's bohemian district. The Vakhtangov Theater is there. It was a favorite haunt of Bulat Okudzhava (1924–1997), the beloved poet, singer, and writer whose statue appears at the corner of Plotnikov and Arbat Streets and is a hangout for students, would-be artists, tourists, and tramps. Next to Okudzhava's statue is Moo-Moo, a popular restaurant chain in Moscow, with a giant black-and-white polyethylene cow standing out front.

The Arbat explodes with curiosities and Soviet kitsch. Old and new are jammed together helter-skelter like a modernist collage: Kiosks sell portraits of Lenin and huge quantities of army-surplus gas masks, Soviet army medals, knives, hats, and belts, alongside matryoshka dolls, scarves, and other folk-art keepsakes. A fire-eater entertains a circle of edgy onlookers; a child violinist plays out-of-tune Tchaikovsky near a row of sedated small animals put on sale by their lethargic owners—bunnies, kittens, chinchillas, puppies. A boa constrictor winds itself around the shoulders of a young impresario whose sole purpose is to be seen. An enormous black-and-white Great Dane, swaying its bony hips, is held close on a choke chain by his owner; lovers embrace opposite the golden statute honoring Gozzi's Turandot in front of the Vakhtangov Theater, while hauntingly beautiful women in designer clothes and high heels slip through the crowd like apparitions, past a scruffy guitar player sitting on a wooden box playing the "Moonlight Sonata" and a group of punk rockers with spiked hair, chains, black leather, tattoos, and amplifiers. A diminutive and elderly Chinese man sways back and forth on the arm of a slim young woman as he leads an entourage of sightseers. His head is dwarfed under the enormous black plush Red Army hat he has just purchased.

The next morning, a former KGB general shows up at my hotel to discuss his memoir, which Yale has been considering for publication. He is gray-haired, a little stooped, and frail after a recent heart operation, conducted in Spain and paid for by his wealthy son living abroad. He is remarkably handsome, genial, soft-spoken, and a master of the major European languages. At his apartment some years before I had seen copies of Dick Francis novels, Flaubert, and Graham Greene on his well-stocked shelves. He likes fine cognac and fish and chips, which he would eat regularly while stationed in London as a KGB resident in the 1970s.

He looks about the crowded lobby of the Arbat Hotel and then at the ceiling.

"Do you see the beautiful design? This was always a very fine hotel. I have many memories here. Many memories. You don't know, do you?"

"What?" I ask.

"Why, Jonathan, this is the old party hotel. This is where they would put up foreign dignitaries. It's one of the presidential hotels now. First-rate. I met with an old friend here. I was his handler, you see."

He smiles, frowns, his tone changes. "It is essential we meet here, unfortunately. Since Roza [his wife of many years] died, I haven't kept it up well and have little to offer you, but that isn't the reason. The fact is my apartment is bugged. I know it. They know I know it. It's an annoyance, nothing more, but why should I give them that satisfaction? They do it to let you know they're still around."

"Is it bugged here?"

His answer was a mirror of Naumov's some years before. "Certainly. But probably nobody is listening just now." He stifles a laugh.

"It's partly just a habit," he explains. "They want to know everything, but they don't know why. Information is leaking out—they don't know what or how, and they don't know how to stop it, or even if they should, but there are powerful forces in this country that want to be prepared in the event something might happen.

"But mainly it's still a kind of . . ."—he searches for the right word—"a kind of implied intimidation."

"But why?"

"Nobody knows."

As we step into the elevator, a repairman gets in with us. The general eyes him carefully, and when we exit on the sixth floor he says, "You have to be very careful these days. They're watching everywhere. Undoubtedly, they know all about our little meeting." But our meeting is about *nothing*. Still, they want to know. Stalin, too, wanted to know about nothing. He wanted to know about the toothbrushes his Politburo members used; he wanted to know if you preferred white or red telephones; he wanted to know your habits, your expressions, your taste in women, wine, and clothes. And all these nothings became something over time.

Two days before, a minor incident had occurred that put me a bit on guard and seemed connected, but in ways I could not fathom. Twenty minutes after I had checked into my room at the Arbat, the telephone rang.

I answered.

"I wish to welcome you to Moscow," said a familiar voice on the other end of the line.

"Thank you very much," I said to my friend, this same former KGB general I was now meeting in the lobby of the Arbat. "But how did you know I was in Moscow and staying here?"

"Why, Jonathan, you yourself told me."

"I told you? When?"

"When? When we spoke last week on the telephone."

Indeed, we had spoken and, if I remembered, I said I'd be coming to Moscow this week and would call him when I arrived. I didn't remember giving him the name of my hotel or the date and precise time of my arrival.

"Maybe so, maybe so," I conceded.

I have nothing to conceal. I have nothing to worry about, I said to myself, remembering my encounter with General Staroshin years before. But then I realized how *my* thoughts instantly and invisibly began to travel the same pathway as those of Sofia Petrovna after she learned her son had been arrested: "In our country innocent people aren't held. Particularly not Soviet patriots like Kolya. They'll clear the matter up and let him go." Indeed. It is the first turn the mind takes when it is unable to conceive the inconceivable fact that what it thinks *may not matter.*

I went to sleep that night dismissing my KGB general and his elevator mechanics as the residue of his own bad habits—and yet perhaps the creeping revanchism that Yakovlev feared was truly under way. The next day I visited the Stalin exhibit at the Museum of the Revolution, where a large assortment of historical materials on Stalin and the Stalin period were set out in roughly chronological order: posters praising Stalin side by side with denunciations. Nothing in the exhibit—no handout or narrative posted on the wall—indicated how to judge the man or his accomplishments. As Naumov had said regarding my textbook idea, no guiding point of view was evident. Stalin the hero of the revolution, the hero of industrialization, the hero of the Great Patriotic War stood next to horrific images from the gulag, forced collectivization, and the famine of the 1930s.

The purpose may have been to confront the viewer with the injunction, "Judge for yourself." But this act of seeming high-minded social responsibility evades responsibility. Was Stalin, in fact, a hero of the revolution? Was he a hero of the Great Patriotic War—or was he responsible for one of the greatest military blunders of all time in allowing Hitler to invade unopposed on June 22, 1941? Can any of Stalin's accomplishments be justified in light of the horrors he produced? These are not simple questions to answer, and they are certainly not, as the exhibit suggests, self-evident. Nor will the answers depend on balancing the moral, psychological, and physical horror he inflicted with the social good he may have accomplished.

In the lobby of the museum the carpets breathe out stupefying dust and decay with every step. The old lady attendants keep a fierce eye on the two or three tourists who have made their way to the otherwise empty exhibit hall. Henry Ford's accomplishments could be on display, not those of Josef Stalin. A recent survey found that more than half of the Russian population still thinks favorably of Stalin. Behind the exhibit's "objectivity" and "balance" is something larger, the memory of a time when the Soviet people stood atop a high mountain looking down, an exalted time of triumph and unimaginable power, albeit consecrated by an ocean of blood.

Outside, the image of the past instantly disintegrates. The spectral faces of the workers on the Belomor Canal are washed away in the tide of Nike T-shirts and Reebok sneakers, Volvos, Mercedes-Benzes, and Audis, *Vogue* magazine and Marlboro cigarettes, Gucci shoes and silk suits, Pizza Hut and McDonald's, cellphones and computers, the fancy new bicycles, the pornography and Dzak-Pot gambling casinos and gentlemen's clubs that light up the city after dark and put to shame the innocent pranks of the shy Little Bo Peep of years past.

Over the weekend I visit the dacha of Vladimir Pavlovich. He is paler and frailer than when I saw him last, almost a year ago. He wears a blue-and-white striped flannel shirt and carries his portable Panasonic telephone in his front pocket. Valentina Ivanovna is heavier, but also frailer, than when I last visited. It is hard for her to walk and bend down. She has prepared a long time for my visit with blini and *khachapuri*, cakes, smoked salmon, caviar, borsch, and numerous other treats from her generous kitchen.

This is the magical time of year when mushrooms appear everywhere and never in the same place twice. Behind their house grow mountain ash with bright red berries, wild currant and gooseberry bushes intermixed with small brush. After a week of solid rain, the cool air sparkles in the golden afternoon sun.

To walk off our lunch, Valentina Ivanovna and I stroll to the river. A friend who once lived nearby moved to Leningrad some time ago, she tells me. The NKVD, she divulges, may still own the property on which a children's sanatorium now stands not far from the river. Leningrad? The NKVD?

"They change their names so often it hardly matters what you call them," she chuckles.

The slender *topol* trees, Russian aspens, are beginning to lose their leaves, but it is still a few weeks before the "golden snow" begins that will flood her garden with the beauty that precedes its winter death. "What more do I need?" she asks.

At dinner, Vladimir Pavlovich tells a story about a man in a small village who had an ugly daughter he couldn't marry off. One day a matchmaker came to persuade the man that this homely girl without looks or dowry should marry the grand Prince Pototsky. The stupefied father at first refused to give his consent to such a nonsensical arrangement, but after considerable persuasion by the matchmaker, who cited all of his daughter's fine qualities and domestic skills, the father finally consents to the union. Delighted, the matchmaker jumps to his feet and claps his hands. "Now," he exclaims, "the deal is half done! If only Prince Pototsky will agree."

So much in Russia today is like this, Vladimir Pavlovich comments: if only Prince Pototsky will agree. Behind the mask of normal conversation, he observes, remains the residue of a witticism that made the rounds in the 1930s: A man looks into the mirror while shaving and thinks, "One of us is a traitor."

"Only the complete de-Bolshevization of the country will save Russia from sliding backward," Alexander Yakovlev tells me the next day in his office for our final round of meetings before I leave again. "The struggle today is not over how to fix the economy—we know how to do that. It is over who controls the economy." Before the murders of Politkovskaya and Litvinenko, Yakovlev assured me that a fierce power struggle was under way that would elicit all the most lethal tactics from the government to ensure its victory.

People in the West do not understand that the universal corruption in Russia is *not* an attack on the government or a sign of weakness, Yakovlev continued. Quite the contrary; it is the very means by which the central government further destroys the rule of law and thereby can gain indisputable power for itself. The rule of law is a much greater enemy than Khodorkovsky or Berezovsky. Putin's appearance in September 2003 in New York City, opening up the first Russian gasoline station in the United States, was not a random goodwill gesture. It signaled the extent to which his government has laid claim to the country's vast fortunes in oil, natural gas, diamonds, and gold. The "capitalist barons"—the oligarchs, like Berezovsky—are now being brought to account for their corruption, which the government once encouraged—an old Stalinist ploy. Ivan the Terrible is once again sweeping away the boyars.

The son of a peasant, Yakovlev remembers the time before collectivization when the people had potatoes, but didn't have socialism, he tells me. Afterward they had socialism but no potatoes. Putin may not be a bad man, Yakovlev emphasizes, but his promise of potatoes may come at too high a price. He distrusts the people, an age-old characteristic of Russian government, and relies exclusively on elites. In the end, Yakovlev fears that Putin may simply not be able to cope with the massive forces bearing down on him, because his support base is too small. An important sign of Putin's difficulties is the absence of transparency in his administration. He has wrapped himself in secrecy, closed down the only liberal television station, and eliminated elections for the upper chamber of the Russian parliament—all of which no one intent on democratic reform would have done. No wonder, then, that the bombings of the five apartment buildings in 1999 are suspected widely of being the work of the KGB, and the assassinations of Anna Politkovskaya in October 2006 and the ex-KGB officer Alexander Litvinenko in November 2006 of having Putin's tacit approval.

The secrecy and conspiratorial nature of the Soviet regime was in some ways its most lethal aspect, as Yakovlev rightly understood. It informed all aspects of government functioning both in its internal affairs and foreign policy decisions. A chilling document has recently come to light, dated October 20, 1951, and composed by S. D. Ignatiev, the head of the MGB. Ignatiev sent this memorandum to the Politburo of the Central Committee because of his concern for how relatives of victims of the purges of the 1930s should be informed of the condemned person's fate. Ignatiev wrote that the MGB had been receiving numerous complaints from the relatives of the condemned wondering about the disposition of their cases. Since many of the condemned, all of whom had been shot the day after their trials, had been arrested over ten years previously, the answer that they were exiled for ten years without the right of communication could no longer satisfy the relatives. Why did their relatives need this information? It was not the basic human need to know what had become of a loved one (what Molotov in the conversation with Eisenstein called "psychologism"), Ignatiev notes; this information was needed in order to dispose of property, take new spouses, or establish guardianships, which often necessitated written notification.

In his memo, Ignatiev outlined the procedure he recommended for the MGB, with the sanction of the Central Committee. Relatives should be told that the condemned person had died at the place to which he or she had been sent for incarceration, never that the condemned had been sentenced to *vyshaya mera nakazaniya* (VMN)—the supreme measure of punishment, or shooting, usually carried out within twenty-four hours of the verdict.

> In order to preserve the extreme secrecy [*konspiratsii*] in this work, the composition of the death certificate of the condemned for the relatives should be handled by the central apparatus of the MGB USSR [in Moscow], but the declaration of the notification—this should be handled by the corresponding workers of regional MGB organs.

This procedure would ensure that the relative could not ever be certain what happened. Wherever possible, notification should be given orally. Only under circumstances where a legal certificate was necessary should one be prepared. Ignatiev's recommendation was approved by the Central Committee, and until the end of the Gorbachev regime, no one knew what had become of their dead.

By 1951, the bureaucracy of the Soviet state had to begin dealing with its past, something it had never had to do before. For the first time, it became conscious that it *had* a past. In beginning to look backward, Soviet history had entered a new phase, despite the fact that its first impulse was to retain its extreme secrecy [*strogaya konspiratsiya*]. Ignatiev's choice of the word *konspiratsiya* is also telling. *Sovershenno sekretno* is the term used in Soviet documents to denote "top secret." *Konspiratsiya* suggests something more than the secrecy of certain information; it suggests a plot to keep it so. That is also part of the mentality Naumov had spoken of.

Yakovlev's hope was that the past could now be looked at fully and truthfully. As long as the conspiratorial nature of the state could not be fully exposed even to its own citizens, the state could never be truly liberated from its Bolshevik origins.

Yakovlev lamented that although the Russian population enjoys a very high level of education, a grasp of history is not among the people's greatest accomplishments. Knowledge of the history of the Stalinist past and the cold war is particularly lacking. Why? People are still afraid of telling the truth. Perhaps that is the greatest fear of all.

Yakovlev's ambition of building a self-critical, democratic culture in Russia depended, he told me, on reform, but this reform depended on Russia's no longer being isolated from the West. What he saw around him daily, however, was that so much of the recent engagement had brought little more than pornography, cheap material goods, and a race toward the "good life" of pleasure and material comfort for a small elite.

"Russia is waiting," Yakovlev said to me as we concluded our last interview. "We must wait. I have only one thing to ask of the West: Do not forget Russia. It would be a tragic mistake."

Alexander Nikolaevich Yakovlev died on October 18, 2005. He was two months shy of eighty-two years old. His funeral was attended by dignitaries from around the world and by leading Russian diplomats and politicians, as well as hundreds of ordinary people. A year later, at the anniversary of his death, Vladimir Pavlovich sadly observed, nobody came. He had already been forgotten. His passing was like a great stone dropped into the sea. At first, it sent out many resounding waves, but soon they all disappeared.

Yakovlev never saw the publication of the Stalin archives.

Chapter 20

Stalin

Simon Sebag-Montefiore recounts the following exchange:

> [Stalin's] adopted son Artyom Sergeev remembers Stalin shouting at his son Vasily for exploiting his father's name. "But I'm a Stalin too," said Vasily.
>
> "No, you're not," replied Stalin. "You're not Stalin and I'm not Stalin.
>
> "Stalin is Soviet power. Stalin is what he is in the newspapers and the portraits, not you, not even me!"

Stalin was a self-creation, as Sebag-Montefiore suggests, but he was also the creation, as Stalin himself acknowledged, of "the newspapers and the portraits"—of the imagination of the people. He was the image of power projected by them into him. He was the great power brought down to Earth.

Efforts to rehabilitate or condemn Stalin today miss the point. As Kyrill Anderson said to me, "Stalin can't be rehabilitated. He never disappeared." It is not enough to look at Stalin the man or argue his case as if in a court of law, proving his guilt. Many, like Stalin's great-grandson, Jakob Jugashvili, an artist living in Tblisi, Georgia, will insist that "Stalin didn't commit any crimes." Others will say that Stalin of course made many mistakes, was cruel, misinformed, and often barbarous, but that he was nonetheless a "great man" who saved his country and the world from the worse evil of Hitler. "Josef Vissarionovich Stalin . . . it is difficult to find in the history of Russia a man who did more for its greatness and flourishing during his life and who is so unjustifiably slandered after his death."

Stalin saved Russia from Hitler. But he also undeniably opened the door for Hitler through his military and political policies of the 1930s and early 1940s, his destruction of the officer corps in 1937, his distrust of his own intelligence services, his defensive strategies in the western Ukraine, above all in his decision to destroy the German socialists, who might well have stood up to Hitler long before the Nazis trampled and burned the Ukraine, encircled Moscow, and murdered millions of innocent people in the death camps and mobile killing units.

It is not enough to try to bring out his "humanness," as Rodina Publishers attempted with the book *Iosif Stalin v ob'yatiyakh semyi* (Josef Stalin in the embrace of his family: from the personal archive), through photographs of Stalin with his daughter in his arms; Stalin relaxing, hat askew, with Voroshilov and others after a boat ride in Sochi; letters to Nadezhda Alliluyeva, his second wife, or to his mother. It is not enough to argue, as does I. Pykhalov in his 2001 book *Vremya Stalina: Fakty protiv mifov* (the time of Stalin: facts against myths), that the crimes of which Stalin is accused are vastly overstated and the result of little more than the desire for personal gain by various careerists or opportunists who hope to destroy Bolshevism. Denial of Stalin's crimes in Russia has a counterpart in the denial of the Holocaust in the West, and the debate over Stalin's role in history has nothing to do with this or that fact—Pykhalov was right on that score.

Stalin is a certain kind of transpersonal power arising out of a particular configuration of the modern totalitarian state in which the individual has become an abstraction. It is a power that binds all individuals together, but leaves them empty of meaning, ciphers who can be "filled" with meaning only by the state, as Babel was by his confession. It does not oppose the "self" of individuals; it creates it and offers its own brand of transcendence, in which the empty, individual ego, like the skin of Bukharin's sausage, is filled with the plenitude of the state's multifarious relationships. This power does not come from any individual's valorous deeds, the consent of the people, or even a coup d'état. As Stalin noted in his November 7, 1937, toast, "A great deal is said about great leaders. *But a cause is never won unless the right conditions exist. And the main thing here is the middle cadres. . . . They don't try to climb above their station; you don't even notice them.*" Great men do not make history; history makes great men, as Marx taught.

Stalin admired Ivan the Terrible. But the power he wielded was qualitatively different. Ivan's power was invested in him by the church. He searched for allies, created new laws, destroyed his enemies, and was certifiably insane by the end of his life. High quantities of mercury were found in his body after his death. Stalin killed the innocent together with the guilty; but unlike Ivan the Terrible, he did not throw cats and dogs from the Kremlin windows; did not attempt to rape his daughter-in-law; and though he allowed the Nazis to kill his son Jakob, he acted out of principle and did not beat his son's brains out with his staff, as did Ivan the Terrible.

Stalin required enemies more than friends. The power of his regime depended on them because his regime was based on violence—in Lenin's formulation, "the violent overthrow of the bourgeoisie"—and the legitimization of this violence. "The proletariat needs state power," Lenin wrote, "a centralized organization of force, an organization of violence, both to crush the resistance of the exploiters and to lead the enormous mass of the population—the peasants, the petty bourgeoisie, and semiproletarians—in the work of organizing a socialist economy." Enemies legitimate the use of violence; violence legitimates the state.

The violence is not sanctioned by any individual, as with Ivan the Terrible. It is sanctioned by the collective, by a transpersonal abstraction. Who is petty bourgeois, who is a semiproletarian, a kulak, or a counterrevolutionary at any particular moment is never fixed. New ones will have to be invented once the old are destroyed, unlike the boyars, the powerful landowners Ivan the Terrible had to eliminate. The rule of law could extend no further than such abstractions would allow. Such abstractions enabled Lenin to write in his March 19, 1922, decree that "it is precisely now and only now, when in the starving regions people are eating human flesh, and hundreds if not thousands of corpses are littering the roads [most of whom belonged precisely to 'the enormous mass of the population' that Lenin thought needed the protection of the state], that we can (and therefore must) carry out the confiscation of church valuables with the most savage and merciless energy." Instead of vowing to aid "the starving regions," and the people, mostly peasants, who suffered there, Lenin seeks to *use* their suffering to build the state. Yakovlev understood this when he cautioned that the rampant corruption of present-day Russia does not weaken the government; it indirectly strengthens it by weakening the rule of law, thereby reducing restrictions on the government's range of permissible actions. The Stalinist state provides *total* freedom—not the freedom of a parliamentary democracy that comes encumbered with responsibilities and limitations.

> Here, look at you—blind men, kittens, you don't see the enemy; what will you do without me—the country will perish because you are not able to recognize the enemy.

Stalin uttered these prophetic words to members of the Politburo in December 1952 as he was preparing to unleash his final great, conspiratorial enterprise, the doctors' plot. Recognizing the enemy in this case, as in others, meant inventing one. The plot against the Jewish doctors was intended to root out Jews from the professions—medical, scientific, scholarly, artistic, literary, journalistic, military, and security—purge the security services of so-called "Zionist" agents in league with Israel and the United States, rid the Politburo of rivals, such as Molotov, and reassert Stalin's supreme grip on the Soviet state. However, of the six doctors originally charged in the plot against the life of Andrei Zhdanov, only one was Jewish, Sophia Karpai, the EKG technician who did not even attend Zhdanov in the last phase of his illness. Nevertheless, Jewish doctors were blamed for Zhdanov's death, Israel was blamed and through Israel the United States. Russian Jews feared mass deportations to concentration camps then being built, but Stalin died under suspicious circumstances before being able to put these alleged plans into effect.

Whether the plan for mass deportations was real or not, Jews were the principal target of the last days of his regime. Many believe that this plot was the result of Stalin's inveterate anti-Semitism, but a deeper analysis demonstrates it had nothing to do with his personal hatreds; it had everything to do with his need to reconsolidate what he perceived to be the unitary power of the Soviet state after World War II.

Every period of Stalin's rule after Lenin's death in 1924 crystallized around an enemy: Trotsky, kulaks, urban wreckers, the "counterrevolutionaries" and "spies" of the 1930s, Hitler, the United States and Britain after the war, and finally the Jews and the blind kittens of his own Politburo in the years before his death; Every stage of Stalin's political career was defined by enemies, and as his famous November 7, 1937, toast reminded those who heard it, anyone was a potential enemy:

> We will mercilessly destroy anyone who, by his deeds or his thoughts—yes, by his thoughts—threatens the unity of the socialist state. To the complete destruction of all enemies, themselves and their kin! *(Approving exclamations: To the great Stalin!)*

Bukharin, already in prison when Stalin made that toast, reiterated its essential theme when he wrote to Stalin in December of that same year, begging for his life: "This purge encompasses (1) the guilty; (2) persons under suspicion; and (3) persons potentially under suspicion." Everyone was "potentially" suspect; therefore, the purge had an everlasting place in Soviet society. Everyone would always be suspect—even diners innocently chatting at Vensky Dvor, or foreigners ringing home to their families seven thousand miles away, or former KGB officers attempting to make sense of their life experience, or journalists attempting to write the truth, or scholars who might want to grapple with the truth of the Soviet period.

But the key to understanding Stalin—not the man but the power—is that he connects the merciless punishment not with opposition to "socialism" or "communism" or his regime, but to "the unity of the socialist state"; that is, to the integrity of the nation as it had been established by the tsars from the Baltic to the Pacific, from Siberia to the Crimea.

How remote all this seems from Moscow in 2006, now reputed to be the most expensive city in the world, where lunch for one at a simple restaurant in the downtown area can cost upward of $50. Teenagers walk down Tverskaya Boulevard with stylish new cell phones pressed to their ears; they stop before the windows of luxury shops that could easily be found on Madison Avenue; they treat themselves to ice cream and coffee at a wide spectrum of new Italian, French, or German cafés and coffee bars. Fine sushi restaurants can be found beside pizza parlors and restaurants advertising "Old

Russia" and serving the finest prerevolutionary lamb. Uzbek, Turkish, Georgian, and Azerbaijani restaurants have proliferated, and Moo-Moo with its great polyethylene Holstein is now joined by other enterprising chains throughout Moscow: Shesh-Besh, Shashlyk-Mashlyk, Yolki-Palki.

All this is clear evidence that Vladimir Putin's plan to "consolidate the vertical power of the government" is paying off; the oligarchs are intimidated, in jail, or in exile, and much of their carefully constructed empire has fallen into government hands. The ruble is more or less stable, and vast wealth is beginning to pervade Russian society, or at least the top strata of Moscow society.

When I recently visited RGASPI (formerly RTsKhIDNI and formerly the Central Party Archive), Kyrill Anderson called me over to a window. He motioned across Bolshaya Dmitrovka Street, where two men in leather jackets stood before the recently opened Stefano Ricci clothing store with submachine guns, much like the *militsiya* guarding government buildings in 1992 and 1993. A moment before, Anderson told me, they had escorted all the customers outside.

"What's going on?"

"An oligarch has shown up," Anderson said. "It's typical. These are his guards. Look at the cars." And in fact there were several long, black Mercedes parked out front. "They can't just go in and buy clothes. They take over the entire store." Just below us, on the face of the archive, Marx, Engels, and Lenin (the three blind men, as Vladimir Naumov calls them) also look out upon the scene.

Little of Moscow's new opulence improves the lives of ordinary people. An archivist in RGASPI made 10,000 to

12,000 rubles per month (approximately $400). Ukrainian archivists are better paid, Anderson told me, and a janitor in the metro makes more. Property values are sky-high, perhaps higher than in New York City, yet scruffy packs of wild dogs can be seen sleeping in rough heaps along the sidewalks and in the parks. Outside the center, one feels the oppressive weight of years of destitution and neglect in the unkempt squares and shabby high-rises whose inner courtyards are lined with graffiti-covered doorways, where mangled children's play equipment rusts amid broken glass and twisted wire and broken-down Ladas, hoods raised, are still propped up on cinder blocks awaiting repair.

The contrasts between opulence and poverty are astounding, even by the standards of London or New York. A glass of beer may cost $7 but the salary of a university professor may be no more than $150 per month. Under these circumstances, it is no wonder that despite Putin's efforts to "normalize" daily life, Russian society is still experiencing deep uncertainties about the future. As one liberal-minded young historian said to me, "Stability must come before everything else."

Though showing some improvement, the countryside has many pockets where matters are worse still. Economic depression, social malaise, and severe depopulation, particularly of men, continue in many villages unabated. "The villages are dying," one young woman whose mother lives about three hundred miles outside Moscow lamented. In her mother's village, in the absence of men, the elderly women must harvest the potatoes themselves and band together to drag the heavy sacks into their cellars, or try to recruit men from surrounding villages. In some areas paper money is not even used to purchase goods—there isn't any. In July 2006, a suggestive, if dubious, article appeared in a Moscow newspaper purporting to be about a man who had petitioned the state to allow him to marry his cow. Why? There were no marriable women left in his village and he needed companionship.

However, the essential dislocation in Russian society is not simply between rich and poor, democrat and xenophobe, nationalist and communist, haves and have-nots. Economic stratification indicates more than how much money one has in one's pockets; wealth is not simply a matter of worldly goods, prosperity, and physical well-being. It signifies a much deeper division. Russian poverty is the past. Wealth is the future. Between past and future lies a perilous gulf, as radical and threatening as the dislocations of 1917.

When the empress wrote, on May 22, 1918, that "Lenin gave the order that the clocks have to put [*sic*] 2 hours ahead (economy of electricity) so at 10 they told us it was 12," she recorded, even if she didn't recognize, a threat to the most basic frame of reference. The next day and for several days thereafter she wished to cling to the old continuities, even in her reference to the Tsarevich, as "Baby," who was twelve at the time. "Supped at 8, but Baby only went to his room at 10 (8) as too light to sleep. Played bezique—to bed at 11 (9)."

When Kafka's Gregor Samsa wakes up to discover that he has been turned into a giant beetle, he tries to restore order in his life by vainly attempting to "get up, because my train leaves at five." But when he glances at his alarm clock he understands for the first time that something is terribly amiss:

"Father in Heaven!" he thought. It was half past six, and the hands were moving ahead peacefully; in fact, it was later than half past, it was almost a quarter to seven. Could the alarm have failed to ring? From the bed he could see that it was correctly set for four; surely, it had also rung.

The alarm had rung for the royal family long ago but, as with Gregor, they too did not hear it. By July 17, 1918, the transformation was complete.

What time is it in Russia today? Has the alarm already gone off without anyone's hearing it? Both the drive toward the future and the pull of the past can be observed on every street corner—for each "answering blow" and New Russian *Vogue* there is a shapeless babushka, an old grandmother, twig broom in hand and stockings rolled up to her knees. An advertisement for a major Moscow bank expresses this dilemma well: its slogan, "Come with us into the future," has beneath it a traditional Russian knight upon his massive charger, lance poised in attack. The future will lead back to the past, the advertisement suggests, where strength, courage, and honor await us.

At a performance of the Moscow Circus in 2006, I witnessed an act that in its very guilelessness provided a window into some of these contradictions. "My Old Circus, My Love," as the colorful brochure calls it, was founded in 1880 and has an honored place in Moscow cultural life. At the performance I attended, probably half the audience consisted of foreign tourists; many if not most were American and of these many were Jews.

When the chimpanzees came on stage, their antics immediately produced hilarity. One of them appeared wearing a white yarmulke along with awkwardly improvised *payos*, and danced the hora around the stage to traditional Jewish music. The foreigners in the crowd fell silent. My first thought was the scene in *Cabaret* with the Jewish gorilla. Was I supposed to find this funny—the little Jewish chimp dancing around the ring? But should I become upset while my Russian friend, with whom I had gone to the performance, found nothing objectionable? When I later pointed out to my friend that no other "religious group" had been mocked, he said, but the Jews aren't a religious group. In Russia, they're a national group and there were other national or social groups represented by the chimps: a peasant girl and a Gypsy, in particular. This was true, but it missed the central point.

The age-old problem is that Jews were the object of hatred in Russia not because they were a different nation but because they were Jewish. The recent speculation of the Orthodox Church and Pamyat about the "ritual murder" of the tsar's family did not have to do with the national aspirations of the Jews, but with their alleged religious practices. The allusions to *The Protocols of the Elders of Zion* during the interrogations of Jewish security officers in 1952 at the time of the doctors' plot, and the fact that *The Protocols* now circulate widely as an established text among political extremist groups in Russia that have allied themselves with the Orthodox Church, further suggest that the so-called national character of the Jews merely disguises a religious stigmatization going back a thousand years.

I pointed out to my friend that an Arab can be a Christian and an Armenian can subscribe to the Armenian Apostolic Church or the Armenian Evangelical Church, but a Jew is always Jewish. A Jew cannot be a Christian, though an Israeli can be—unless you subscribe to the Nazi race laws. In any case, the *payos* and the yarmulke were religious rather than national symbols and no ape appeared dressed as a Russian patriarch, Polish priest, or Muslim imam. No Soviet *vozhd* was ridiculed. It's doubtful that the skit was *intended* to be anti-Semitic, but that was just the problem. The anti-Semitism was invisible even to my Russian friend, who was Jewish. The circus act was so innocent, so charming, so outlandish, and so public that it was difficult to see the line between comic parody and racist message. It seemed to fall directly on this line, much like Stalin's signature on the original plans for the Moscow Hotel.

Most of the racist rhetoric in Russia today is directed at the so-called Caucasians—Georgians, Chechens, Ossetians, and the like—but there's plenty left over for Jews. To this day, the Holocaust remains a relatively unknown and untaught aspect of twentieth-century Russian history, and Holocaust denial remains alive in the very fertile cultures of Russian racist thinking and fascist propaganda; according to Alexander Yakovlev there are nearly two hundred openly anti-Semitic daily newspapers. The fascist parties openly call for restrictions on Jews in all walks of life proportional to the percentage of Jews in the general population. David Duke's *Jewish Supremacism: My Awakening on the Jewish Question*—an updated and thinly disguised version of *The*

Protocols of the Elders of Zion—was published in Russia in 2000 with an introduction by Boris Mironov, a former official in the Yeltsin administration, and was sold in the lobby of the State Duma, the lower house of the Russian parliament, in Moscow.

At a political rally in 1998 to commemorate the eighty-first anniversary of the revolution, General Albert Makashov, a self-proclaimed anti-Semite and a member of the Communist Party, shouted, "I will round up all the Yids and send them to the next world!" Elsewhere he characterized the Jew as a "bloodsucker feeding on the misfortunes of other peoples. They drink the blood of the indigenous peoples of the state." In 2000, there was an attempt to condemn the outbursts of Makashov, who was an elected member of the Duma. A total of 170 deputies voted for condemnation, 120 deputies voted against, and the censure was rejected. In 2001, a motion to condemn anti-Semitism was rejected again by the Duma, and in April 2001, Vladimir Zhirinovsky and other deputies protested effectively against observing a minute of silence to commemorate the victims of the Holocaust on Soviet soil—approximately one-half of all Jews murdered by the Nazis.

The Jew as ape dancing the hora is not simply the gentle invention of the Moscow Circus. A version of it can be found in Babel's *Red Cavalry*. Bivouacked in the house of a Jewish woman after a pogrom in the Ukraine in 1920, the narrator finds a dismal and dispiriting scene.

> In my room I find a ransacked closet, torn pieces of women's fur coats on the floor, human excrement, and

fragments of the holy Seder plate that the Jews use once a year for Passover.

"Clear this up!" I said to the woman. "What a filthy way to live!"

The two Jews rose from their places and hopping on their felt soles, cleared the mess from the floor. They skipped about noiselessly, monkey-fashion, like Japs in a circus act, their necks swelling and twisting.

Hopping about "monkey-fashion" like "Japs in a circus act," their necks "swelling and twisting" while the woman's father lies dead with his face cleft in two in the next room is the unfortunate archetype behind the light-hearted pranks of the Moscow Circus.

The ambiguous innocence of the Moscow Circus's world-famous monkey show had a more sinister, if also ambiguous, echo in a box of chocolates on display at the duty-free shop at Sheremetyevo Airport. "Souvenir from Russia" is printed in English at the top of the box, produced by Dilan, a Moscow chocolate manufacturer that also produces boxes of souvenir chocolates with wrappers depicting the glories of St. Petersburg, Russian Palekh lacquer art, Gzhel porcelain, and portraits of Russian tsars. The box I happened upon in the duty-free shop is labeled simply *plakaty*—posters. The back of the box reproduces a 1930s poster of Stalin showing him at the helm of the ship of state. The wheel is inscribed with the capital letters *CCCP*—USSR. Above the wheel, to the left of Stalin, in the direction of his gaze and set in the background of the red Bolshevik flag are the words: "The Captain of the Country of Soviets Leads Us from Victory to Victory!"

Stalin's powerful hands grip the wheel. Above his head to the right, the sky is blue, but he peers intently toward the bottom left-hand corner where dark storm clouds gather. Benign, confident, steady, Stalin steers the ship of state into this uncertain future.

The other side of the box displays the chocolates individually wrapped in miniature reproductions of other famous Soviet posters. Mixed in are some wrappers with reproductions of World War II American posters, such as the famous one of Rosie the Riveter with her fist clenched, flexing her bicep and accompanied by the caption: "We Can Do It!"

Together these images testify to the happy moment when Soviet and American interests were united against a common enemy—the enemy that must lurk among the storm clouds gathering on the other side. In the bottom left corner, however, another iconic figure appears: the bourgeois capitalist wearing a shiny black bowler, his pudgy, beringed hand grasping a pile of gold coins. The piggy black eyes set into the fat, neckless head, the thick brutish nose, and the sensuous lips raised above a cavernous mouth suggest the cynical identity of this bourgeois as none other than the traditional Jewish banker whose heartless greed is ironically emphasized by the heart-shaped, gold pendant dangling from a massive gold chain on his enormous belly.

Is the subliminal message of this juxtaposition that the common enemy of both Stalin, the Great Helmsman, and Rosie the Riveter, the heroic American worker joined with him against Nazism, was in reality not Hitler but international Jewry? The usurious Jew clutching his pile of gold is at the bottom of everything? Certainly, this is the conclusion General Albert Makashov would draw. One can shake it off with a laugh—as might have been intended—and say, look at how foolish the past was, how far we've come: this box of sweets is making light of the great bugaboos of the Russian past. The Great Leader on one side and the Great Enemy on the other. We're beyond all *that*, it seems to say. But are we? Unfortunately, this is precisely the message of the article in *Russkoe Voskresenie* I obtained back in 1992, which presented Hitler and Stalin as upright leaders lured into war by Jewish control over the world economy, and from time to time this message still breaks out of its rhetorical wrapper in street demonstrations and public political debates.

Stalin's greatness is indisputable. All those who followed were mere pipsqueaks, as Stalin himself put it: "blind men, kittens" who let their country perish because they could not see the enemy. This little box of chocolates provides a simple reminder of who that enemy was and, for many, still is. I witnessed a striking example of this when I visited the home of the retired KGB general I met at the Arbat Hotel, who wished Yale to publish the story of his extraordinary life.

At the time of the revolution, his father had been an officer in the White Guard and his grandfather had been a successful merchant in a small city not far from Moscow. Had this information ever made its way to his superiors, over the course of his nearly fifty years in the KGB, he would have been expelled, if not arrested and shot. He kept his origins well hidden—even from his wife—and achieved considerable eminence in the KGB as a man of great linguistic and social abilities. After World War II he was given the task of translating for Raoul Wallenberg at his last interrogation, and when Churchill's son, Randolph, came to Moscow to visit Stalin after the war, he translated for him as well. Once, he told me, he translated for Stalin himself at a meeting at which many hostile foreign journalists asked questions about Soviet postwar policy. He remembered how Stalin eventually sent these journalists home with their tails between their legs, having answered every question they asked with "irrefutable logic." He had been stationed in Germany for many years and had risen to become the head of the German department of the KGB.

"Germany was our Garden of Eden," his wife, the daughter of a famous KGB officer, lamented as she came out from the kitchen. Her English was excellent, but she had to shout because the television was kept on and at a very high volume, something I didn't understand until much later as a measure against the electronic bugs in the apartment. "It is such a pity. Such a pity. We were about to show the world what we could accomplish. Those cowards!"

"What do you think of Yeltsin?" I asked.

She took her hand and put it under her throat and jerked upward.

"He should be hung?"

"Ha!" she laughed. "Upside down!"

"Please, please, dear. That's enough," the general called out. "Enough. Do you hear?"

"And Gorbachev?" I persisted.

She made the same silent gesture with her hand.

"And Khrushchev?"

The same.

"Not one was any good?"

"Not one," she said with the bitterness of someone who has been cheated out of her inheritance. "Not one."

"Enough, dear. Enough!" the general shouted over the television.

His wife disappeared back into the kitchen to finish preparing dinner while the general and I discussed his book.

All at once, I asked, "What do you know of the Kutuzov file?"

The general looked at me sharply, but said nothing.

"Does it exist?"

"How do you know of this?" he demanded, and for the first time there was a harsh edge in his voice.

"I heard of it. Does it exist?"

"Yes."

"Where is it?"

"It is in a place where you will never find it." After regaining his composure, he continued. "Imagine," he said with real amazement, "Wallenberg wanted to become the president of Hungary after the war. It was impossible," he said, shaking his head. "Nobody wanted him."

I was incredulous.

"It's true. He had wild, inflated ideas."

"Is the man who interrogated him still living?"

"Yes," the general said.

"Has he told the story of this interrogation?"

"No."

"Why?"

"He doesn't wish to lose either his pension or his life. The truth of Wallenberg will never be told."

At that moment a tremendous crash came from the kitchen and I could hear the general's wife screaming. Soon an enormous parrot soared into the sitting room, flew toward the curtains, circled, and landed on my head.

"You evil bird!" the general's wife cried, dashing out of the kitchen with a long stick in her hand. "Come here, you evil bird!" She waved the stick over my head and I thought she intended to hit the bird; instead, she merely began to coax it back onto its perch.

"It's very beautiful," I said, after calm had been restored and the bird had hopped onto the general's knee.

"It is an evil bird." The general's wife pronounced "evil" as "eeveel," which made the epithet even more menacing.

"No, no. Now that's enough. Do you know what kind it is?" the general asked, turning to me.

"I believe it's an Amazon," I said, "but I've never seen one like this with this blue coloration—it is most unusually beautiful."

"Yes, it's a blue Amazon," he said. "Castro gave it to me as a present. But look closely at its chest. Do you see anything?"

"There appear to be three white flecks. Three stars?"

"Yes. Highly unusual. My rank at the time, you see. It was very thoughtful. Very valuable." The bird stepped dutifully onto its perch and returned to the kitchen with the general's wife.

The glory of their Garden of Eden; the glory of the blue Amazon with the three pale stars on its breast; the glory of holding the destiny of nations in your hands, translating for Stalin, translating for Wallenberg; the drama of hiding one's lineage in a life-and-death game with the most ruthless and wily security service in the world—and now to be sitting with the volume of the television turned up in a cramped apartment, unsure of how to pay for his next medical operation, with a dwindling pension, in a dwindling nation whose borders no longer included the city of Kiev, the cultural capital of ancient Rus, Odessa, or Kharkov and whose influence no longer could mold the destiny of Eastern Europe or even Ukraine, alone with the burning humiliation of having lost the one thing that had given all of their life its meaning: the great socialist state.

Chapter 21

Stalin's Hand

On February 20, 1941, just months before the Nazi invasion, Georgi Dimitrov recorded in his Diary the proceedings of an evening session of the Central Committee in which the applications of a number of prospective members were voted down, including that of the wife of Molotov, Polina Zhemchuzhina, whom Stalin eventually arrested in 1949.

> What happened to Zhemchuzhina was especially striking. (She made a good speech.) "The party rewarded me, gave me encouragement for good work. But I let things get out of hand; my deputy (as people's commissar of the fishing industry) turned out to be a spy, so did a woman friend. I failed to demonstrate element[ary] vigilance. I drew a lesson from all that. I declare that I will work to the end of my days honestly, like a Bolshevik."

Dimitrov notes that during the voting, one member abstained: Molotov. "Perhaps because he is her husband; even so, that was hardly correct," Dimitrov comments. Vladimir Naumov relates a similar story about Stalin's longtime personal secretary, a general in the Red Army and member of the Central Committee, Alexander Poskrebyshev, whose wife had been arrested. Poskrebyshev came to Stalin and threw himself at Stalin's knees, begging that his wife's life be spared. "Get up," Stalin said. "We'll find you a new wife."

Perhaps apocryphal, this story reveals the mentality out of which the Stalinist system took shape. The party is at the center of the nation and the nation must be at the center of your life. It *is* your life. Your life has meaning only within the larger, transpersonal collective. Without it, one is a non-person—a bedbug, vermin, a traitor. An enemy. By abstaining at the session of the Central Committee that voted against his wife, Molotov acknowledged the primary importance of his relationship to his wife—a bond potentially more important than the bond with the party. At that moment, he did something "that was hardly correct" and revealed, in Bukharin's words, that he was "a potential enemy."

There is not a far distance from Molotov's being a potential enemy of the state because of his relationship with his wife to entire classes of people becoming potential enemies. During the time of the doctors' plot, M. D. Ryumin, the chief interrogator and then deputy minister of the MGB, told one of the defendants:

> In Moscow there live more than a million and a half Jews. They have seized the medical posts, the legal profession, the union of composers and the union of writers. I'm not even speaking of the trade networks. Meanwhile of these Jews only a handful are useful to the state, all the rest—*are potential enemies of the state*. (February 1952 face-to-face confrontation between M. D. Ryumin and I. B. Maklyarsky. My italics.)

They are potential enemies because of their sentiments for the new state of Israel and through Israel for The United States.

This line of thinking eventually caused the MGB to coerce the following confession from Yakov Broverman, one of the Jewish MGB officers arrested in connection with the doctors' plot.

> I referred contemptuously to Russians, and in every way praised Jews, elevating their intelligence and abilities, declaring in this regard that, really, *by virtue of their history Jews were chosen to rule over the world*. Accordingly, [Broverman and another Jewish MGB officer] expressed the view that it was necessary for Jews, in the USSR and in other countries, to take the example of American Jews who had penetrated into all chinks of the economic and political life of the country, exercising influence over the foreign and domestic politics of the American government.

Broverman's testimony corresponded almost precisely with that given by another Jewish MGB officer, L. L. Shvartsman, a fact that confirms that the so-called confessions were being linked in anticipation of a show trial. Stalin died and the trial never took place. Thus did *The Protocols of the Elders of Zion*, the discredited nineteenth-century tsarist forgery, make its way back into the heart of the Soviet regime. It is a short step from Broverman's extorted testimony to David Duke's variations on this theme for sale in the lobby of the Russian State Duma.

When Vladimir Naumov asked me in the fall of 2001 whether Yale might be interested in Stalin's personal archive, I instantly said we would be. We discussed a list of possible topics, from Stalin's relations with Western intellectual leaders to the origins of the Cold War and his manipulation of the Great Terror. I began to see documents from this archive on the terror and knew these materials would provide the links missing up to now in our understanding of how this event unfolded and the extent of Stalin's personal involvement. I saw a letter from Upton Sinclair to Stalin in the late 1930s begging for the life of a young Soviet film producer who had worked with Sinclair in Mexico. To Sinclair's respectful plea, Stalin responded in neat handwriting on a slip of paper that reminded me of the narrow strips I found Naumov cutting out so long ago in his study. He wrote that while he was grateful for Mr. Sinclair's words on behalf of this producer, the case had already been disposed of by the security services and was out of his hands. But there is a distinction between what Stalin did, what he said, and what he thought. And what Stalin thought has always been an enigma. What he *really* thought. Was he merely a power-hungry opportunist? Was he a true believer, a fanatic? Was he a statesman, a gangster, or a Caucasian chieftain? Was he all of these things? How did he weld his beliefs into action? Was there a logic of any sort to the terror?

Who was Josef Stalin?

I asked Vladimir Naumov once why he thought Stalin succeeded when others, like Trotsky, had failed. Stalin's own explanation, recorded in Dimitrov's diary, was that he respected and relied upon the "middle cadres." Naumov's explanation was different. "He was crueler than anyone else," he told me, by which Naumov meant that he was freer. He felt no restraints. As a result his power was absolute.

Stalin did not build pleasure palaces for himself; he did not fancy racehorses or expensive cars. In the exhibit on Stalin at the Museum of the Revolution, magnificent testimonials of the world's adoration of Stalin were on display, including a ceremonial headdress presented to Stalin on behalf of the "Indian Tribes" of North America, who made him an honorary chief. Daggers from the Caucasus; pipes of all shapes, sizes, and designs—one with the claws of an eagle clutching a meerschaum bowl from the United States; an armadillo cigar holder from Brazil; a telephone in the shape of the globe with a hammer-and-sickle receiver; mother-of-pearl trays and jade bowls from Korea; opulent oriental lacquer screens; a magnificent fur coat from the U.S. Furriers Union, kimonos and samurai swords, chess sets carved from the horns of antelopes; and brass cigarette holders made from machine-gun bullets.

Stalin received these gifts from nearly every country in the world, but he never wore the coats, he never smoked the pipes, he never adorned his living quarters with the screens or bowls. He was not ascetic, but he had no need for them.

Though he valued "the middle cadres," he mercilessly destroyed them in the terror along with the party elite. No one was safe. Stalin was master of the house. He demanded selfless devotion. This meant that those around him could have no independent will, no conscience, no attachments or loyalties to anything but the state, and the state was Stalin.

Thoughtlessness and chatter—these are the entryways for enemies. . . . Party, Soviet, social organizations must conduct an uncompromising, relentless struggle with thoughtlessness and complacency, to educate Soviet people in the spirit of the most stringent maintenance of state secrets in the spirit of the highest revolutionary vigilance. Wherever a Soviet man works—in a state institution, in an economic organization, in a business, in a kolkhoz, in transportation, in a scientific institution—everywhere and in every way he must remember and unshakably fulfill the demands of the party and the Soviet state—to be vigilant.

Comrade Stalin, mercilessly thrashing the idiotic sickness of thoughtlessness, spoke at the February–March Plenum of the Central Committee of the Party in 1937:

"And when we are finished with this idiotic sickness, we will be able to say with complete confidence that we are afraid of no enemy, neither internal nor external; their attacks do not frighten us, because we will destroy them in the future as we destroy them now, as we destroyed them in the past."

This was not written in 1937 but appeared on January 15, 1953, as an editorial in *Izvestia* under the title: "To Raise Political Vigilance." There is no question that Stalin approved it. The hunt for enemies both real and potential continued to the very end. He died approximately six weeks later, on March 5. Just as his own enemy was a broken blood vessel in his brain, the country's enemy was within. Not

Jewish doctors, not Trotskyists, not German or American spies, not kulaks or White Guard soldiers, but thoughtlessness, an "idiotic sickness." It was weakness in the nature of man himself that was the greatest enemy.

In the end it is the freedom to be weak, not strong: the freedom to make a mistake, "to write badly," in Babel's words. The "idiotic sickness" of being confused and thoughtless, of finding oneself in a miserable hallway without beginning or end and realizing that life proceeds "slowly and incorrectly." Babel knew there can be no art and no human civilization without it. There would be no eating of the fruit of Eden, no wandering in the desert for forty years, no forgiveness for sinners, no redemption of King David or resurrection of Christ. Nor would there be the shining, quotidian ironies Babel loved, such as the one at the end of the story "Dolgushov's Death," in which to soothe Lyutov's wounded pride, his companion, Grishchuk, took a wrinkled apple from under the cart seat. "'Eat it,' he told me, 'Do please, eat it.'" This wrinkled apple of knowledge, taken not from a tree in Eden but from under a dirty cart seat that represents the crumpled hopes and ordinary dreams of imperfect people is a sign of the human world Stalin found most threatening.

In Stalin's personal archive, now housed in RGASPI, it is possible for the first time to trace the pathways of Stalin's thought. There is a bitter irony in the fact that this archive has found its way into RGASPI. This archive, of which Kyrill Anderson is now the director, was founded in 1921 as the Marx-Engels Institute by David Borisovich Ryazanov

(1870–1938), a "nonfactional" social democrat who joined the Bolshevik Party in 1917. Born in Odessa and fluent in German, Yiddish, French, and other European languages, Ryazanov was a committed social democrat and connoisseur of Marx and Engels. One unfortunate consequence of his passion for Marxist thinking was that he didn't think much of either Lenin or Stalin. He never mentioned them in his public speeches and was indifferent to their theoretical pronouncements. He organized the Institute largely to enshrine German social democracy, and the young Communist regime gave him a generous budget to collect the works of Marx and Engels. Working like a fanatic, he would often buy an entire collection simply for one or two documents. When he couldn't purchase the documents he wanted, he would copy them. Thus the Institute has one of the principal collections in the world, containing many unique documents: other copies in European collections were either lost or destroyed at the beginning of World War II. In particular, originals of many handwritten manuscripts by Marx were lost at sea when the ship carrying them from their Amsterdam archive to safety in the United States was sunk by a German submarine.

Anderson told me that in response to the growing repression, Ryazanov instituted a kind of human rights watch and saved the lives of approximately three thousand imprisoned employees. He protected people, including some he didn't particularly like, such as the widow of I. G. Shcheglovitov, the minister of justice in the tsar's government who instigated the famous anti-Semitic, blood-libel case in 1912 that became known as the Beiliss affair, in which Mendel Beiliss was accused of murdering a thirteen-year-old Ukrainian boy to use his blood for matzohs—the same charge the Orthodox Church investigated in regard to the execution of the Romanov family in 1918. Paradoxically, the widow of Shcheglovitov in 1928 had been fired from all her previous jobs because of her husband's connection to the tsarist regime.

Lenin tolerated Ryazanov, calling him a *bukvoyed* (literally, "a word eater"; figuratively, a hairsplitter or pedant), but Stalin hated him. Ryazanov's relations with the government were not helped by the fact that Boris Nikolaevsky (a Menshevik opponent to Lenin's regime), who was arrested in 1919–1920, was a close confidant and gave the present site to the archive. In addition to disdaining the theoretical contributions of Lenin and Stalin, Ryazanov had a reputation for being rude and high-handed. Once when a high-ranking Central Committee member came to see Marx's manuscripts, Ryazanov took out a letter by Marx, waved it in front of the party boss, and said, "There is your Marx, now go." He didn't allow women into the Institute in summer unless they wore stockings, and he would put on white cotton gloves to check for dust on the staircases and window ledges.

But what really incurred Stalin's wrath was Ryazanov's failure to mention him in his speeches before the Central Committee plenums. In 1929—the year of Stalin's newly invented fiftieth jubilee—he failed to send the *vozhd* special birthday greetings. Ryazanov was fired from his position in the archive and sent into exile in Saratov by the NKVD, though clearly with Stalin's approval. In 1937, he was arrested; a year later he was shot.

The Lenin Institute was not established until 1923, a year before Lenin's death. It was originally a separate body attached to the Central Committee and merged with the Marx-Engels Institute only in 1931. Lev Kamenev was its first director. When it was first opened, Lenin gave two weeks for all the monuments to the tsar in the neighborhood of the building to be demolished and replaced with monuments to Bolshevik leaders. The original of the statue of Lenin sitting in the entrance of the archive was commissioned and placed in a courtyard behind the building. By the 1930s, most of the names of Bolshevik leaders inscribed on these new monuments had been erased or changed.

In 1954, the famous equestrian statue of Yuri Dolgoruky was installed facing pedestrian traffic, but with its back to Lenin's monument, which to some signified a new relationship between the Soviet government and its Leninist-Stalinist origins. Not long afterward an elderly art historian pointed out that no *knyaz* (prince) of the tsar would ever have ridden a horse such as the one under Yuri Dolgoruky. It was a gelding. The appropriate appendages were commissioned and, as Anderson told me, the first sex change in Soviet history was performed publicly on Dolgoruky's horse behind the Lenin Institute.

Unlike the Marx-Engels Institute that enshrined Social Democracy, the Lenin Institute was founded to commemorate Lenin; another difference was that unlike Ryazanov's Institute, it didn't purchase the materials in its collection. Rather, it raided all the archives of Lenin's works throughout Russia and brought materials back to Moscow. The Lenin Institute was political and not opened to the public;

its purpose was to control the history of the party. The conjoining of the research institute with this political body in 1931 had important consequences.

As Anderson said to me, Stalin well understood Orwell's formulation that "he who controls the past controls the future" and made great use of the combined Marx-Engels-Lenin Institute. Throughout the turmoil of the 1930s and 1940s, the archive was used primarily to change the picture of the past. The archivists, who were intent on protecting an accurate historical record, lost the struggle with the politicians, who wanted to manipulate it. Eventually, all the archivists were chosen by the Central Committee. Much material was kept secret, even from most of the archivists—such as the six thousand secret Lenin documents that formed the basis for *The Unknown Lenin*, published by Yale University Press in 1997, and the caricatures that members of the Politburo drew for their own amusement.

Today, the institute founded by David Ryazanov preserves the personal materials of the man who had him shot in 1938. Its name has changed three times in the last fifteen years, but Lenin's large portrait still hangs on the wall above the long table in Naumov's office, and although the fresh flowers were replaced by plastic ones and then by none, Lenin's statue—a poor copy in Anderson's opinion—remains at the head of the entryway off the downstairs lobby.

Many cream-colored and dark brown folders are laid out on Naumov's long table. Some are quite thick; others contain only a single item. Inside one the user record notes that its contents had been inspected only once, in the 1970s, by a researcher. Most of them have never been looked at. Opposite where I stand is a bookcase containing many of the books we have published together over these fifteen years; I stand where I once sat when Vladimir Petrovich Kozlov first welcomed me to the archive; behind me is another bookcase; above the door at the end of Naumov's office Lenin's portrait still hangs on the wall; the faded drapes over the windows overlooking Bolshaya Dimitrovka have not been replaced; the chairs have not changed; the light fixtures are the same. All these things have grown familiar, but for the first time these silent folders, like shells washed up after a storm, are laid out before me containing the fossilized remains of one of the great terrors of the earth: Joseph Stalin's personal archive.

The folders selected and brought out for my inspection were from Fond (file) 588, Opus 3, the designation for the books and manuscripts found in Stalin's personal library after his death. On an earlier trip, I had inquired about the library only out of curiosity: I wanted to know what sort of literary taste Stalin had. Would there be the same assortment of books I had noticed, for instance, in the library of the KGB general whose house I had visited? Had Stalin read *Madame Bovary*? Or did he have a taste for American detective stories?

None of my academic advisers to the project expected there would be much here appropriate for the projected series of publishing materials from the Stalin archive. Nobody was prepared for what we found. We discovered that this was neither an institutional nor an official library; it was not merely eclectic either. It did not reflect "official" taste, with complete editions in uniform bindings of Marx,

Engels, Lenin, and so forth: that is, the kind of library one might find in a government office filled with books no one had read. Nor were there examples in it of idle reading on rainy afternoons, collections of poetry inscribed by lovers or adventure novels to take his mind off his daily affairs. Stalin's personal library was a working library, containing everything that related to Stalin and little or nothing that might have related to Djugashvili. At a certain point, it seems, Djugashvili ceased to exist.

To see the works of this library is somehow to be brought face-to-face with Stalin. To see the words his eyes saw. To touch the pages he touched and smelled. The marks he made on them trace the marks he made on the Russian nation. Not mediated through the Central Committee or proxies, these marks preserve the vehemence of his hand as it touched the paper through his pen, his impatience and exasperation with his enemies, his expressions of approval at finding the right turn of phrase or the correct formulation written by those he admired.

All the works in his library pertained to affairs of state, including a copy of Machiavelli's *The Prince* that was stolen, it seems, by a government official in the 1990s who had privileged access to these materials. I had not realized what an avid and comprehensive reader Stalin was. I had not realized what kind of reader he was. He did not read detective novels, comic books, or romances while leaving the serious philosophical or political writings to his aides. Quite the contrary. Though David Ryazanov thought little of Stalin's theoretical accomplishments, it is clear that Stalin set himself to master these concepts as he would master the nation he governed. It is clear that he saw the nation as a set of ideas as much as a set of economic or material facts.

As I looked at page after page of Stalin's corrections, annotations, and commentary, I realized that while he professed a worldview set radically against metaphysics and Kantian idealism, Stalin was an idealist in the sense that he believed completely in the primacy of ideas. This represents a radical, if almost invisible, reorientation and revision of Marx's philosophy and is the key to understanding Stalin's threat to "mercilessly destroy anyone who, by his deeds or his thoughts—yes, by his thoughts—threatens the unity of the socialist state."

Thoughts were as important as deeds to Stalin despite Marx's historical materialism, which taught that thought follows action, and that great men do not make history but that history makes great men. For Stalin, only correct thinking could produce the historically "necessary" result. He understood that only an act of *will* could effect the "violent overthrow" of the bourgeoisie, and only the party, Lenin's great invention, could lead the masses. Without this will the historically inevitable outcome of class struggle would not be inevitable. Stalin's underlinings, exclamations, and explanations to himself record the power of that will.

Not a single work I inspected was not read *by him*. Not a single work was not copiously annotated, underlined, argued with, appreciated, disdained, studied. In his brilliant biography, Robert C. Tucker observes that Stalin's basic emotion was anger. Perhaps this was so in his dealings with colleagues, underlings, and coconspirators. But alone in his study, away from the exigencies of power, control, and confrontation,

Stalin had a wider spectrum of emotional, psychological, and intellectual responses. We see him thinking, reacting, imagining *in private*. In his careful editing of the work of others, we see that the way ideas were framed mattered as much to him as the content of those ideas.

Unlike Georgi Dimitrov, who knew that Stalin read his diary, Stalin knew that none of his colleagues or adversaries would read his comments or try to make sense of his underlinings and emphases. And yet when I pointed this out to an archivist in Moscow, long familiar with the Stalin period, she shrewdly responded: "Stalin didn't think his colleagues would read this. But he thought history would. Even from before the revolution. He lived for history. He saw himself as a historical actor." He would live beyond himself as an idea.

This understanding gives all the more meaning to Stalin's marginal notes, his appreciation of a graceful or powerful turn of phrase, his seizing of a particularly salient formulation. His volumes of Lenin are marked up from cover to cover like those of a graduate student on fire. Here and there, in the margin, he writes *"stil"*—"style"; from time to time, he jots down his ideas as points one, two, three, outlining for himself the structure of the argument. Again and again, in his edition of Lenin's *The State and Revolution*, Stalin underlines Lenin's justification of the dictatorship and the premise that the Soviet state can arise only through the "violent overthrow" of the bourgeois state and can be maintained only through violence against the remnants of the bourgeois oppressors. He is teaching himself how to write, organize his thoughts, and express himself.

In addition to his books, there are also manuscripts that contain his revisions of works presented to him by the Central Committee and other agencies. Among these are *The Short Course in the History of the VKP(b)* and *The Biography of Josef Stalin*. Both are so thoroughly revised and amended they could be considered works *by* Stalin. Each demonstrates the same scrupulous attention to details of style and rhetorical effect as in the transcript of his meeting with Sergei Eisenstein about *Ivan the Terrible*. Now, however, Stalin is not correcting the representation of a sixteenth-century tsar—he is correcting the representation of himself and the account of the process whereby he became Stalin and, moreover, how he will be known.

The Central Committee wrote in *The Short Course*:

"The VKP(b) [Communist Party (bolshevik)] grew, became strong and was tempered in a stubborn, principled struggle with the enemies of Marxism-Leninism."

Stalin corrected this passage to read:

"The VKP(b) grew and became strong in a principled struggle with the petit bourgeois parties."

He eliminates the mechanical redundancy of "became strong and was tempered in" and "stubborn, principled struggle." He makes "the enemies of Marxism-Leninism" specific in "the petit bourgeois parties."

The directness and concreteness of his thinking stands out in contradistinction to the hackneyed rhetorical flourishes of the Central Committee. But what is the substantive value of this minor emendation? It is more condensed, eliminating clichés and redundancies, but it also erases something else. By correcting the notion that the VKP(b) was either tempered or stubborn, Stalin rids the description of an implicit moral evaluation and depicts the VKP(b) as a force of history to which moral judgments or qualifications do not apply.

It was *necessary* that the Bolsheviks would struggle against "the enemies of Marxism-Leninism," and such a struggle, cruel as it might be, was also necessary—there was nothing tempered or stubborn about it. "Ivan the Terrible was very cruel. You can show that he was cruel, but you have to show why it was essential to be cruel," Stalin said to Eisenstein in 1947. In 1939, at the conclusion of the great purges in *The Short Course*, he is writing about himself. He was cruel because it was necessary that he be cruel, not because he was stubborn. Eisenstein began the screenplay for *Ivan Grozny* after World War II at a time when Stalin and the Central Committee recognized the need "to restore to Russian history the authentic face of Ivan IV, which has been distorted by aristocratic and bourgeois historiography." In 1939, Stalin understood the need to restore—or invent—the authentic face of the party and thereby of himself.

Who were Josef Stalin's enemies? Certainly the bourgeoisie, the blood-sucking capitalists, the Americans, the Zionists; but perhaps his greatest enemy was God—not the "big god almighty," but the "godlet," as Mayakovsky might have put it, of weakness, indecisiveness, irresolution, instinctive feelings of mercy in the face of hard political realities, the thoughtlessness identified in the 1953 article in *Izvestia* in the days leading to the climax of the doctors' plot, and the "universal chicken-heartedness" that Venedikt Erofeev writes of in *Moscow to the End of the Line*.

> Oh, if only the whole world, if everyone were like I am now, placid and timorous and never sure about anything, not sure of himself nor of the seriousness of his position under the heavens—oh, how good it could be. No enthusiasts, no feats of valor, nothing obsessive! Just universal chicken-heartedness. I'd agree to live on the earth for an eternity if they'd show me first a corner where there's not always room for valor.

This was not the world Stalin envisioned. It is antithetical to the essence of the history of the Bolshevik Party Stalin outlined in *The Short Course*. Here, Stalin takes great care to identify his enemies. Stalin saw the enemy. He identified it. He crushed it because it was the enemy. His prose is concentrated, concrete, attentive to every detail so as to provide a unified conception. The prose *is* Stalin and it is in the linking of these details that he will be found—not the Stalin who sat in his Kremlin office, but the other Stalin who "is Soviet power," who "is what he is in the newspapers and the portraits."

Stalin's preoccupation, if not obsession, with enemies is particularly evident in a passage in *The Short Course* where he revises three paragraphs written by the Central Committee concerning the struggle with the Mensheviks in 1903. The original text submitted to Stalin read:

The Mensheviks struggled against the creation of a fighting proletariat party with sharply defined boundaries, a clear program, with a hard line of political behavior, and with strong discipline. The Mensheviks struggled against the creation of such a proletarian party which could have given the proletariat contol over the bourgeois-democratic revolution and in the future have led to a socialist revolution.

Stalin rewrote this paragraph as follows:

The Mensheviks banded together with the "economists" and worked closely with them in the party. The opportunism of the Mensheviks was meanwhile demonstrated in their approach to certain questions. The Mensheviks were against the fighting, revolutionary party of the Lenin type. They were for a vague, disorganized, rump party. With the help of Plekhanov they seized *Iskra* [a party journal] and the TsK [Central Committee], using these centers for their fractionist goals.

Stalin's specificity and concreteness again vividly contrast with the Central Committee's much blander and more theoretical prose. Stalin introduces the historical figure of Plekhanov, the legendary Russian revolutionary; he mentions the party journal *Iskra*; he employs the word "fractionist" to describe the Menshevik program; but the most important aspect of this rewrite is that Stalin ascribes a motive for the Menshevik behavior that is absent in the Central Committee draft. The motive was "opportunism," a recurrent motif throughout the *Short Course*. They were not guided by principle but by expediency. They didn't see what was necessary; they saw what was useful. The motive contains their "thoughts." It is as close to a moral judgment as Stalin will allow. The language of enemy warfare has almost entirely eclipsed a moral vocabulary. Individuals are neither good nor bad, neither virtuous nor sinful. They are either "principled" or "opportunists." They adhere to what is necessary, what history dictates or what the state compels; or they follow their own self-interested motives, as echoed in Pykhalov's condemnation of present-day critics of Stalin as "careerists." The battle is not between this person or that person and the state; it is between *any* person and the state.

For Stalin, individuals were always the problem, the cause—never the system. If the Five-Year Plan goals were not fulfilled, individuals were to blame, never the unrealistic goals, the insufficient resources, or the ineffective economic system in which they were forced to function. This is perhaps the deepest paradox of his regime: in a world in which individuals had ceased to matter, all blame was assigned to them.

Insight into the fundamental premises of Stalin's thinking process is provided in another chapter of *The Short Course*, which he wrote himself rather than edited. This is the chapter on "dialectical and historical materialism." The chapter is approximately forty pages in manuscript. Stalin read, reread, corrected, re-corrected, crossed out whole pages, added many others, and was engaged in the most minute details of how this definitive formulation of the Soviet dogma was being prepared for general consumption, or as he wrote at the outset, "not in philosophical terms but in simple, generally understood words," before crossing out the sentence.

Translations of *The Short Course* are available on the Internet, so it is not necessary to reproduce the body of the text here, but what is not on the Internet or in any other edition of the work—in Russian or any language—is Stalin's painstaking effort at reducing a complex system of thought to "generally understood words." Thus, the first sentence that had initially read:

> The philosophy of Marxism-Leninism is called dialectical materialism because it is a method of studying nature, life, society, thought; its method of understanding of all existence is dialectical; and its explanation of the phenomena of nature, life, society, thought, its theory is materialist.

Stalin altered this sentence to the following:

> The philosophy of Marxism-Leninism is called dialectical materialism because it is a method of studying the phenomena of nature; its method of understanding these phenomena is dialectical; its explanation of the phenomena of nature, its theory, system, worldview is materialist.

He improves the parallelism of the sentence and he eliminates "life, society, thought" twice. He introduces "system, worldview" at the end to emphasize that this is not simply a method of thinking, but a structure encompassing the whole—"life, society, thought" have no independent places within it. The word "dialectic," Stalin notes, comes from the Greek word for dialogue, "which meant to conduct a conversation, to conduct a polemic. By dialectic they understood in ancient times the art of achieving the truth through the path of disclosure by means of contradiction and the judgment of the opponents and the overcoming of their contradictions." Truth is the result of overcoming contradiction. However, the fundamental premise of dialectical materialism is that everything is connected and everything is constantly in motion. There is no escape from the battles of contradictions—whether between the bourgeoisie and the proletariat or between Trotsky and Stalin. No object can be seen or understood outside of its world of interconnections; no object, person, or idea—whether the idea of a tree or the idea of justice—can exist outside its historically determined relationships. This is a way of thinking that clears the path for a kind of relativism far deeper than individual subjectivism or Nietszche's "perspectivism." It poses a philosophical challenge that cannot be resolved by pointing to the political or social consequences it has engendered. Abstract, universal concepts such as justice or truth disappear in this sausage of existence. Only proletarian justice as opposed to bourgeois justice, only proletarian truth as opposed to bourgeois truth, remains.

Throughout this section of *The Short Course*, Stalin injects the phrase "contrary to metaphysics," as in the sentence, "contrary to metaphysics, the dialectical method sees the world not as consisting of [things in a state of] rest and immobility, frozen and unchanging, but as consisting of unending motion." Whose metaphysics is never specified, but Stalin's intent is clear: the average reader will be directed away from "theories" or "abstractions" such as truth or justice, and will be forced to plunge wholly into the endless "material" of life, the social and political relationships that define reality. Everything else is "metaphysics."

Elsewhere Stalin neatly taped together a three-part gatefold of comments and revisions, marked with different colored pencils as one might find in a Montessori School project. The careful aligning of the sheets of paper, the precise underlining and insertions of side comments, suggests the sheer pleasure he must have taken in the artful exposition of his thoughts. Here he was constructing, building, placing each word in careful relation to another. He took this work seriously. He took the material work of taping the slips of paper together as seriously as plotting an action against a political enemy. The design of the Moscow Hotel, the design of the theory of Soviet Marxism, the design of his own thoughts, and the design of the state were as integrally, essentially related to Stalin as were the three centimeters of swelling in the tsarevich's knee and the collapse of the Russian empire to Empress Alexandra.

In his copies of Lenin's *The Proletarian Revolution and the Renegade Kautsky* and *The State and Revolution*, we find Stalin very clearly searching for principles. On page 16 of *The Proletarian Revolution*, Stalin underlined the passage in which Lenin defines the dictatorship of the proletariat.

> The dictatorship does not necessarily mean the destruction of democracy for that class which constitutes the dictatorship over other classes, but it necessarily means the destruction ... of democracy for that class over which or against which the dictatorship is constituted.

On page 17, he underlines an equally forceful description of the dictatorship:

> The dicatatorship is power depending directly on force, not bound by any laws.

> The revolutionary dictatorship of the proletariat is power won and supported by the force of the proletariat over the bourgeoisie, power not bound by any laws.

On the top of page 18, he summarizes in half-words, like a graduate student:

1. The dict—ship, as the domination of the pr—at over bourg, relying on revolutionary force.
2. The dict—ship as a type of gov—ment .

At the bottom of page 18, he underlines another passage.

> The proletarian revolution is impossible without the forceful destruction of the bourgeois state machine and the change to a *new* [machine] which, in the words of Engels, has not already appeared in its own form of governance.

What is fascinating about this underlined passage is that Stalin drew a broad line through the text "in the words of Engels" as though he objected to Lenin's quoting Engels for this thought. Most evident in these few pages is the way that Stalin not only underlined and emphasized Lenin's text but also was seizing it, appropriating it, putting it into his own words; in short, doing with Lenin's words what he appeared to want Lenin to do to Engels'—cross out the source by making the words his own: exercise the *will* of supreme authorship.

Stalin had an orderly, methodical mind, but he didn't simply make lists and sort things into meaningless, bureaucratic categories. One senses the driving will of the man in every stroke he makes on the page. He lunges after and consumes Lenin's words and formulations, like a ravenous fish. He searched for relations—for instance, between the Mensheviks and the "economists" or between the Mensheviks and Plekhanov; but he also searched for motives. His mind worked syllogistically from premise to conclusion. Facts mattered less than the force of these deductive relationships from which intentions and thoughts could be revealed. His proofs of the existence of enemies were as internally coherent as any scholastic proof of the existence of God. If there is something machinelike in the relentless movement of Stalin's mind, there is also something subtle, complex, and powerful. It is not enough to characterize Stalin or those around him, such as Yezhov, as Robert Conquest did when he wrote that these men possessed "a sense of allegiance to the mystique of an organization" like "leading gangsters" for whom "the Party was indeed *cosa nostra*—'our thing.' "

The enigma and the tragedy of Stalin is precisely that he was *not* a mere materialist on the one hand, or a gangster on the other. He was no Genghis Khan or Pol Pot piling up pyramids of human skulls in a bloody orgy. He was not a raving anti-Semite; he was not a racist, sadomasochist, or closet homosexual; he was not impotent or afraid of women; he didn't hate his children; he was not a delusionary fanatic. He did not have syphilis or epilepsy. He is not the only man whose wife tragically committed suicide. He was always of a paranoid cast of mind, but probably no more so than Richard Nixon. In his writings and the marginal comments he made on the books he read one sees the energy of a man looking out upon a new world, seizing it, and making it his own. Stalin's lifelong ideological commitment was not simply a framework for action, or "allegiance to the mystique of an organization"; it expressed his discovery of a truth that, for him, tied his world together: truth, justice, freedom, democracy, peace—in the passage from Ehrenburg's March 11, 1953, article in *Pravda*: "the peaceful structure of a happy life." It was his framework for *knowledge*, the telescope by which he saw the future and the past, through which he saw himself. And through which he wanted others to see him.

He was Stalin. He was never who he was. As he told his son Vasily, "You're not Stalin and I'm not Stalin." Stalin is power, the unique power flowing from the Soviet state. How could Stalin be Stalin when, in accordance with his dialectical materialism no "thing" exists in itself but is the nexus of an infinite set of relations? Stalin's idealism consists in his utter certitude in the power of these ideas, paradoxically, in the power of the *idea* of historical materialism. It was the power of these ideas that crushed Sofia Petrovna into madness and brought Anna Akhmatova to understand that, "No, this is not me, this is someone else who's suffering." Like Stalin, Akhmatova too was no longer who she was. Such is the mesmerizing nature of this power that draws everything into itself—victim and victimizer—that sweeps the self clean of individuality and uniqueness. It is the center of the silence that Babel and so many others tried to express. It is an obliterating wind.

The transpersonal nature of Stalin's power is brilliantly depicted in a constructivist poster from the 1930s that shows a crowd of ordinary Soviet citizens—some serious, some smiling—with individual expressions and features. Each holds up his hand as a pledge to honor the slogan of the poster: "Let's fulfill the plan of the great work." Rising above these faces and all the individual hands is the greater outstretched arm of Soviet power. But if you look closely you see that the hand of each individual is but a miniature of this same gigantic hand, cutting diagonally across the poster against the red background.

One could read this poster as saying that Soviet power flows out of the unity of purpose of each individual, that the great hand of the people is nothing but a collective hand. But this is not quite correct, because the great hand as well as all the smaller ones of which it is composed is not connected to the bodies of the individual workers but rises up out of the workers from some detached and abstract entity. The forest of individual hands and faces contained within the one great Soviet arm is not connected to an actual body. Therefore, one must read the poster backward as saying that each individual flows out of the unity of Soviet power—the unity that Stalin spoke of in his November 7, 1937, toast. Each hand is but the one hand. Each hand is no one's hand.

This is Stalin's hand. The hand of the people out of which his power comes. The power of that hand is not easily forgotten or dispelled; it is still somehow there, its imprint visible in Mariana's hawklike vehemence over her Russian pills and the soft dreaminess of her portrait in my room; in her almost pagan superstitiousness and her demand to nail down the cost of everything; in the tender, pastel yellows, greens, blues, and pinks of the façades of Moscow's public buildings and the broken glass and twisted iron of the unattended courtyards and living spaces; in the bathroom mirror that swings violently at the slightest touch, the plumbing that never works, the broken elevators and the twig brooms with which the dismal Moscow streets are swept, and the broom of terror with which Stalin swept his country clean in the purges of the 1930s.

It is in this unity and power of the state that Stalin is to be found, and in his unswerving loyalty to *that. That* is strength, honor, glory, redemptive grace. In the service of it one can do anything. And therefore one must. But that unity and power cannot exist without the disfigured, broken reality in which most Soviet people lived the slow and incorrect unfolding of their lives. The terror could not have existed without the petty, damaged life of Sofia Petrovna. As if in dialectical relation to each other, Stalin died on March 5, 1953, and Akhmatova on March 5, 1966.

Just as the Romanov dynasty came to an abrupt and shameful end, so did Stalin's. Weakness again proved stronger than strength. The cover of *Russkoe Voskresenie*, which Jeff Burds gave me on my first trip, amply expressed this sense of shame. Underneath the swastika and the Orthodox cross on the masthead is the Jew-devil, with bristly tail, long hooked nose, and bugged-out eyes, dressed in the Stars and Stripes, holding the cur Yeltsin, grimacing on all fours, and the cur Gorbachev, with a resigned expression on his chubby, effeminate mug. Under the cartoon is the caption: "Shame on the intelligentsia who betray the people."

Before his death, Alexander Yakovlev told me that he had been called in to see Gorbachev when the civil disturbances in Lithuania took place in January 1991 in an attempt to remove the Soviet-backed government. Russian tanks were surrounded by unarmed but angry Lithuanian demonstrators. Gorbachev asked a simple question: "Should we shoot?"

Yakovlev answered that if a single Soviet soldier fired a single bullet on the unarmed crowds, Soviet power would be over. Gorbachev thanked him and ordered the army to stand down. What Yakovlev told me he didn't say to Gorbachev but thought as he left the office was that if they didn't shoot, Soviet power would also be over. The process had gone too far; the ethos had changed.

Today, Vladimir Putin and his successor must wrestle with the multiplicity of forces tearing at the heart of his country: nationalism, xenophobia, wounded pride, lawlessness, the ecological disaster in the Russian villages, lakes, rivers, and forests, the need to transform a centralized command economy into a free market, the very real threat of depopulation and the vulnerable borders in the Far East, the insurgencies from the Caucuses, the insensate greed of the oligarchs, and the disaster of the once great Soviet Army. It was enough to see the posters raised on May 9, 2007, the traditional Day of Victory celebrating the end of World War II, in downtown Moscow to realize that Putin is not beloved by many on the Russian far right.

Among posters demanding "Russia for the Russians," and others denouncing "Jewish fascism! Today there is nothing worse," and yet another, "Today: the Jewish question. This is a question of power or the dishonor of Russia. It is the question of life or the destruction of the Russian people!"—among these was one with the caption "The kike mut on the throne," showing a doglike Putin held in place on the throne of Russia with a steel collar around his neck. On one side stands the Jew-devil, and on the other a Russian dog sellout to the United States with a bushy tail and a sack of U.S. dollars at his belt. Between fifty thousand and seventy thousand members of the Russian Nationalist Socialist Party are active in Russia today, most of whom are in Moscow.

As the sale of David Duke's book on white supremacy in the lobby of the Russian State Duma demonstrated, the membrane dividing the center from the periphery—the moderate, liberal, thoughtful core of Russian society from those who march through the streets with provocative racist banners—is very thin, very porous, very vulnerable. The ethnic, religious, linguistic, and political tensions in present-day Russian society are as deep and unresolved as they were fifty years ago. The unrelenting turmoil in Chechnya, Georgia, Ukraine, and Kosovo makes this all too clear. Putin's aim to preserve the unity of the Russian state and to prevent this turmoil from causing further disintegration satisfies the deepest needs of his society. Not to consolidate power and root out enemies is to risk chaos.

A strong, centralized state unconstrained by law is the age-old, instinctive Russian response to the dilemma of its ungovernable size and inherent cultural tensions. What is most worrisome is not that Dimitry Medvedev, Russia's newly elected president, will govern for the next four years but that as Putin's handpicked successor and proxy, his election preserves only the appearance of legality. Many will argue that for Russia at this time stability is more important than laws, and there is some truth to this. But once the new Russia begins to go down a path of institutionalized lawlessness—and it is already fairly far along—it will not be possible to reform itself. Its past truly will overtake its future.

Two elderly women knocked on the apartment door of a friend of mine not long before the parliamentary elections of 2007. They introduced themselves as political activists.

"Do you intend to vote for United Russia [Putin's party]?" one of them asked.

"No," my friend answered, neither she nor her husband would vote for Putin.

"Can you tell us your name?" the other inquired.

"Why do you need me to tell you my name? You can find it out easily enough. You already know it. What is the matter with you?"

"Are you afraid to tell us your name?" was the reply.

Today, the country may not be returning to Stalin, but there are many indications that it is searching for him and for an acceptable version of the tradition of thinking Stalin celebrated in his November 7, 1937, toast: the unity of the great Russian state. At the heart of this centralized state is the hand of that 1930s poster—Russia's answer to Adam Smith's "invisible hand" of the free market. But this is the hand of unlimited power that rises over and above the individual, rather than the hand that emerges out of the millions of hands of free citizens pursing their individual ends, preoccupied with their own limited self-interest.

Since 1991 more journalists have been murdered in Russia than in any other country in the world during this same period. The very public murder and silencing of Alexander Litvinenko in 2007 sent a message to the entire world that watched him die on television as he succumbed to polonium poisoning: do not cross us. But who is us? No one knows for sure.

In January 2007, the air is cold, but not nearly as frigid as in January 1992. It is fifteen years since I first came to Moscow, almost to the day. I have familiar haunts now and old friends. I have made the acquaintance of an elderly historian who struggled all his life to reveal the truth of the Nuremberg trials to the Russian people. When he first submitted his dissertation in the 1970s, he was told by his adviser to burn the manuscript. He didn't, and the Gorbachev regime gave him a chance to publish it. I met my friend at a newly opened, stylish restaurant near the Arbat, across Plotnikov Street, not far from my hotel, a place appropriately named Déjà Vu.

Not many people are in the restaurant when we arrive. French cabaret music from the 1930s plays over the loud-speakers. Because my friend is elderly, I ask that the volume be lowered, and the volume is immediately turned down. The menu is somewhat expensive and French. Gone are the fried aborigines of years past. The service is attentive without being intrusive. We are left alone to talk, but not abandoned by our waitress who, in the early 1990s, would have simply retired to a back room at some point, never to be seen again.

I order roast duck and my friend orders fish. Our main courses are served on elegant white platters, garnished with baby carrots, beets, parsley, and mashed turnips. The merlot is excellent. We discuss our mutual project, now nearing completion after many years of interruptions and frustrations, a major new study of Stalin's prewar diplomacy. I ask how his other research is going.

He smiles broadly and raises his hands, palms up. Though retired, he is still a prominent member of a major institute and is cited on the honorary advisory boards for many of the volumes of documents published under the aegis of the Russian State Archival Service. He is known as a meticulous scholar, honest, truthful, balanced, precise. But recently he has run afoul of the institute and, according to what he's heard, of the Putin government as well. In a recent article, he wrote a sentence with which no Western scholar would disagree: that the Soviet Army had occupied Lithuania for a period of time prior to the outbreak of war between the Soviet Union and Nazi Germany in 1941. A torrent of abuse came down on his head as a consequence. He was officially reprimanded for what was considered slander against the Soviet Army. He was told in so many words that if he ever wrote anything of the sort again, he would be kicked out of the institute and lose his pension and the subsidy for his apartment—at the age of seventy-six—and his daughter's job might also be in jeopardy. Déjà vu indeed.

"It is a return to the 1970s," he said. "There is nothing to do about it."

In October 2007, I met at RGANI, the Russian State Archive of Contemporary History, formerly the Archive of the CPSU Central Committee, with Nataliya Georgievna Tomilina, the director, to whom I was introduced by Vladimir Naumov many years before. For almost fifteen years, and according to ritual, after our business is complete, Nataliya Georgievna offers tea and cookies. We talk about my family in New Haven whom she met years ago when she visited Yale; about conditions in her archive and at the Yale Press. She once held my now sixteen-year-old son on her lap and wants to know when he will come to Moscow. Someday, I assure her, he will. I know he will.

Is there time for a bit more tea? she asks.

"Da, pozhalusta," I say, leaving the old tea bag in the cup.

Nataliya Georgievna discards it and adds a new one. "Tea must be strong," she says; and I remember the strict instructions Isaac Babel once gave friends on how to prepare a proper cup: let it brew five minutes and always use fresh tea.

"Without tea where is our strength?" is an old Russian proverb—simple and beautiful as the sky. As I begin to collect my things, preparing to leave, I look across the room and see behind various screens and pieces of furniture the large, multicolored map of the pre-1991 world that has hung in this office opposite our meeting table ever since I first came to the archive. Many years ago, after we had concluded the agreement to publish the collection of documents on the Kirov assassination, Nataliya Georgievna's staff and I had our photographs taken in front of this map. Several of those in the picture are now retired, Nikolai is dead, and the volume on Kirov has still not seen the light of day.

Today, we discuss three new projects, including one on the year 1956—a critical moment in the cold war, with Khrushchev's secret speech denouncing the cult of personality, followed by the Polish and Hungarian revolts, and the Suez Crisis. How did 1956 happen? Was Khrushchev's speech one man's inspiration or the outcome of a tide of change? Had this change begun invisibly during Stalin's reign? How did it register in the minds of people across the Soviet world? Did 1991 begin in 1956?

If so, what is the West's claim to "winning" the Cold War?

Between 1956 and 1991 are thirty-five years; between 1917 and Stalin's death in 1953 are thirty-six years. The entire duration of the Soviet period therefore falls into two roughly equal periods, with a brief interregnum from 1953 to 1956: Lenin and Stalin; then Khrushchev, Brezhnev, and the rest. The first half ended in the death of Stalin, and the second in the death of the Soviet empire. The first began with a revolution against the tsar, and the second with a revolt against the cult of personality. Each phase lasted roughly a generation.

Khrushchev's speech, on February 25, 1956, at the Twentieth Party Congress, rocked the universe of the party and clearly helped precipitate turmoil throughout the Soviet bloc at that time. The Polish uprising began in June 1956 and the Hungarian Revolution followed in October, while the Suez crisis boiled over into an international confrontation. In August 1956, the Central Committee learned that Pasternak had sent his novel *Dr. Zhivago* to the Feltrinelli publishing house in Italy after he could not get it published in Russia. Soviet attempts to block foreign publication proved futile, and the entire affair turned into a huge international embarrassment for the Soviet Union. In the course of the fiasco over the foreign publication of *Dr. Zhivago*, the culture department of the Central Committee reviewed the manuscript and wrote a lengthy report. Among its various findings, the report commented specifically on the effect of Khrushchev's speech on writers.

> The most important questions of international and domestic life hardly find any reflection in the Party literary circles in Moscow. The most striking material to be found is that in which the perversions of the cult of personality are unmasked, thereby signifying the necessity of a deep internal perestroika. This process of internal perestroika will not be swift or painless.

The use of the word "perestroika" in this memo, dated December 1, 1956, is astonishing. It anticipated Gorbachev's program by almost thirty years and proves that the origin of reform had nothing to do with Reagan's Star Wars, blue jeans, military budgets, or the advent of rock 'n' roll among Russian youth. It had everything to do with another displacement in the consciousness of the people brought about by the shock of Khrushchev's criticism of Stalin. Perhaps in this instance, contrary to Marx's theory, consciousness preceded action.

Khrushchev's speech on February 25, 1956, which disoriented loyal communists around the world, had the force of Lenin's decision to move the clocks up two hours in 1918: "At 10 they told us it was 12." This thunderbolt, however, did not simply come out of the blue, out of Khrushchev's own initiative. It, too, had its origin in a process as painful as the writing inscribed on the bodies of the victims of Kafka's "machine like no other" in *In The Penal Colony.* When the Explorer says that he can't make out the meaning of the machine's writing, the Officer laughs:

> "It isn't model calligraphy for schoolboys. One has to study it a long time. . . . Naturally, it can't be any simple script; you see, it is not supposed to kill at once, but only after a period of twelve hours on the average . . . And so there must be many, many ornaments surrounding the actual letters."

One such ornament came on February 1, 1956, just three weeks before Khrushchev's speech. At a session of the Presidium of the Central Committee the question was raised as to whether it would be possible to discuss the cult of personality at the forthcoming party congress. A transcript of this meeting relates the discussion of top leaders concerning the rehabilitation of party members executed in the purges of the 1930s. They speak about a man named Rodos, a vicious interrogator during the terror, shot in 1956. Khrushchev says: "The guilty are higher. Semicriminal elements were drawn into carrying out this business. Stalin is guilty."

A B. Aristov (1903–1975) asks Khrushchev, "Do we possess enough courage [*muzhestvo*; manliness] to tell the truth?" Khrushchev replies, "Yezhov, certainly, was not guilty; he was an honest man."

But if Yezhov was not guilty, who was? Only Stalin? How convenient to pin everything on Stalin, as if the great outstretched hand in that poster of the 1930s did not contain everyone's. Who in reading the account of this conversation could find his way out of the labyrinth or read the truth encrypted in its script? Khrushchev's Twentieth Party Congress speech was a "secret" speech and contained many unspoken secrets of its own.

Aristov's question hangs in the air today.

I say to Nataliya Georgievna that I'm anxious to move forward with the documents pertaining to 1956. There is so much work to be done—gaining contractual approval from Rosarkhiv, raising money, finding translators, hiring editors, selecting and annotating documents, checking and rechecking every source and word.

Nataliya Georgievna finishes her tea and holds up her hand as if to make a toast.

"So now," she urges with a smile, "as Comrade Stalin said: 'Let's get to work.'"

Notes

Pg. 1: **I threw myself . . ."** A. A. Akhmatova, *"Requiem,"* in *Anna Akhmatova: Stikhotvoreniya, poemi, proza* (Yekaterinburg: U-Faktoriya, 2005), section 5, lines 3–7. My translation.

Pg. 1: **"The immortal name . . ."** *Rech' tovarisha V. M. Molotova*, *Pravda*, March 10, 1953, 2. My translation.

Pg. 2: **"These words . . ."** *Pravda*, March 11, 1953, 4. My translation.

Pg. 3: **"My great guilt . . ."** Yezhov's statement before the USSR Supreme Court, February 3, 1940, in J. Arch Getty and Oleg V. Naumov, *The Road to Terror: Stalin and the Self-Destruction of the Bolsheviks, 1932–1939*, translations by Benjamin Sher (New Haven: Yale University Press, 1999), 560–562.

Pg. 3: **He has been called** See Oleg V. Khlevniuk, *The History of the Gulag: From Collectivization to the Great Terror*. Foreword by Robert Conquest; translations by Vadim A. Staklo. (New Haven: Yale University Press, 2004). Khlevniuk estimates approximately 20 million victims went through the Gulag system alone.

Pg. 6: **"Everything should take . . ."** Venedikt Erofeev, *Moscow to the End of the Line*, translation by H. William Tjalsma (Evanston, IL: Northwestern University Press, 1992), 14.

Pg. 8: **According to Stalin's biographer** Dmitri
Volkogonov, *Stalin: Triumph and Tragedy*,
translation by Harold Shukman (Rocklin, CA:
Prima Publishing, 1992), 5–6.

Pg. 9: **"Things aren't going badly . . ."** Katerina
Clark, Evgeny Dobrenko, Andrei Artizov, Oleg
Naumov, *Soviet Culture and Power: A History
in Documents, 1917–1953*, translation by Marian
Schwartz (New Haven: Yale University Press,
2007), 83.

Pg. 10: **"There was such . . ."** From Pasternak's conversation with Zoya Maslennikova (sculptor who
worked in 1930s on Pasternak's sculpture portrait).
Zoya Maslenikova, "Portret Borisa Pasternaka,"
Sovetskaya Rossiya (Moscow), 1990. I am grateful
to Evgeny Dobrenko for bringing this passage to
my attention and for his translation.

Pg. 11: **"I think that here . . ."** Richard Pipes, *The Unknown
Lenin: From the Secret Archive*, translation by
Catherine A. Fitzpatrick (New Haven:
Yale University Press, 1996), 152–153.

Pg. 12: **"Among the prisoners . . ."** Khlevniuk, 173–175.

Pg. 14: **" 'Beat them!' "** Jonathan Brent and Vladimir P.
Naumov, *Stalin's Last Crime: The Plot Against the
Jewish Doctors, 1948–1953* (New York: HarperCollins,
2003), 218–219.

Pg. 14: **They did as Stalin** Brent and Naumov, 228.

Pg. 41: **"the great worldwide hope . . ."** Andrei Platonov,
The Potudan River, translation by Clarence Brown,
in Clarence Brown, editor, *The Portable Twentieth
Century Russian Reader* (London and New York:
Viking Penguin Inc., 1985), 119.

Pg. 52: " 'So these are . . .' " Franz Kafka, *The Trial*, translation by Breon Mitchell (New York: Schocken Books, 1998), 57.

Pg. 53: "To the members . . ." Alexander Vatlin and Larisa Malashenko, editors, *Piggy Foxy and the Sword of Revolution: Bolshevik Self-Portraits* (New Haven: Yale University Press, 2006), 164.

Pg. 53: **In the drawing** Vatlin and Malashenko, 198.

Pg. 54: **Stalin declared that** Brent and Naumov, 238–239; 334.

Pg. 62: **Inside the six-page** *Russkoe Voskresenie*, No. 7/15, 1.

Pg. 68: **"reach for the shoemaker's"** Vladimir Mayakovsky, "*The Cloud in Trousers,*" in *The Bedbug and Selected Poetry*, edited by Patricia Blake, translations by Max Hayward and George Reavey (Bloomington: Indiana University Press, 1975), 107–109.

Pg. 73: **"To my sweet . . ."** Alexandra Feodorovna, *The Last Diary*, edited by Vladimir A. Kozlov and Vladimir M. Khrustalëv, notes edited by Alexandra Raskina, translations by Laura E. Wolfson, introduction by Robert K. Massie (New Haven: Yale University Press, 1997), 1.

Pg. 73: **On Monday, January 1** Ibid., 3.

Pg. 74: **22 May** Ibid., 156.

Pg. 76: **Rumor here going** Mark D. Steinberg and Vladimir M. Khrustalëv, *The Fall of the Romanovs: Political Dreams and Personal Struggles in a Time of Revolution* (New Haven: Yale University Press, 1995), 331.

Pg. 76: **The image of that execution** Ibid., 352.

Pg. 92: **Two such were telegrams** Harvey Klehr, John Earl Haynes, and Fridrikh Igorevich Firsov, *The Secret World of American Communism* (New Haven: Yale University Press, 1995), 29–30.

Pg. 108: **"A great deal is said . . ."** Georgi Dimitrov, *The Diary of Georgi Dimitrov, 1933–1949*, edited by Ivo Banac (New Haven: Yale University Press, 2003), 65–66.

Pg. 141: **"Dear Comrade Stalin . . ."** Ibid., 387.

Pg. 142: **"To Walter [Tito] . . ."** Ibid., 423.

Pg 143: **"We consider it our duty . . ."** Ibid., 434–435.

Pg. 144: **Much new documentation** Brent and Naumov, 11 and following.

Pg. 149: **"The advantage of . . ."** Dimitrov, 450–451.

Pg. 150: **"We stayed till . . ."** Ibid., 452.

Pg. 150: **By 1950 Stalin** Brent and Naumov, 235–248.

Pg. 157: **"The only possibility . . ."** *Puti Russkogo Vozrozhdeniya* (Moscow: *Russkii vestnik*, 1993), 5. My translation.

Pg. 162: **It engulfed the country** Getty and Naumov, 588.

Pg. 163: **"about a *full* . . ."** Ibid., 557.

Pg. 165: **"Furthermore, if we . . ."** Nikolai Bukharin, *Historical Materialism: A System of Sociology*, introduction by Alfred G. Meyer (Ann Arbor: University of Michigan Press, 1969), 98.

Pg. 172: **The dead men** Isaac Babel, *1920 Diary*, edited by Carol J. Avins, translation by H. T. Willetts (New Haven: Yale University Press, 1995), 3–4.

Pg. 172: **"I am exasperated . . ."** Ibid., 40.

Pg. 172: **"A terrible truth . . ."** Ibid., 41.

Pg. 172: "Now everybody's trembling . . ." Ibid., 32.

Pg. 173: "Everything destroyed . . ." Ibid., 33.

Pg. 174: "What I feel . . ." Ibid., 49.

Pg. 177: "Frank Mosher . . ." Ibid., 18.

Pg. 178: "probably at the instigation..." Vitaly Shentalinsky, *Arrested Voices: Resurrecting the Disappeared Writers of the Soviet Regime*, introduction by Robert Conquest (New York: The Free Press, 1996), 60.

Pg. 178: "a monstrous anomaly..." Shentalinsky, x.

Pg. 179: "I'll never be . . ." Ibid., 15.

Pg. 181: The *Red Cavalry* story Isaac Babel, *The Collected Stories*, translation by Walter Morison, introduction by Lionel Trilling (New York: Meridian, 1960), 200.

Pg. 182: "The question . . ." Brent and Naumov, 136.

Pg. 183: "revenge both on his wife . . ." Shentalinsky, 59.

Pg. 189: "Why can't I . . ." Babel, *Diary*, 56.

Pg. 191: "With Gorky I . . ." Isaac Babel, *Sochineniya tom vtoroi* (Moscow: Khudozhestvennaya literature, 1990), 382. My translation.

Pg. 193: It is now known Oleg Khlevniuk in conversation with author, January 2008, Moscow.

Pg. 195: The mountain had been Varlam Shalamov, *Kolyma Tales*, translation by John Glad (New York: W. W. Norton & Co., 1982), 178.

Pg. 204: According to KGB Pavel Sudoplatov, *Special Tasks: The Memoir of an Unwanted Witness—A Soviet Spymaster*, with Jerrold L. and Leona P. Shecter, Foreword by Robert Conquest (New York: Little, Brown & Co., 1994), 270–273.

Pg. 205: "It's nothing . . ." Erofeev, 15.

Pg. 210: "You can decide . . ." Anna Politkovskaya, *Putin's Russia*, translation by Arch Tait (London: The Harvill Press, 2004), 2–3.

Pg. 231: He instructed Ignatiev Brent and Naumov, 130.

Pg. 243–47: transcript of conversation with Eisenstein Clark, Dobrenko, Artizov and Naumov, 440–445.

Pg. 250: "[Sofia Petrovna] was . . ." Lydia Chukovskaya, *Sophia Petrovna*, translation by Aline Worth, revised by Eliza Kellogg Klose (Evanston, IL; Northwestern University Press, 1988), 92.

Pg. 251: "must smash [her] memories . . ." from *Requiem*, in *The Word That Causes Death's Defeat: Poems of Memory* (New Haven: Yale University Press, 2004), translated by Nancy K. Anderson, section VII, lines 5–8.

Pg. 251 "For a little while . . ." Solzhenitsyn, 152, 178.

Pg. 264: "In order to preserve . . ." V. N. Khaustov, V. P. Naumov, N. S. Plotnikova, *Lubyanka: Stalin i MGB SSSR, 1946–1953* (Moscow: Mezhdunarodnii fond "demokratiya," 2007), 366 my translation.

Pg. 267: "[Stalin's] adopted son . . ." Simon Sebag-Montefiore, *Stalin: The Court of the Red Tsar* (New York: Vintage Books, 2003), 6.

Pg. 268: "Stalin didn't commit . . ." private e-mail to author, June 2007.

Pg. 268: "Josef Vissarionovich Stalin . . ." I. Pykhalov, *Vremya Stalina: fakty protiv Mifov* (Leningrad: Neotek Elektro, 2001), 3.

Pg. 271: "Here, look at you . . ." Brent and Naumov, 171.

Pg. 272: "We will mercilessly . . ." Dimitrov, 65.

Pg. 273: "This purge encompasses . . ." Getty and Naumov, 557.

Pg. 276: "get up, because . . ." Franz Kafka, "The Metamorphosis," in *The Metamorphosis and Other Stories*, edited and translated by Stanley Appelbaum (New York: Dover Publication, Inc., 1996), 12.

Pg. 280: "In my room . . ." Isaac Babel, *Collected Stories*, 42.

Pg. 288: "What happened to Zhemchuzhina . . ." Dimitrov diary, 148–149.

Pg. 289: "In Moscow there . . ." Brent and Naumov, 256.

Pg. 290: "I referred contemptuously . . ." Ibid., 253.

Pg. 293: "And when we are finished . . ." My translation.

Pg. 294: " 'Eat it . . .' " Isaac Babel, *The Collected Stories*, translation by Walter Morison, introduction by Lionel Trilling (New York, Meridian, 1960), 90.

Pg. 294: **Ryazanov** . . . I am grateful to Kyrill Anderson for much of the following information about the history of RGASPI.

Pg. 312: **It is not enough** . . . Robert Conquest, *The Great Terror* (New York: Oxford University Pr., 1990), 15.

Pg. 323: "The most important . . ." V. V. F. Afiani, N. G. Tomilinoi, *Boris Pasternak i vlast: dokumenty, 1956–1972* (Moscow: Rosspen, 2001), 72, My translation.

Pg. 324: "it isn't model . . ." Franz Kafka, "In the Penal Colony," in *The Metamorphosis and Other Stories*, 60.

Pg. 325: "Do we possess . . ." A. Artizov, Yu. Sigachev, I. Shevchuk, V. Khlopov, *Reabilitasiya: kak eto bylo, dokumenty prezidiuma TsK KPSS i drugie materialy, mart 1953-fevral 1956* (Moscow: Mezhdunarodnyi fond "demokratiya," 2000), 308–309. My translation.

Acknowledgments

I owe a real debt to Karen Pritzker, who brought one of my articles to the attention of James Atlas, my editor and publisher. Karen believed there was a story here to tell. Jim's constant support and inspiration made it possible to tell that story; he significantly helped to shape it and offered astute criticisms. I prize his editorial judgment.

In Russia, Vladimir Pavlovich Naumov has been a friend, teacher, guide and inspiration. I want to thank Vladimir Pavlovich and his wife, Valentina Ivanovna, for the warm hospitality their house has offered me for many years. I would like to thank Sergei Vladimirovich Mironenko, Kyrill Mikhailovich Anderson, Oleg Vladimirovich Naumov, and Nataliya Georgievna Tomilina for enabling Yale University Press to forge historic contracts with their archives; Vladimir Petrovich Kozlov, head of ROSARKHIV, had the vision to support these contracts and allow the Annals of Communism project to thrive. I would like to thank George Soros, who invited me to Prague in 1991 for a conference where the idea of the Annals series was born. William F. Buckley Jr. helped save the project at a crucial moment by raising a significant amount of money for Yale Press after the NEH had turned the Press down for a major grant and no other sources of funding could be found. Bill was a true friend to this endeavor. Samuel Lipman, one of the project's earliest supporters, sadly did not live to see the first volumes published. Peter Maffitt has been a consummate friend of Yale University Press and the Annals of Communism series from its inception and his constant incitement and enthusiasm has helped spur the project forward. I wish to thank Margarita Yakusheva for her many years of excellent work as my translator in Moscow.

At Yale University Press, Vadim Staklo has been the steadfast, special project manager of the Annals series for many years. John Ryden, former director of the Press, said one word in October 1991 without which it could not have begun: "Go." John Donatich, present director, continues to tolerate my periodic disappearances to Russia and Eastern Europe and has become a real collaborator.

Oleg V. Khlevniuk, Ambassador Jack Matlock, Joseph Epstein, Isabel Jaen-Portillo, John Lukacs, Rachel Shteir, Evgeny Dobrenko, and Arthur Krystal all read the manuscript at various stages and helped correct many errors of both substance and style. I wish to thank Cathy Ciepela for helping me track down an important quote from Pasternak, and William Odom for checking the section on our meeting with the KGB genenal. David Murphy has continuously helped guide my thoughts about security and intelligence matters in post-Soviet Russia, and conversations with Gary Saul Morson over many years have stimulated my thinking about Russia's past and future. Olga Varshaver offered acute observations at a penultimate stage and helped fill in gaps of both fact and chronology. Marci Shore read the entire manuscript with great care and helped me in many ways great and small with matters of tone and substance.

I wish to express my thanks to the helpful, enthusiastic, and intelligent staff of Atlas & Co.: John Oakes, Lukas Volger, Alexander Rothman, Lauren LeBlanc and Janet Min Lee, as well as to Martha Cameron, my excellent copy editor, who improved the manuscript in many ways.

I am deeply grateful to all. But my deepest debt is to my wife, Franny, who showed me the point of coming home.